THEORIES OF DEVELOPMENT

Capitalism, Colonialism and Dependency

JORGE LARRAIN

Polity Press

Copyright © Jorge Larrain 1989

First published 1989 by Polity Press in association with
Blackwell Publishers
Reprinted 1992, 1994

Editorial Office:
Polity Press
65 Bridge Street,
Cambridge CB2 1UR, UK

Marketing and production:
Blackwell Publishers
108 Cowley Road,
Oxford, OX4 1JF, UK

238 Main Street
Cambridge, MA 02142, USA

ISBN 0–7456–0710–1
ISBN 0–7456–0711–X (pbk)

British Library Cataloguing in Publication Data
A CIP catalogue record for this book is available from the
British Library.

Library of Congress Cataloging in Publication Data
A CIP catalogue record for this book is available from the
Library of Congress.

Typeset in 11 on 13 pt Times by Design Types
Printed in Great Britain by Redwood Books, Trowbridge, Wiltshire

CONTENTS

PREFACE AND ACKNOWLEDGEMENTS

I have been teaching Sociology of Development courses at the University of Birmingham for many years but my research and writing have been mainly concentrated on more general theoretical issues concerned with ideology and historical materialism. I always knew that one day I would wish critically to survey the evolution of theories of development in the light of the experience gained in my previous theoretical explorations. After all, it can be argued that historical materialism itself is, in many ways, a theory of development and that, given its theoretical propositions about the social determination of knowledge, it should have many interesting things to say about other theories of development and their evolution. The decision finally to go into this project was influenced by two main factors.

On the one hand, I detected a growing sense of crisis within development studies. Dependency theory had been an attempt to criticize and replace both orthodox Marxism and modernization theory, which seemed equally to operate with a simple logic of determination. And yet its promise had foundered because, in taking the logic of difference and heterogeneity which divided the developed from the underdeveloped world to an extreme, it had ended up falling into a new kind of simple determinism. If, before, capitalism had been considered to be an inherently developing force, now it was supposed to be an inherently underdeveloping factor. The reaction against such a view was swift and devastating, as the success of the 'articulation of modes of production theory' and then of B. Warren's ideas bore witness, but unfortunately it also meant a return to the facile optimism of the old economic determinism and to the anachronistic critique of old modes of production. In neither case could capitalism be blamed for underdevelopment. Development studies seemed to be swinging from one unsatisfactory extreme to the other.

On the other hand the 'demise of dependency theory', acknowledged by almost everyone, including many Latin American academic circles, personally challenged me in two ways. First, the most articulate critics of dependency theory were European Marxists who rarely distinguished between its various strands and carried out their critique from a very orthodox and/or Althusserian position which I found profoundly mistaken. At the centre of their onslaught was a refusal to see anything specific in the situation of 'peripheral countries'. Second, the best of dependency theory came from Latin America, my own continent, and I felt that although it had to be examined critically, greater care and attention had to be used in the task. If that was done, I hoped, perhaps one would find that the reports about its death had been greatly exaggerated. I wanted an answer to the question as to whether there was any significant contribution to be rescued from the passing of dependency theory.

This book represents an effort to grapple with these issues through the discussion of theories of development and their evolution from classical political economy onwards. It intends to show the sense of their progression, which is determined by the very evolution of the capitalist mode of production. But at the same time it seeks to emphasize that the logic of determination cannot be conceived in general and abstract terms, as if the capitalist system were perfectly homogeneous all over the world. Difference and heterogeneity within a basically common capitalist framework must result from the specificity of historical processes of class struggle. The book wants to show how the best strand of dependency theory succeeds in reconciling the general determinants of the capitalist system with the specificity of the Latin American situation in a way which abstract orthodox or Althusserian Marxism cannot hope to achieve.

Given my motivations and objectives, the book is naturally addressed to those academics, scholars and social scientists in general who in various ways and from different disciplines have been involved or are interested in development studies. Academics more specifically interested in Marxist debates may also, I hope, find this book of some interest. However, because in the pursuit of my objectives I examine systematically and critically the most relevant theories of development, many university and polytechnic undergraduate students may find it useful as a source of information and assessment related to their courses in the sociology of development.

Development theories are not only large in numbers but also usually straddle, with different emphases, various disciplines such as economics, political science and sociology, not to mention psychology and geography.

Additionally, they are sometimes constructed for, or have a particular correspondence with, the more or less specific problems of geographical areas such as Latin America, Africa, the Middle East, South East Asia, and so on. My personal perspective and also the limitations of space make it impossible adequately to cover all but the ones most relevant to my own work. Ultimately, most books on development present a more or less arbitrary selection and discussion of theories depending on the preferences, discipline and background of the author, and the geographical areas or countries in which she or he has developed an expertise. For my part it should be clear that I tend to take what can be vaguely and imprecisely described as a sociological approach and therefore will concentrate on those theories which are most representative of the so-called 'sociology of development'. Besides, I have an obvious preference for theories and examples whose background is Latin American.

This book was partly written during a study leave in Chile. I am grateful to FLACSO (Latin American Faculty of Social Sciences) for letting me have free access to its library in Santiago. Without the goodwill of its two librarians my task would have been much more difficult. I also wish to thank Dr R. Gwynne for his patience in reading the manuscript and commenting on its contents. I owe special thanks to Professor Anthony Giddens for his early comments and suggestions on the first outline of the book, for his valuable editorial advice and for his constant encouragement.

INTRODUCTION

THE ORIGINS OF THE CONCEPT OF DEVELOPMENT

Any study of the concept of development must take into account its historically determined character. Although it can be argued that some forms of economic development and social change have existed in most societies throughout history, consciousness of the fact that societies develop and the conception that economic development should be promoted are relatively new phenomena which arise in precise historical circumstances. The very concept of development appears rather late, in close connection with the emergence of capitalism and the critique of feudal society. This is because, before the arrival of capitalism, there existed mainly agricultural societies whose productive forces – limited by feudal property relations – changed very slowly over the years and whose economic output was consequently relatively stagnant.[1] It was capitalism that for the first time allowed productive forces to make a spectacular advance, thus making it possible for the idea of material progress and development to arise. The agent of this process and of the new concept of development is the bourgeoisie inasmuch as it 'cannot exist without constantly revolutionizing the instruments of production, and thereby the relations of production, and with them the whole relations of society.'[2]

Capitalism emerged from the contradictions of feudal society, in particular from the class struggles which led to the breakdown of serfdom and the undermining of peasant ownership of land.[3] These processes culminated in the conscious political struggles of the bourgeoisie which sought to dismantle those medieval institutions that presented such obstacles to the increase in productivity as the restrictions on free trade and on the personal freedom of workers, the restrictive practices of guilds, the prohibition of charging interest on loans, and so on. The first formulations of the new conception of development (or progress, as it was more usually called then) can be found in the work of classical political economy which represented the interests of the rising bourgeoisie. It was in the struggle of the British bourgeoisie against the remnants of feudalism that the idea of development was born. There is, then, a connection between the conception of development and the development of specific social conflicts.

This relationship between the concept of development and historically determined social processes (which is only a particular formulation of the more general principle of the social determination of knowledge) can be applied to the subsequent development of political economy and indeed to the general evolution of theories of development. Marx was the first to propose such a connection in the case of political economy when he argued that 'the development of political economy and of the opposition to which it gives rise keeps pace with the *real* development of the social contradictions and class conflicts inherent in capitalist production.' [4]

Marx sought to show that for as long as working-class struggles were 'undeveloped' or 'latent', political economy could remain a genuine scientific enterprise. Its emphasis on the 'real relations of production' attracted the opposition of Sismondi and others who stressed the importance of distribution. As soon as working-class struggles became more widespread and threatening, 'vulgar' political economy substituted apologetics and political expediency for scientific research and dealt with appearances only. But it then attracted a sharper and more general criticism, especially in Germany: 'So far as such criticism represents a class, it can only represent the class whose vocation in history is the overthrow of the capitalist mode of production and the final abolition of all classes – the proletariat.' Marx clearly situates his contribution in this perspective and goes on to show how the German bourgeoisie has tried and failed to 'kill' *Capital*.[5] It can be said, therefore, that Marx saw his own contribution as determined by the development of class conflicts.

I want to argue that this crucial relationship must be extended to cover, more generally, the development of development theories throughout the history of the capitalist mode of production. However, as capitalism becomes increasingly internationalized and a thoroughly integrated world market is created, development theories will respond not just to the class struggles and social contradictions of isolated capitalist countries but to the contradictions and conflicts emerging in the world capitalist system, especially those derived from the decolonization process, the emergence and challenge of socialist countries and the increasing separation between peripheral and central capitalist countries.

Within this framework I would like to do three things. First, to situate the concept of development and map out the evolution of development theories in relation to the development of real contradictions and conflicts inherent in the increasingly internationalized capitalist system. Second, critically to appraise the main theories of development from the point of view of their ideological and conceptual underpinnings. I expect theories to range from the simply ideological conceptions that, by remaining at the level of appearances, mask and talk out of existence the social contradictions of capitalism; through others which rigorously analyse the relations of production which lie behind the appearances of the market but wrongly treat them as self-evident necessities imposed by natural laws, to those which accurately deal with the inner relations of the world capitalist system and explore their likely forms of change. Third, to identify the central categories and concepts which allow us a better understanding of contemporary development processes, especially those which allow to grasp the productive processes which lie at the centre of development 'in definite historical form'.[6]

DEVELOPMENT THEORIES AND PHASES OF CAPITALISM

I start from the premise that theories of development do not emerge at random but are closely bound up with the evolution of the capitalist system. This means that one must study theories of development not only as conceptions of such and such an author of such and such an academic tendency, but also as products of a particular period of development of capitalism and its specific characteristics. In order to provide a general overview of this process of evolution and correspondence between theories of development on the one hand, and the development of capitalism on the other, I shall distinguish three main stages in the history of capitalism:[7] (1) Age of competitive capitalism (1700–1860); (2) Age of imperialism (1860–1945); (3) Late capitalism (1945–today).The diagram shows the historical progression of the most important theories of development and their correspondence with the three stages of capitalism:

ROUGH HISTORICAL MAP OF THE MAIN THEORIES OF DEVELOPMENT
(WITH ESPECIAL REFERENCE TO LATIN AMERICA)

CENTRE	PERIPHERY

Competitive Capitalism (1700–1860)

Classical political economy
(Smith, Ricardo)

Historical materialism
(Marx, Engels)

Age of Imperialism (1860–1945)

Neo-classical political economy
(Marshall, Walras, Jevons)

Classical theory of imperialism
(Hilferding, Bukharin, Luxemburg, Lenin)

Late Capitalism (1945–1980)

1945–1966 Expansion

Theories of modernization	ECLA's analysis
(Hoselitz, Rostow)	(Prebisch)

Theory of imperialism refurbished
(Baran)

1966–1980 Deceleration and Crises

Neo-liberalism	Dependency theories
(Friedman)	(Frank, Cardoso)
World system and unequal exchange	Unequal exchange theories
theories	(Amin)
(Wallerstein, Emmanuel)	

Articulation of modes of production
(Rey)

Age of competitive capitalism

From the moment it got off the ground and up to the 1860s, capitalism was mainly geared to the production of final consumption goods by a multitude of small firms which 'bought and sold in competitive markets, used rudimentary, labour-intensive technologies and simple organizational forms, and made rather low-quality products.'[8] This is the stage during which the new industrial bourgeoisie had to struggle to rid Europe of the last vestiges of feudalism and to gain political power. This is also the time when capitalism, from its emergence in Great Britain, began rapidly to expand all over the world. British goods at the beginning and European manufactures soon after are exported everywhere. Yet as Marx pointed out, 'during its first stages of development, industrial capital seeks to secure a market and markets by force, by the *colonial system*.'[9] Investment abroad by the new industrial countries takes the form of public loans and is mainly directed to the construction of railways and other means of communication in order to open up the world to trade. Yet non-industrial, peripheral countries still maintain local control of raw material production and of capital accumulation.

In so far as the conception of development is concerned, two main currents of thought emerged during this time, namely, political economy and the thought of Marx and Engels. In correspondence with the early struggles of the bourgeoisie as it sought to destroy the remnants of feudalism, the thought of classical political economy arose to propound the idea that the development of productive forces or economic progress under the control of privately owned and increasingly accumulating capital was the natural course for humankind; it was only that in the past it had been obstructed by artificial fetters. The new conquering bourgeoisie and its ideological representatives in classical political economy were quite confident that once the artificial obstacles were abolished capitalism would impose itself as the only and absolutely necessary mode of production.

Adam Smith and David Ricardo, the two main representatives of classical political economy, believed that international trade had important consequences for capital accumulation. For the former, international commerce both helps overcome the limitations of the internal market by allowing a country to sell its surplus production abroad and extends the division of labour, thus increasing productivity. For the latter, international commerce is crucial to bypass the limitations of internal agricultural production in order to lower the value of labour and increase profits. Countries are better off from the point of view of accumulation if they specialize in the trading of goods which can be produced with comparative advantages.[10]

As we have already seen, classical political economy emerged at a time when the open antagonism of capital and labour was not yet fully developed. So writers conceived of capitalism as the absolute form of production which can 'never enter into contradiction with, or enfetter, the aim of production – abundance. . .'[11] They interpreted any contradiction within capitalism as either an accident or a necessary law of nature. Thus for Ricardo crises were accidental and for Malthus the poverty of the working class was necessary. Yet as soon as the contradictions of capitalism began to surface and the class struggles conducted by the working class progressively assumed a more systematic and threatening character, 'vulgar political economy deliberately becomes increasingly *apologetic* and makes strenuous attempts to talk out of existence the ideas which contain the contradictions.'[12]

Simultaneously with the vulgarization of political economy, the critique of Marx and Engels came to the fore in the wake of the new struggles of the working class. Marx and Engels, too, see in capitalism a historical necessity because as the most advanced mode of production in history, it is capable of promoting the development of productive forces to an unprecedented degree. Yet they refused to consider capitalism as the natural and absolute mode of production and saw in the development of its inner contradictions the possibility of its demise and replacement by a more advanced mode of production. As the history of the theories of development corresponds with the development of capitalism and its basic contradictions, one can expect to continue to find in the new stages, following the ups and downs of the class struggle, a fundamental opposition between those theories which roughly support the capitalist system and those which are critical of it and seek its replacement by socialism. Yet as the historical circumstances change, so do the theories and the ways in which they confront to one another.

The age of imperialism

During this stage the competitive capitalism of small firms is replaced by the monopolistic control of the market by huge cartels and firms which use 'corporate forms of business organization'. The manufacturing of intermediate or capital goods becomes the most important and dynamic sector of production, requiring considerable investment by bigger firms which get their capital from an enlarged banking system.[13] As a result capital gets increasingly concentrated and centralized and is controlled by big financial institutions. The process of export of capital from the industrial centres to the periphery becomes widespread, seeking mainly the organization of large-scale production of raw materials. Consequently, in many cases peripheral countries lose national control of both raw material production and capital accumulation. This is a period of rapid economic development and technological progress. Capitalism is now firmly established as the predominant mode of production in the world and the bourgeoisie, having acquired political power in most industrial countries, now feels secure and no longer sees itself in struggle against traditional institutions of the past.

In this context, the bourgeois concern with the problem of development, and the necessary institutional changes to achieve it, is lost. As the capitalist mode of production has struck firm roots and shows an inherent dynamism, development is taken for granted. Classical political economy is abandoned and replaced by the neo-classical approach whose main concern is the theory of equilibrium. Walras, Jevons, Menger and Marshall are its main representatives. Neo-classical thought is mainly concerned with micro-economics inasmuch as it focuses its attention on the behaviour of individual economic units and firms in order to ascertain how they determine what to produce, in what quantities and at what prices within the general equilibrium. Unlike classical political economy which took the point of view of production, neo-classical thought emphasizes the sovereignty of the consumer in the market. Equilibrium will be reached when each consumer gets maximum satisfaction within a general equation whereby supply meets demand. The basic assumption is that the market is 'perfect' (each individual has complete information about, but cannot on its own modify, prices), and that production techniques and the preferences of the consumers are given.[14]

Whereas classical political economy and Marx gave a central place in their theories to the class structure of the capitalist mode of production and dealt with individuals only in so far as they represented and were determined by class relations, neo-classical thought tends to consider only individual economic agents (producers or consumers) who make rational choices in order to achieve the optimum satisfaction of their needs.[15] Classes, and more generally, the whole socio-political institutional set-up of society are disregarded as if they did not have any relevance for economic analysis. Separated from the socio-political context, it is no wonder that development was thought of as a process which presents no major problems and which evolves almost automatically as knowledge and technology gradually expand. As Meier and Baldwin put it, 'first, neo-classical economists consider development to be a gradual and continuous process. Second, they emphasize the harmonious and cumulative nature of the process. Third, they are generally optimistic concerning the possibilities for continued economic progress.' This is why 'the problem of economic development tended to subside into the background of economic discussion'[16] and economists turned their attention to smaller-scale problems.

In so far as international trade is concerned, neo-classical economists did not go much further than classical political economists. They fully accepted Ricardo's theory of comparative advantages. However, because the logic of Ricardo's theory entailed that in the long term the development of any society altered the relative values of raw materials (especially food) and manufactures so that the prices of the former tended to increase and the prices of the latter tended to decrease, they were ready to transpose this conclusion, which Ricardo arrived at in the context of a national economy, to the international context, in order to maintain that countries specializing in the production of food and primary products would benefit more from international trade as manufactured goods become cheaper. As Palloix has pointed out, they forgot that international trade, and more specifically the import of cheap food, was for Ricardo the only way to reverse this trend and stop the relative decline of industrial prices in England.[17] So the producers of primary products have no guarantee that in the exchange between raw materials and manufactures the former have a long-term advantage.

The changes in the structure of capitalist development which had occurred by the end of the nineteenth century also prompted Marxist thought to adapt and enlarge its traditional analysis. This is the origin of the classical theory of imperialism which was developed by Bukharin, Rosa Luxemburg, Hilferding and Lenin during the second decade of the twentieth century. The theory of imperialism seeks to account for the new features of capitalism such as the appearance of monopolies as the result of the concentration of capital, the creation of finance capital which is controlled by big banking institutions, the export of capital to non-industrial countries and the territorial division of the world among the advanced capitalist countries. They do not innovate in so far as the Marxist concept of development is concerned, but rather follow the early vision of Marx and Engel which takes it for granted that the forced expansion of capitalism abroad by means of colonial conquest and the export of capital will eventually bring about the industrialization of those territories. To this extent the classical theory of imperialism, too, believes that the inherent characteristics of capitalism contribute to development; only, paradoxically, it develops some doubts as to whether capitalism still has the same dynamism in Europe itself!

Both neo-classical economics and the theory of imperialism were reconditioned during the new circumstances which emerged in the late 1920s and early 1930. In the wake of a series of depressions which culminated in the world crisis of 1930, the thought of Keynes shook neo-classical theory, particularly in respect of the need for the state to intervene to counteract the worst effects of depressions and secure full employment. He realized that without state intervention it was possible to reach a situation of equilibrium compatible with high unemployment. Keynes was confident in the ability of capitalism to continue to produce wealth, and only felt that economic science had shown little imagination in devising rational policies which the state could follow in order to correct the deficiencies and problems which arise during a recession. However, from the point of view of the theory of development many assumptions of neo-classical thought were still maintained. As Weaver has pointed out, 'in both the neoclassical (micro) theory of price formation and resource allocation and the Keynesian (macro) theory of aggregate economic performance, ignoring non-economic phenomena is appropriate for discussing commodity and exchange relationships.'[18] Keynesian economics, to a large extent, continues to abstract from the social relations which constitute the economic structure and condition economic growth.

The theory of imperialism, in its turn, began to be reinterpreted little by little in order to accommodate the plight of colonized countries which did not show much evidence of having been put on the path of industrialization and development by their colonial powers. The first step was to concede that for as long as the colonial bond was not broken, the development of third world countries would be temporarily arrested. This change of perspective, officially sanctioned during the 6th Congress of the Third International in 1928, was to affirm that imperialism is an obstacle to the development and industrialization of colonial countries. The idea was that independence would remove the major outstanding obstacle to development in these countries, namely, colonialism, and that consequently either a national capitalist economy would be able to resume its developing mission or an alliance with the Soviet Union would make it possible for these countries to leap over the capitalist stage altogether in order to pursue a socialist path of development.[19] Still there is practically no consideration of the effects of imperialism on backward but formally independent countries. The study of imperialism remains almost exclusively confined to colonial or semi-colonial situations.

Late capitalism

During this stage the most dynamic sector of the capitalist system is the production of modern consumer goods (cars, fridges, TV sets, etc.) which is controlled by big transnational corporations. The production of raw materials ceases to be carried out almost exclusively in third world countries and is shifted on a massive scale to the industrial centres.[20] International capital in the metropolitan centres is mainly exported to other metropolitan centres, but in so far as a proportion of it goes to the newly independent third world, it is no longer interested only in raw material production but, above all, in the production of modern consumption goods which can be sold internally at monopolistic prices or exported cheaply to the metropolis. This stage can be subdivided into two phases. The first one, from 1945 to 1966, is mainly a phase of economic expansion, rising profits and accelerated development. The second, from 1966 until the present, is a phase of decelerated growth and of rapidly succeeding and increasingly threatening recessions.

Expansion　After the second world war an important process of decolonization starts all over the world and new independent nations emerge everywhere. The new wave of nationalism in the third world coupled with the expansion of socialism brought about by the Russian war effort are a matter of great concern for the Western industrial societies. The issues of social progress and economic development are practically forced back into the agenda. For the first time the poverty and economic difficulties of less developed countries come to the fore and are recognized as genuine problems by the developed world. In this context, development can no longer be taken for granted, and a renewed academic interest in the study of the necessary conditions for, and obstacles to, development arises in the metropolitan centres. The direct investment by international companies accelerates some processes of industrialization in the third world which nevertheless remain heavily dependent on the metropolitan centres, both technologically and financially. Due to the payment of royalties and interests, the repatriation of profits and the payment for imported capital goods, the net flow of capital favours the metropolitan centres. The new developing nations suffer from chronic deficits in their balances of payments, from inflationary processes and widespread unemployment.

Theories of modernization emerge which seek to explain the process of development as a transition between two models or ideal types, the traditional society and the modern or industrial society. During the transition process, changes occur in different sectors and structures of society which are not synchronized, and hence a mixture of traditional and modern institutions and values is to be expected which characterizes a developing or modernizing society. This transition is accomplished first by the developed countries, and the newly developing nations are supposed to follow the same pattern of change. The theories of modernization, therefore, seek to identify those areas and social variables which should experience some specific changes in order to facilitate the process of transition of the latecomers.

Some theories emphasize economic factors. Rostow,[21] for instance, describes various economic stages within which certain crucial areas and rates of investment are necessary in order to progress to the next stage. Other versions stress psychological motivations. McClelland,[22] for example, argues that economic growth requires the development of the motivation to do well in a class of entrepreneurs, the so-called 'need for achievement'. Still other theories underline a more complex set of sociological variables. Hoselitz[23] and Germani,[24] for instance, describe development as the necessary change from emotive, primary and diffuse social relations to neutral, secondary and specific social relations, from prescriptive to elective actions, from ascribed and particularist roles to achieved and universalist roles, etc. Invariably, though, these theories are teleological and take the advanced capitalist Western societies as a model for all developing nations. The new nations are bound to go along the same road and should expect to find the same problems as those experienced by Western societies in the nineteenth century. The diffusion of capitalist values, economic attitudes and institutions is deemed to be indispensable for development and therefore close contact with Western societies, especially through unrestricted international trade, should be promoted.

At the opposite extreme, the Marxist theory of imperialism, in a third evolutionary step, is further refurbished to account for the situation of backwardness and underdevelopment after the abolition of direct colonial rule. For the first time the theory of imperialism focuses on the internal effects of the introduction of capitalism in third world societies and carries out analyses which go beyond the problems brought about by the more or less arbitrary decisions of colonial powers. Paul Baran[25] makes the most important contribution from this point of view by arguing that in formally independent countries imperialist powers enter into alliance with the local oligarchies and as a result vital economic resources are partly syphoned off to the metropolis and partly squandered in luxury consumption, thus preventing accumulation and development. Economic development everywhere, but particularly in backward capitalist countries, comes into conflict with the economic and political order of imperialism. Imperialist countries are opposed to the industrialization of the underdeveloped countries, and consequently they try to maintain the old ruling classes in power. Development in the third world can only be achieved through a determined struggle against the internal conservative forces which are propped up by imperialism.

The novelty which appears during the first phase of this stage, however, is the fact that, in addition to the traditional confrontation between bourgeois and Marxist theories of European or North American origin, for the first time in the history of the concept of development some original contributions to the debate are produced in the periphery of the industrial world, specifically in Latin America. Later, during the second phase of this stage, African and Asian authors will also make important contributions. This shows the rising consciousness of third world societies in general about what they see as their disadvantaged situation in the world economic system and expresses their political will to achieve a better deal within the emerging post-war international system. The first contributions reflect the intellectual maturity achieved by the Latin American continent which, unlike Africa and Asia, had achieved its independence from colonial rule during the first quarter of the nineteenth century and had already experienced the problems of starting an import-substituting industrialization during the first half of the twentieth century.

In the late 1940s, the Economic Commission for Latin America, ECLA, an international organization created by the United Nations, under the chairmanship of Raul Prebisch, an Argentinian economist, develops a body of thought which challenges some of the assumptions of the theory of international trade.[26] ECLA, too, wants to promote the modernization and industrialization of Latin America, but sees some problems stemming from international trade. According to their analysis, the terms of trade are consistently deteriorating for raw material exporters because they sell their products at international prices which are below their real value, whereas central countries sell their industrial products at prices above their real value. There is therefore unequal exchange between centre and periphery, a terminology which they were the first to introduce. This means that most developing countries must export an increased amount of raw materials each year in order to be able to continue to import the same amount of industrial goods. ECLA's solution is to suggest that since the exchange of raw materials for industrial products is unfavourable for the producers of the former, Latin American states should promote, plan and protect an import-substituting industrialization in order to become less dependent on the industrial centres. The difficulty in this proposal is that the very import substituting industrialization itself depends on the expanded export of raw materials to pay for the necessary imports of capital goods and technology.

Deceleration and crises   By 1966 a new phase sets in which is characterized by a slowing down of economic growth and a falling rate of profit in industrial nations. Simultaneously, most processes of industrialization in Latin America have lost their dynamism and are unable to go on into the phase of substituting internal production for imports of capital goods. This crisis contributes to create unemployment, inflation and increased political instability, which will end up in the widespread emergence of military dictatorships, starting with the 1964 military coup in Brazil and followed by coups in Argentina, Peru, Bolivia, Chile and Uruguay. These regimes, with few exceptions, will seek to enhance the participation of international capital as a way of overcoming the structural limitations of the industrialization processes and will adhere to the new neo-liberal and monetarist thought which is becoming influential in the industrial centres at the time.

These new neo-liberal theories in the metropolitan countries attack the Keynesian policies prevalent since the 1940s. If growth and development have become sluggish it is because of excessive state interference, high taxation to support the heavy burden of welfare state policies and, in general, encroachments on free trade and free markets. Economist like Milton Friedman propose to abolish controls and protectionist tariffs, cut down on public expenditure and keep a tight monetary grip. Neo-liberalism does not contribute much that is new to the debate about underdeveloped countries, but it insists, following Adam Smith, that it is a mistake to try to industrialize by protecting inefficient ventures behind high tariffs, and that the free interplay of market forces should allocate resources. What had been the central plank of ECLA's recommendations and of the Latin American industrialization policies for several decades comes under severe attack.

At the opposite extreme, new theories arise in Latin America which are critical of both the theories of modernization and ECLA's policies. These are the theories of dependency. They draw in part on the classical theory of imperialism but challenge some of its assumptions by focusing more specifically on the problems which the world capitalist system causes in the periphery. Both ECLA and the Marxist orthodoxy since 1928 have regarded the national bourgeoisies as progressive and considered industrialization to be a process fundamentally antagonistic to and opposed by the imperialist centres. The new theories of dependence are sceptical about the liberating role of national bourgeoisies and propose that the processes of industrialization in the third world are the vehicle of imperialistic penetration and of a new kind of dependence on transnational companies.

There are various kinds of dependency theory. The best known is that of A. G. Frank.[27] It has a great intellectual impact partly because it is the first to appear but more fundamentally because it radically questions what has hitherto been a received truth of both Marxist and bourgeois theories, namely, that capitalism is essentially a mode of production able to promote development everywhere. Frank rejects this idea and maintains that capitalism is to blame for the continuous underdevelopment of Latin America since the sixteenth century. He conceives of capitalism as a world system within which the metropolitan centres manage to expropriate the economic surpluses from satellite countries through the mechanisms of the international market, thus producing simultaneously the development of the former and the underdevelopment of the latter. Third world countries are underdeveloped because they are dependent within the world capitalist system. Hence development can only occur when a country breaks out of the system by means of a socialist revolution.

Despite its appeal and widespread impact, Frank's theory has been severely criticized. First, because it defines capitalism in terms of orientation to the market and not as a mode of production. Second, because it over-emphasizes the exploitation of certain countries as a whole and pays less attention to the exploitation of their working classes. Third, because it confuses dependency with underdevelopment, whereas it can be shown that some countries like Canada are dependent and developed. A less well-known but more sophisticated theory of dependency is that of Cardoso and Faletto.[28] For them dependency must not be used as a blanket concept which can explain all the evils of underdevelopment everywhere. For a start they propose that even within Latin America the situation of dependency is not the same for every country and that although the conditions of the international market and the strategies of international capital may be common, they are negotiated in different ways by different countries depending on their internal class struggles. This means that there is a specific mode of articulation between internal class structures and the mode of incorporation into the world market. Thus in certain countries a path of dependent capitalist development is possible whereas in others stagnation may result. The advantage of this approach is that it allows the study of concrete situations of dependency instead of uncovering a single universal mechanism of exploitation applicable to all peripheral countries.

ECLA's analysis and the various dependency theories which emerged in Latin America in the 1950s and 1960s became quite influential in the academic world of the industrial centres and in other underdeveloped areas. The new theories which arise in the 1970s show that influence. The most representative are the theories of unequal exchange of A. Emmanuel and Samir Amin and the theory of the world system of I. Wallerstein. They all start from certain basic intuitions taken from the ECLA and Frankian analyses. For Wallerstein[29] all the states within the capitalist system cannot develop simultaneously by definition because the system functions by virtue of having unequal core and peripheral regions. But he adds an interesting feature: the role of being a peripheral or semi-peripheral nation is not definitive. Core countries and peripheral countries can become semi-peripheral and vice versa. What remains is the unequal nature of the world system.

Emmanuel[30] and Amin[31] try to formulate and found in more rigorous Marxist terms the theory of unequal exchange. For them the problem is to show why and how in the exchange of commodities between central and peripheral economies, the former appropriate part of the value produced in the latter. They locate the problem in the low level of salaries and the poverty of productive forces in the periphery. Because of these circumstances the developed countries sell commodities to the periphery at prices that exceed their value, and buy from them commodities at prices below their value. So every transaction means a transfer of value from the underdeveloped country to the developed one, which means that the rate of accumulation of capital is reduced in the former and enhanced in the latter. Thus unequal exchange results in unequal development. A major theoretical conclusion of Emmanuel's approach is to maintain that internal class antagonisms have become marginal in the industrial centres and have been replaced in importance by the conflict between rich and poor nations. In the developed world the working class has been definitively integrated into the system and shares in the exploitation of the third world. The classical theory of imperialism detected this phenomenon (Lenin's theory of the labour aristocracy, for instance) but mistakenly believed that integration was only a temporary occurrence.

P.P. Rey[32] and other French authors like Meillassoux and Dupré react against unequal exchange mainly because, like Frank's theory, it bases its analysis on the international market and pays no attention to the internal modes of production of the periphery. Their theory has been appropriately called the 'articulation of the modes of production'. Unlike Frank, Rey rejects the idea that it is capitalism itself that lacks dynamism in the periphery; the problem is that some pre-capitalist modes of production in those regions proved to be far more resilient and impervious to the attack of capitalism than feudalism was in Europe. In other words it is no good blaming capitalism on its own; the success of capitalism depends on the nature of the pre-capitalist modes of production it is articulated with. The problem of underdevelopment is therefore the result of a more protracted and difficult transition to capitalism due to the fact that the processes of modernization and urban industrialization in the periphery are dependent for a long time on pre-capitalist modes of production in the countryside. Capitalism could emerge internally from feudal Europe because the feudal lords, acting in their own interests, simultaneously served the interests of the bourgeoisie by forcing the peasants out of their lands. In other regions capitalism could not evolve from the native modes of production because their ruling classes fiercely opposed it. Hence their resistance had to be broken by force and this is the task that colonialism tries to carry out with only partial success.

1

Early Capitalism: Classical Political Economy and Marx

The expression 'classical Political Economy' was introduced by Marx to differentiate between the scientific and the vulgar stages of the economic thought developed by the representatives of the bourgeoisie:

> Once and for all I may here state, that by classical Political Economy, I understand that economy which, since the time of W. Petty, has investigated the real relations of production in bourgeois society, in contradistinction to vulgar economy, which deals with appearances only, ruminates without ceasing on the materials long since provided by scientific economy, and there seeks plausible explanations . . .[1]

Political economists like Adam Smith, Ricardo, Malthus and John Stuart Mill constructed their theories with the conscious purpose of influencing the formation of policies and the political decisions of the day.[2] In this they shared the new bourgeois perspective according to which knowledge was not only a passive contemplation of the truth, as it had been in the theocentric conception of the Middle Ages, but was mainly geared to changing reality and nature to suit the happiness of human beings. Adam Smith, for instance, saw in the productive and accumulative character of capitalism a solution to the profound historical crisis of feudalism which originated in the fact that the surplus created by the feudal society was squandered by unproductive workers and the aristocracy, thus condemning society to be stationary.[3] In particular he wanted to oppose the Mercantilist ideas that identified wealth with gold and silver and the physiocratic ideas that considered industrial labour as unproductive. Smith was particularly concerned with struggling against all narrowing of competition or encroachment on free trade. Ricardo, in his turn, developed his theory of value in the context of the controversy about the tariffs imposed by the Corn Laws which impeded the free import of corn. For Ricardo the struggle against protectionism was crucial in order for capitalist profits and their progressive accumulation as capital to be maintained.

Both Smith and Ricardo started from the premise that the capitalist society they wanted to defend and promote was divided into classes. Adam Smith contends that

> the whole annual produce of the land and labour . . . constitutes a revenue to three different orders of people; to those who live by rent, to those who live by wages, and to those who live by profit. These are the three great, original and constituent orders of every civilized society . . .[4]

The interests of both landowners and workers is directly connected with the general interest of society since both rent and wages rise with the prosperity and increased wealth of the society. This is not so in the case of manufacturers because the rate of profit tends to fall with the development of society, and therefore they seek to narrow competition, which is against public interest.[5] This does not necessarily mean that Smith is against the interests of the industrialists, but it does show that Smith was writing at a very early stage of the development of capitalism, when the memory of the feudal obstacles to free trade was still fresh. As Dobb has argued, Adam Smith's

> doctrine can be properly understood only as a reflection of a period of transition, whose problems essentially consisted in clearing the ground for industrial investment and expansion, which he identified with the sweeping away of obstructive and sectionally-protective regulation . . . [6]

For Adam Smith development means the extension of the division of labour and the application of machinery to the productive process so that an increase in the productivity of labour could be achieved.[7] Insofar as the objective of economic development is concerned Adam Smith proposes that

> The riches, and so far as power depends upon riches, the power of every country, must always be in proportion to the value of its annual produce, the

fund from which all taxes must ultimately be paid. But the great object of
the political economy of every country is to increase the riches and power
of that country.[8]

The objective is then to increase the riches and those riches are a function
of the annual product. So Smith defines economic activity in material
terms, the physical production of material goods. It is important to
understand that, for Smith, productive work is only that which allows the
accumulation of material wealth and that, conversely, material wealth
has value only in so far as it embodies human labour :

> There is one sort of labour which adds to the value of the subject upon which
> it is bestowed: there is another which has no such effect. The former, as it
> produces value, may be called productive; the latter, unproductive labour.
> Thus the labour of a manufacturer adds, generally, to the value of the
> materials he works upon, that of his own maintenance, and of his master's
> profit. The labour of a menial servant, on the contrary, adds to the value of
> nothing.
> ... the labour of the manufacturer fixes and realizes itself in some particular
> subject or vendible commodity, which lasts for some time at least after that
> labour is past. It is, as it were, a certain quantity of labour stocked and stored
> up to be employed, if necessary, upon some other occasion.
> ... The labour of the menial servant, on the contrary, does not fix or realize
> itself in any particular subject or vendible commodity.[9]

So, in Smith's view, one of the factors which promotes development is
an increasing proportion of the work force dedicated to productive work,
which is precisely the reverse of the situation in feudalism. But in
addition to this, and most important, there must be an increase in
productivity through the division of labour which is achieved through the
expansion of the market and international trade.[10] However, Smith was
not consistent in his labour theory of value and endeavoured to show that
profit and rent were also components of value with independence of
labour. As Clarke has pointed out, the purpose of this retreat was to justify
the distribution of the national product and to show the natural harmony
of interests among the main three classes of society. So although the
originality of Smith's contribution to social science must be stressed 'for
he was the first to analyse systematically the emergent capitalist society
in terms of the fundamental class division between capitalists, landowners
and wage-labourers',[11] he failed to analyse the relationships between

these classes in terms of the labour theory of value which he himself outlined.

David Ricardo, too, started from the existence of classes in society and saw as the role of political economy the determination of the laws of distribution according to which 'the produce of the earth . . . is divided among three classes of the community, namely, the proprietor of the land, the owner of the stock or capital necessary for its cultivation, and the labourers by whose industry it is cultivated'.[12] He further elaborates and perfects the idea that the value of a commodity is the result of the amount of labour incorporated into it, measured by the time taken to produce it. So for him, profits, wages and rent, the rewards of the main three classes of society, could only come out of the fixed magnitude of value produced by the available labour force, whatever the pattern of distribution. Ricardo found in the labour theory of value the clue to ascertain the way in which distribution was carried out.

Whereas Smith firmly believed that the interests of the three classes were essentially harmonic and saw it as 'natural' that the greater part of capital was directed to agriculture because there it mobilizes a greater proportion of productive labour,[13] Ricardo presented the interests of capitalists and landowners as diametrically opposed and sided with the former. Landowners benefit from the fact that, as population grows, it is necessary to cultivate progressively less fertile land with diminishing returns. This pushes up rent and increases the price of corn which leads to a necessary rise in wages in the towns. This in its turn affects industrialists who see their profits diminish as value is transferred to the landowners. It is in the interest of manufacturers to lower the price of food in order to lower the cost of labour, thus boosting accumulation. To the natural bottleneck presented by the limited supply of fertile land, Ricardo added the fact that the Corn Laws prevented the importation of cheaper corn and the Poor Laws artificially increased the demand for corn and stimulated the growth of population. This is why Ricardo attacked the landowners, who in order to maintain high rents, opposed the repeal of the Corn Laws.

Ricardo, then, understood development as a process of self-sustained accumulation of capital and growth which could be arrested only by the limitations of available land. Schumpeter refers to this conception as 'pessimist', 'stagnationist' and revealing a 'complete lack of imagination'.[14] But he does not give enough weight to the fact that Ricardo conceded a central place to the free import of corn as the essential counterbalancing force to diminishing agricultural returns. As Ricardo put it, referring to food and raw materials, 'let these be supplied from abroad in exchange for manufactured goods, and it is difficult to say where the limit is at which you would cease to accumulate wealth and to derive profit from its employment.'[15] A year later he reiterates: 'I contend for free trade in corn on the ground that while trade is free, and corn is cheap, profits will not fall however great be the accumulation of capital.'[16] However, the fact that both Adam Smith and David Ricardo conceived of, and wanted to fight against, a possible 'stationary state' of society, clearly corresponds to the situation of an early bourgeoisie which is still struggling to impose its rule and which is unsure of the eventual results of its struggles. As Marx put it:

> The Classics, like Adam Smith and Ricardo, represent a bourgeoisie which, while still struggling with the relics of feudal society, works only to purge economic relations of feudal taints, to increase the productive forces and to give a new upsurge to industry and commerce.[17]

CLASSICAL POLITICAL ECONOMY AND BACKWARD NATIONS

Although the main focus of attention of classical political economy is the development of capitalism in Britain and, by implication, in Western Europe, one can find plenty of references in their writings to the situation of the less developed, non-European nations.[18] They refer to them as 'backward countries' or 'unimproving nations'. It cannot be said that classical political economists constructed an elaborate theory about, or carried out any systematic analysis of the nations they considered to be backward and unimproving, but they certainly tried to explain the causes of their backwardness, and were especially interested in assessing the impact and consequences of the European colonial expansion on these countries. For most political economists European tutelage through colonialism was the only way to break the millennial pattern of stagnation of backward nations and to initiate them on to the road to progress. However, some of them also saw and denounced some problems in the way in which European countries organized the economic control of their colonies.

Adam Smith for instance vigorously and consistently attacked the monopolistic control of commerce with the colonies established by European nations and denounced their mercantilist policies which looked only for the importation of gold and silver. His concern stems mainly from his resolute opposition to all obstacles to free trade. Thus he could say, referring to the discovery of America, that 'the savage injustice of the Europeans rendered an event, which ought to have been beneficial to all, ruinous and destructive to several of those unfortunate countries.'[19] Monopolistic colonial trade discouraged consumption and industrial development in the colonies because they had to pay higher prices for their imports and received less for their exports. Yet for Smith the colonial monopoly of trade was not only bad for the colonies but also particularly bad for the colonial powers that instituted it because it promoted an unnaturally high rate of profit for the monopolistic sector and an artificially high price system which led to a distorted and inefficient allocation of national resources. This would prevent the more rational and advantageous utilization of capital thus curtailing the rate of growth of the whole economy. As Smith put it, the monopoly of colonial trade 'depresses the industry of all other countries, but chiefly that of the colonies, without in the least increasing, but on the contrary diminishing, that of the country in whose favour it is established.'[20]

However, it would be a mistake to believe that Smith opposed colonialism in general. He distinguishes between the economic and the political aspects of it. In opposing the monopolistic control of trade by the East India Company he nevertheless accepted that the company should continue to govern India for the British crown in order to guarantee free trade. For Smith colonial trade was advantageous for both the colonies and the colonial powers as long as there was no monopolistic control of it. As he put it,

> We must carefully distinguish between the effects of the colony trade and those of the monopoly of that trade. The former are always and necessarily beneficial; the latter always and necessarily hurtful. But the former are so beneficial, that the colony trade, though subject to a monopoly, and notwithstanding the hurtful effects of that monopoly, is still upon the whole beneficial, and greatly beneficial; though a good deal less so than it otherwise would be.[21]

Smith's assumption was that if free trade were to be assured, the colonies would have no problem in developing normally. So he did not really question the British rule in America and India, he only challenged its monopolistic economic policies and the specific way in which they were enforced. Therefore Adam Smith did not blame colonialism or colonial trade for the backwardness of non-European countries. True, the colonial monopoly of trade was more hurtful to the colonies than to Europe, but

colonial countries were backward and stationary before they were
colonized just as China is backward without having been colonized.
Backwardness for Smith had to do with internal factors which favour
agriculture over industry and internal trade over foreign trade:

> As the political economy of the nations of modern Europe has been more
> favourable to manufactures and foreign trade, the industry of the towns,
> than to agriculture, the industry of the country, so that of other nations has
> followed a different plan, and has been more favourable to agriculture than
> to manufactures and foreign trade.[22]

The consequence of this was spelt out clearly: 'When a landed nation
. . . oppresses, either by high duties or by prohibitions, the trade of
foreign nations, it necessarily hurts its own interest . . .' Perfect freedom
of trade, the lack of barriers against foreign industry was for backward
nations 'the most effectual expedient for supplying them in due time with
all the artificers, manufacturers, and merchants whom they wanted at
home.'[23]

As J.P. Platteau[24] has pointed out, Smith is exceptional among other
classical political economists in that he does not propound as a justification
for colonialism the paternalist conception that European countries have
a civilizing mission to accomplish in the rest of the world. Smith
conceived of the British Empire as a vast commercial enterprise to which
both Great Britain and the colonies should contribute and which should
benefit both on equal terms. At the opposite extreme J.B. Say distinguished
between 'enlightened nations' possessing a 'superior civilization' and
'savage nations' possessing an 'inferior civilization'. The individuals of
the latter were rather passive and resigned, had a marked preference for
leisure and were incapable of any rational reflection and scientific
activity. As all nations must go through the same stages of progress, the
enlightened European countries had the duty and the right to help the
savage nations to become civilized:

> It is 'in the interest of the human species' that the advanced European
> nations must keep and even increase their influence in Asia . . . it is evident
> that 'with its despots and superstitions, Asia has no good institutions to lose'
> but 'she could receive many good ones from the Europeans'.[25]

Unlike Smith, Say believed that colonies were a burden rather than a
positive factor in the development and prosperity of the metropolitan
countries. Besides, for Say, in principle all peoples had the natural right

to govern themselves. So he thought that ideally, in the interest of both parties, colonized countries should become independent. Yet colonialism was justified as a temporary measure for as long as backward countries remained immature and were being educated in European values and customs.

Similarly, in his *History of British India* , James Mill took the view that India was uncivilized by comparison with Britain, and in arguing against the fictional accounts of the first travellers which described a fabulous ancient Indian civilization he averred that 'every thing . . . bears clear, concurring, and undeniable testimony to the ignorance of the Hindus, and the low state of civilization in which they remain.'[26] The same applied to China and other Asiatic societies. In describing the moral character of Indians and Chinese he maintained that

> both nations are to nearly an equal degree tainted with the vices of insincerity; dissembling, treacherous, mendacious, to an excess which surpasses even the usual measure of uncultivated society. Both are disposed to excessive exaggeration with regard to every thing relating to themselves. Both are cowardly and unfeeling. Both are in the highest degree conceited of themselves, and full of affected contempt for others. Both are, in the physical sense, disgustingly unclean in their persons and houses.[27]

Ricardo, impressed by Mill's account, wrote to him exclaiming: 'What a frightful obstruction to improvement does the immoral character of the people of India present!'[28] For Mill the main cause of this situation was political, especially bad laws and the despotic character of government which destroyed morality and the motivation to work in the population. As with Say, the only possibility of changing this picture was, for Mill, the benign and enlightened tutelage of Europeans, even if they must resort to some forms of authoritarianism. Again, Mill did not see much economic advantage for the colonial power to be derived from its civilizing task. Colonies were a burden rather than a means for European nations to become rich.

It is true, on the other hand, that there was among classical political economists a clear perception about some of the excesses committed by colonial powers and about some fundamental differences in the prosperity of various colonies which were related to the way in which they were administered. Smith, for instance, tried to explain the relatively successful development of the British North American colonies in comparison with the sluggishness of the British colonies in Asia and the Spanish and Portuguese colonies in South America, in terms of the more liberal policies pursued in the former which facilitated greater autonomy and trade, and the more restrictive and monopolistic commercial practices imposed on the latter. Malthus used similar arguments. Yet they never questioned colonialism in itself and there was a tendency to over-emphasize the critique of the Spanish and Portuguese forms of colonization in contrast with the supposedly more enlightened British approach.

This was very noticeable in Malthus who concentrated on the differences between North and South American colonies. In the latter he accused Spain and Portugal of cruelty, violence, maladministration, and so on, to the point that he could invert the moral invectives of Say and James Mill: 'Whatever may be the character of the Spanish inhabitants of Mexico and Peru at the present moment, we cannot read the accounts of these countries without feeling strongly that the race destroyed was, in moral worth as well as numbers, superior to the race of their destroyers.'[29] The English North American colonies, on the contrary, 'far outstripped all the others in the progress of their population. To the quantity of rich land which they possessed in common with the Spanish and Portuguese colonies, they added a greater degree of liberty and equality.'[30] That Malthus's point was not so much to praise the moral value of the natives as to attack the character of the Spanish colonizers in contrast with the talents and tact of the British colonizers was shown by his multiple remarks about the indolence, ignorance and improvidence of the Indians. These bad habits are fostered by the natural richness and fertility of the soil in those countries. The easier it was to make a living, the greater the tendency to leisure.[31] In order to break this propensity to leisure new needs should be stimulated, especially through international trade. As he put it,

> The greatest of all difficulties in converting uncivilized and thinly peopled countries into civilized and populous ones, is to inspire them with the wants best calculated to excite their exertions in the production of wealth. One of the greatest benefits which foreign commerce confers, and the reason why it has always appeared an almost necessary ingredient in the progress of wealth, is, its tendency to inspire new wants, to form new tastes, and to furnish fresh motives for industry.[32]

This concern with the motivation of the inhabitants of backward countries was also shown by John Stuart Mill. According to him backward societies had a very weak 'effective desire' to accumulate, to work harder and to save. Like Malthus he attributed this lack of motivation to the favourable natural conditions in backward countries which generate the development of only limited needs in the population. But he also followed his father's belief that oppressive political institutions were partly responsible for discouraging the right attitudes. This was, in J. S. Mill's view, the main problem in India before the British conquest. Unlike J. Mill and Say, J.S. Mill saw colonization as advantageous for European nations, because it allowed the possibility of investing capital abroad and of getting cheap food stuffs, thus helping to counteract the tendency for the rate of profit to fall. Yet he resolutely rejected the idea that British existence and prosperity simply depended on getting new markets abroad or that colonial countries suffered economic damage under European rule. Colonialism for J.S. Mill was not only not antagonistic to the interests of non-European nations but also benefited the colonies more than the metropolitan countries. Although he criticized the most blatant errors committed by the British rule in Ireland and India, he saw colonial rule as necessary, especially for immature non- European countries. As he put it,

> Independence and nationality, so essential to the due growth and development of a people further advanced in improvement, are generally impediments to theirs. The sacred duties which civilized nations owe to the independence and nationality of each other, are not binding towards those to whom nationality and independence are either a certain evil, or at best a questionable good . . .[33]

Most classical political economists, even those who were critical of some of the colonial practices, justified colonialism on the grounds of its civilizing role and as the only way of stimulating the needs and material aspirations of the backward peoples. The benign and enlightened tutelage of Europe was necessary for the backward nations to initiate their road to progress. On their own, the economies of backward nations were stagnant and could not advance the development of productive forces. This was mainly due to the wrong attitudes of most of the people in these nations: they had a preference for leisure, they did not want to work harder and save for the future. Ricardo once said that if for any reason the wages of Irish workers went up, they would work less because with less effort they would satisfy their meagre needs. This was applied in general to all backward nations. The lack of motivation was not innate but the result of a variety of reasons such as hot climates, natural fertility of the land and, above all, oppressive despotisms which did not reward effort and discouraged trade and industry. All this could only be changed, in so far as it was changeable, through the diffusion of values, international trade and, in general, the civilizing mission which colonialism secured.

THE CRITIQUE OF POLITICAL ECONOMY

It is well known that Marx formulated his analyses of the capitalist mode of production as a critique of political economy. However it would be a mistake to believe that Marx simply rejected classical political economy as a whole and in every respect. On the contrary, he respected its scientific achievements and took from it a good number of key concepts while criticizing its ideological shortcomings. Hence the aforementioned distinction between classical political economy and vulgar political economy. Marx simply dismissed the latter as 'the evil intent of apologetic'[34] which consists 'in the falsification of the simplest economic relations.'[35] The balanced treatment of classical political economy by Marx was a concrete application of his complex theoretical conception about the relationships between ideology and science. It can be maintained that Marx dealt with classical political economy both in terms of science and in terms of ideology. On the one hand, political economy achieved scientific status in so far as it was able to penetrate the veil of appearances created by the operation of the capitalist market to discover the real relations which lay in the process of production. Thus for instance Marx said that

> Ricardo's theory of values is the scientific interpretation of actual economic life . . . Ricardo establishes the truth of his formula by deriving it from all economic relations, and by explaining in this way all phenomena, even those like rent, accumulation of capital and the relation of wages to profits, which at first sight seem to contradict it; it is precisely that which makes his doctrine a scientific system.[36]
>
> . . . to examine how matters stand with the contradiction between the apparent and the actual movement of the system. This then is Ricardo's great historical significance for science . . . Closely bound up with this scientific merit is the fact that Ricardo exposes and describes the economic contradiction between the classes.[37]

On the other hand, Marx accused classical political economy of having a singularly unhistorical conception of development which was bound to smudge over 'all historical differences and see bourgeois relations in all forms of society.'[38] Political economists conceived of the capitalist mode of production as a natural and absolutely necessary process which in the past had been hindered by artificial institutions.[39] They failed to interpret capitalism as a transitory historical necessity. Two consequences followed from this. First, bourgeois economists regarded their economic categories 'as eternal laws and not as historical laws which are valid only for a particular historical development, for a definite development of the productive forces.'[40] Second, they could not conceive of any contradictions, crises or barriers which could adversely affect the development of productive forces. The sufferings of the early proletariat were interpreted as passing and accidental; poverty was construed as the necessary 'pang which accompanies every childbirth, in nature as in industry.'[41] In so far as classical political economy was unable to understand the limited historical character of capitalism, and tended to dismiss its contradictions as pangs of a natural process, it became an ideological theory which distorted the true character of capitalism.

Marx recognized that classical political economists had the great scientific merit of having developed the labour theory of value, but he accused them of not being consistent in its application. Smith correctly propounded the idea that only labour created value, but when he was confronted with the problem that there was a difference between the value of a commodity in the market and the value of the labour necessary to produce it as expressed in the wage, he abandoned the labour theory of value and resorted to the idea that the value of the commodity was also created by capital and land. This is why Marx said that

> Smith himself moves with great naïveté in a perpetual contradiction. On the one hand he traces the intrinsic connection existing between economic categories . . . On the other, he simultaneously sets forth the connection as it appears in the phenomenon of competition . . . One of these conceptions fathoms the inner connection, the physiology, so to speak, of the bourgeois system, whereas the other takes the external phenomena of life as they seem and appear and merely describes, catalogues, recounts and arranges them under formal definitions. With Smith both these methods of approach not only merrily run alongside one another, but also intermingle and constantly contradict one another.[42]

Ricardo criticised Smith's retreat from the labour theory of value but he did not see, let alone solve, the problem Smith had perceived. He therefore accepted that the value of the commodity was different from the value of the labour necessary to produce it. As Marx put it,

> Ricardo simply answers that this is how matters are in capitalist production. Not only does he fail to solve the problem; he does not even realize its

existence in Adam Smith's work . . . '*They are not equal*', that is 'the quantity of labour bestowed on a commodity, and the quantity of labour which that commodity would purchase' [1. c., p. 5]. He contents himself with stating this fact. But how does the commodity labour differ from other commodities? One is *living labour* and the other *materialised* labour. They are, therefore only different forms of labour. Since the difference is only a matter of form, why should a law apply to one and not to the other? Ricardo does not answer – he does not even raise this question.[43]

Marx's solution was that wages do not express the value of labour but the value of labour-power, a commodity whose peculiar nature allows the capitalist who purchases it to appropriate unpaid surplus value produced by the labourer while formally keeping the equivalence of exchange between capital and labour. This surplus value is the source of capital accumulation. This means that in accordance with a consistent application of the labour theory of value, the accumulation of capital under the capitalist relations of production is based on exploitative relations. The contradictions inherent in those exploitative relations will eventually erect a barrier to the continuous accumulation of capital. Against the belief of classical political economy that capitalist production was natural and absolute, Marx maintained that 'it has its barrier, that it is relative, that it is not an absolute, but only a historical mode of production corresponding to a definite limited epoch in the development of the material requirements of production.'[44]

It is interesting to note that one does not find in Marx a specific critique of the classical political economists' views about backward societies. On the contrary, it is possible to argue that, in a certain manner, Marx and Engels shared with the political economists the belief in the world mission of European capitalism, and occasionally showed similar prejudices as well. Ricardo's comments on the lazy Irish are matched by Engels's remark about the lazy Mexicans, whom Marx, in his turn, labels as '*les dernières des hommes*'. James Mill's description of the moral character of Indians and Chinese as compromised by the vices of falsity and slyness can be compared with Marx's remarks about the 'hereditary stupidity' of the Chinese.[45] True, none of the political economists showed the degree of awareness about the cruelty and arbitrariness of colonialism, or condemned it as forcefully as Marx and Engels did, nor did they have any inkling of the possibility that colonialism might hinder the development of colonies, an idea that Marx and Engels developed after 1860. But on the whole, even when Marx and Engels advocated the independence and self-government of some colonies, their point of reference and their main objective were the liberation of the British proletariat and the advance of socialism in the most developed countries of the world.

THE CONCEPT OF DEVELOPMENT AND HISTORICAL MATERIALISM

Although it should be clear that Marx's concept of development must be studied in the context of his materialist conception of history, the first problem which such a proposition must confront is the fact that there are alternative interpretations of historical materialism which differ in some fundamental respects. It is not possible for me to get involved here in a general discussion about the various interpretations of historical materialism,[46] but at the very least it is important to identify the existence of an orthodox version which was constructed by and received crucial inputs from Engels's *Anti-Dühring*, the theoreticians of the Second International both from the German SPD and the Bolshevik party, and which was finally codified by Stalin.[47] Very briefly, the main elements of the orthodox interpretation are the following:

> First, historical materialism is considered to be an extension or application of the principles of dialectical materialism to the study of society and history. Second, consciousness is a reflection of material reality because being, the material world, is prior to and exists independently of consciousness. Third, productive forces tend to develop throughout history and are the chief determining factor of changes in the economic structure and, through it, of changes in the rest of society. Fourth, history evolves through universal and necessary stages according to the progressive logic of natural-like laws which inevitably lead humankind toward the classless society.[48]

Aspects of this orthodox approach, especially the last two points, have been intellectually strengthened by the recent resurgence of rigorous and logically constructed 'technological determinist' interpretations of Marxism in the Anglo-Saxon world, the best example of which is the work of G.A. Cohen. Although I fundamentally disagree with this interpretation, I accept that it has a strong basis of support in Marx's writings. However such a basis can be easily overrated by unilaterally over-emphasizing one side of what must be recognized as some essential tensions in Marx's thought. These tensions have to do with (a) the conception of dialectic, either as a universal principle of motion in nature or as a negative principle operating only in class societies; (b) the understanding of consciousness, either as a mere reflection of material reality or as anticipatory of a practically constructed reality; (c) the mechanism of social change, either the primacy of productive forces or the primacy of class struggle; and (d) the conception of history, either as a natural process inexorably leading through some stages to a preordained goal or as a non-teleological process practically made by human beings within some limited options. Although all these tensions can be related to Marx's concept of development, the last two seem particularly relevant.

In so far as the mechanism of social change is concerned, the theory that the autonomous growth of productive forces is the key to understanding social change and economic development is well supported by Marx's texts throughout his intellectual evolution. The idea is that each phase in the autonomous progress of productive forces brings about new relations of production which are especially suited for the widespread adoption of the new techniques, and which induce new political institutions and ideas:

> At a certain stage of their development, the material productive forces of society come in conflict with the existing relations of production . . . From forms of development of the productive forces these relations turn into their fetters. Then begins an epoch of social revolution.[49]

> Social relations are closely bound up with productive forces. In acquiring new productive forces men change their mode of production; and in changing their mode of production, in changing the way of earning their living, they change all their social relations. The hand-mill gives you society with the feudal lord; the steam-mill, society with the industrial capitalist . . . There is a continual movement of growth in productive forces, of destruction in social relations, of formation in ideas . . .[50]

However strong and decisive these and many other texts may appear to be in favour of the primacy of productive forces, there are also passages which indicate that for Marx the advance of productive forces is not always the original cause of development and that class struggles should also be considered as relatively autonomous causes of change. Thus for instance in *Capital* Marx describes how the passage from handicraft to manufacture does not entail a previous development, or the introduction of new technology.[51] Furthermore, in *The German Ideology* Marx and Engels seem to argue that the 'material elements of a complete revolution' are two relatively independent factors and not just one: 'on the one hand the existing productive forces, on the other the formation of a revolutionary mass, which revolts'.[52] But even if the weight of textual exegesis favours the primacy of productive forces, I think there are compelling arguments not to accept them as a sound explanation of change.

In effect, productive forces just as much as relations of production are social results or circumstances produced by human practice. As Marx puts it, nature 'builds no machines, no locomotives', productive forces are 'the products of human industry', 'they are *organs of the human brain, created by the human hand*',[53] 'the result of practically applied human energy'.[54] They certainly condition human activities, but human beings can and do modify them, and for Marx this shows 'that circumstances make men just as much as men make circumstances.'[55] Change itself is certainly conditioned by objective circumstances, but it cannot be fully accounted for as a mere effect of objective circumstances: only human practices, class activities and struggles can bring about change in society. Brenner has conclusively shown how in pre-capitalist societies the mere appearance of a new technique is unable to induce the economic actors to adopt it without first changing the property relations into capitalist ones. But the new technique cannot by itself bring about that change in the property relations: they change only as a result of various processes of class struggle.[56]

This is the reason why there is a difference in the pattern of development between Eastern and Western Europe from the fifteenth century onwards. In most of Western Europe the peasantry struggled and broke away from feudal subjection by the mid-fifteenth century, whereas in Eastern Europe they failed to achieve freedom. What is crucial in Brenner's argument is the contention that 'the question of serfdom in Europe cannot be reduced to a question of economics' or to a question of technology. The class conflict between landlords and peasants had different outcomes in different places. In some places it resulted in the breakdown of the old structures, in other places it resulted in their restrengthening. Thus he argues that there is an 'element of indeterminacy' of the results of these class conflicts in different regions. Not that these results are totally arbitrary, but they are

> bound up with certain *historically specific* patterns of the development of the contending agrarian classes and their relative strength in the different European societies: their relative levels of internal solidarity, their self-consciousness and organization, and their general political resources.[57]

The development of peasant solidarity appears to have been far greater in Western than in Eastern Europe, which resulted in a greater ability in the West to resist seigneurial reaction. This is the cause of the economic backwardness in Eastern Europe, a class structure that precludes increased productivity. But not even in the West did the collapse of serfdom lead automatically to capitalism or successful economic development everywhere. It all depended on the degree of success of peasant struggles. In England the peasant revolts of the sixteenth century failed, allowing the English landlords to control most of the cultivatable land. This allowed the emergence of the tripartite class pattern: the landlord, the capitalist tenant and the wage labourer, which transformed agriculture in England.

So, the reason why agrarian capitalism flourished in the eighteenth century in England and resulted in the industrial revolution while agrarian backwardness was prevalent in France must be sought in the structure of ownership of land. Whereas in England land could be concentrated in large estates, in France the peasantry secured proprietorship of the land to a far greater extent. According to Brenner, economic development depended on

> the emergence of a specific set of class or social-property relations in the countryside – that is, capitalist class relations. This outcome depended, in turn, upon the previous success of a two-sided process of class development and class conflict: on the one hand the destruction of serfdom; on the other, the short-circuiting of the emerging predominance of small peasant property.[58]

In showing the crucial importance of class struggles and class structures for the failure or success of economic development in Europe, Brenner's historical studies contribute to strengthen a version of historical materialism which moves away from technological determinism. Hence, the tension in Marx's writings between the primacy of productive forces and the primacy of class struggles in the explanation of social change and development must be resolved in favour of the latter even if it can be shown that on the whole Marx really preferred the former. This is part of the task of reconstructing historical materialism as a theory of practice which I have propounded elsewhere.[59]

In so far as the concept of history is concerned, it is frequently thought that historical materialism purports to have found the general laws of history so that it is possible to determine with the accuracy of natural science both the general course of history and the path of development through which all countries must go. Such an interpretation finds support in some texts where Marx argues that 'the evolution of the economic formation of society is viewed as a process of natural history',[60] that he wants 'to show, by rigid scientific investigation, the necessity of successive determinate orders of social conditions',[61] that 'Asiatic, ancient, feudal, and modern bourgeois modes of production can be designated as progressive epochs in the economic formation of society',[62] and that 'the country that is more developed industrially only shows, to the less developed, the image of its own future.'[63]

However, to assess Marx's theory only on the basis of these texts is an oversimplification and a distortion. It is a distortion in so far as it ignores other texts where Marx seems to be arguing against universal and abstract schemes of historical development. For instance, in clarifying his theory about the genesis of capitalism to Vera Zasulich, he contends that the 'historical inevitability' of this process is *expressly* limited to the *countries of Western Europe.*[64] Furthermore, Marx complains against a Russian critic because

> He insists on transforming my historical sketch of the genesis of capitalism in Western Europe into an historico-philosophic theory of the general path of development prescribed by fate to all nations, whatever the historical circumstances in which they find themselves . . . But I beg his pardon. (He is doing me too much honour and at the same time slandering me too much).[65]

It is also an oversimplification because, paradoxically, one of the 'laws' discovered by historical materialism is that, whereas in pre-capitalist modes of production based on landed property natural relations still predominate, in the capitalist mode of production 'social, historically evolved elements predominate'.[66] This means that before capitalism human beings were far less capable of consciously altering the course of history and they were mostly driven by social and economic forces of which they were not aware and of which consequently they could not seek control.

With capitalism on the other hand the possibility for conscious human participation in shaping the future of society is greatly increased. This means that the outcome of socio-political processes is not determined solely by natural relations but is shaped by conscious human intervention.

True, even in pre-capitalist modes of production, human intervention was crucial because nothing in history can happen without human practice. But it was not a fully conscious human practice in that human beings were unable to understand the real causes of their actions and set themselves goals which could not be achieved. Hence the peasant revolutionary opposition to feudalism in Germany was expressed as, and took the shape of the Christian millenarist heresy of Munzer.[67] Of course it has always been true that human practice frequently produces results which were not envisaged at the beginning and that there are unintended consequences of human actions. This is also true today, but there is a difference: the economy has become an autonomous instance of society and its determining influence can be theoretically and politically ascertained. Hence many contemporary conflicts can be fought over the real issues instead of being perceived as religious differences.

Schmidt has argued that the subject–object relationship has changed in history with varying degrees of relative weight being given to the participation of subject and object: 'under pre-industrial conditions the objective, natural moment is dominant, whilst in industrial society the moment of subjective intervention asserts itself in increasing measure over the material provided by nature.[68] At the beginning the subject's participation is minimal *vis-à-vis* the importance of objective conditions. But this equation changes with capitalism and the subject's participation increases more and more. This does not deny that in any case the subject's participation is conditioned by objective circumstances so that only some options are open for action. Still it is true that within certain material parameters the choices for action have increased and are likely to continue to do so. As the scope of human conscious intervention in history grows, history itself loses its former natural course and can advance in many optional directions to be determined by human practice. So one of the most important principles discovered by historical materialism affirms the impossibility for natural-like relations or 'laws' to govern history after the emergence of capitalism. Still, the ambiguous results of the capitalist mode of production, its immense capacity to produce wealth and simultaneously to engender poverty, its ability to expand the productive forces and to create contradictions not only within one country but also on a world-wide scale, do condition the courses of action open for human beings.

Two important corollaries follow from this analysis. First, even when the appropriate conditions are present, the socialist revolution is not an inevitable historical occurrence but a task for human beings to carry out, a task in which they may fail. Second, the appropriate conditions for a socialist revolution are not bound to occur first in the most advanced capitalist countries. For a long time Marx and Engels believed that a revolution was more likely in Western Europe, because, as it is expressed in the 1859 Preface, 'no social order ever perishes before all the productive forces for which there is room in it have developed.'[69] This is the reason why Marx was still able to write in 1870 that 'England, the metropolis of capital, . . . is at present the most important country for the workers' revolution, and moreover the *only* country in which the material conditions for this revolution have reached a certain degree of maturity.'[70] Yet a few years later, he altered this view. With the occasion of the outbreak of the Russo–Turkish war, Marx was convinced that a revolution was imminent in Russia and he said that 'this time the revolution begins in the East, hitherto the unbroken bulwark and reserve army of counter-revolution.'[71] Similarly, the drafts of Marx's letter to Zasulich and a preface to the Russian edition of the *Communist Manifesto* show that he thought it was possible for a revolution to occur in Russia which would allow the peasant commune to become the regenerating element of society.[72]

H. Wada[73] has conclusively shown that this change of mind was to a great extent due to the profound impression which Chernyshevsky's thought made on Marx, especially the idea that

> when certain social phenomena in a certain nation reach an advanced stage of development, the evolution of phenomena up to this same stage in other backward nations can be achieved much faster than in the advanced nation . . . This acceleration consists of the fact that the development of certain social phenomena in backward nations, thanks to the influences of the advanced nation, skips an intermediary stage and jumps directly from a low stage to a higher stage.[74]

Löwy has characterized this tension in Marx's writings as the opposition between a 'stagist conception' of revolution which maintains that bourgeois revolution and industrial capitalism are the necessary historical pre-conditions of proletarian revolution and a theory of 'permanent revolution' which conceives of an uninterrupted revolutionary process enabling the proletariat to overturn capitalism in the peripheral and backward areas without the need for a prior completed bourgeois revolution.[75] Löwy seems to be unaware of the fact that these poles share a common element: the presupposition about the inevitability of revolution. Both 'stagism' and 'permanent revolution' start with the assumption of the inevitability of a proletarian revolution everywhere. They only differ about the way in which this is supposed to happen. For the stagist perspective, history evolves in a mechanical and unilinear fashion everywhere. For the permanent revolution perspective, history evolves 'through innumerable combinations, fusions, discontinuities, ruptures and sudden, qualitative leaps.'[76] Yet in both cases there seems to be no doubt as to the final result of the historical 'logic', which appears to be preordained.

The conception of a permanent revolution constitutes only a variant of the orthodox 'deterministic' approach to historical materialism which takes very little account of the autonomy of political practice and hence the possibility that socialism may fail to be established. True, Löwy does appear to distance himself from determinism in a couple of places. First, he speaks of 'autonomous political factors' and of history not being 'preordained' by the economic structure.[77] Second, he refuses 'to consider world revolution as a demiurge of the historical process irresistibly asserting itself in every corner of the globe'.[78] However, the first argument seems to be exercised mainly against a conception in which economic structure prevents socialist revolution from occurring in a backward country rather than considering the possibility of such revolution not occurring at all. The idea of permanent revolution expects revolution everywhere, starting with the backward areas. The autonomy of political factors is then only an autonomy 'for revolution' or, as Löwy puts it, 'the international extension of the revolutionary process and the construction of socialism on a world scale'.[79] As for the second argument, it is belied by the general thrust of the book. How can one reconcile his statement about world revolution not being a demiurge of history with this other statement to be found a page before?: 'world revolution has unfolded during the twentieth century through an uneven and combined process.'[80] It is as if 'world revolution' were a subject or force unfolding or expressing itself, like the Hegelian idea, in particular countries at particular times.

The same problem can be illustrated by considering the so-called 'law of uneven and combined development' which seems to me to suffer from the same difficulties as Engels's general laws of dialectic: abstraction and ahistoricity. With this 'law' Trotskyists derive the specific and particular from the general. Thus for instance Löwy argues that in backward countries 'the articulation of modern industry with traditional (pre-capitalist or semi-capitalist) rural conditions' is a consequence of the law of uneven and combined development, and that this is 'the structural foundation for the fusion or combination of democratic and socialist tasks in a process of permanent revolution'.[81] All this can easily lead to substituting general principles for the specificity of historical analysis. The articulation of modes of production or the fusion of democratic and socialist tasks should not be arrived at by the application of a general law but by the concrete historical analysis of specific cases. Löwy's analysis of the four major revolutions of the twentieth century after 1917 is obsessed with making them fit into a 'permanentist' scheme. Thus China, Cuba, Yugoslavia and Vietnam are shown as 'proofs' of Trotsky's permanent revolution theory. There may well be some interesting similarities. But the analysis of these revolutionary processes suffers because of the unilateral insistence on showing how they fit the preordained Trotskyist idea of permanent revolution.

In conclusion, the tension in Marx's writings cannot be described in terms of 'stagism' versus 'permanentism' but is rather the opposition between, on the one hand, a unilinear and universal conception of history which inexorably leads to a preordained end, and, on the other, a conception which is based on human practice and which rejects the interpretation of history as 'a metaphysical subject of which the real human individuals are merely the bearers'.[82] This tension must be resolved in favour of a conception which underlines the increasing scope of human practice and rejects the idea of an immanent drive which leads history towards an inevitable end. But such a conception must take into account the fact that the further back in history one goes, the more important 'natural relations' and 'objective conditions' become. It is only in societies where capital becomes the decisive factor that the social, practical and subjective elements can predominate. Hence, for Marx, capitalism introduced a qualitative change in history. In fact the very concept of development is born out of this crucial change.

THE SCOPE OF MARX'S THEORY OF DEVELOPMENT

The question arises as to whether Marx's concept of development can be simply equated with historical materialism. Two objections can be made to this equation. On the one hand, it may seem too reductionist in so far as historical materialism purports to be much more than a theory of economic development, a general theory of history. On the other hand, the equation may seem anachronistic, inasmuch as any contemporary theory of development seems to entail a necessary reference to formally independent 'backward', 'underdeveloped' or 'less developed' capitalist countries which are economically dependent on more developed ones, a conception hardly in existence in the nineteenth century. True, Marx briefly refers to slave, Asiatic and feudal societies as pre-capitalist social formations which are economically stagnant and dominated either by a landowning aristocracy or by a centralized state bureaucracy. But of course one must not identify a pre-capitalist or 'traditional' society with a capitalist 'underdeveloped society', a mistake so often committed by the theories of modernization.[83]

However, this reference to 'underdeveloped' societies (as different from pre-capitalist societies) is not of itself an essential part of all theory of development. As I argued in the introduction, the very notion of development arose in conjunction with the emergence of capitalism two centuries ago, whereas the idea that certain regions or countries 'underdevelop' by comparison to others is far more recent and corresponds to the new historical circumstances emerging with the process of decolonization after the second world war. Understandably, the early theories of development could not conceive of 'underdevelopment' in the contemporary sense and sought to study pre-capitalist social formations in the context of and as a prelude to the necessary advance of capitalism. On the contrary, post-war theories of development only know of basically capitalist countries, some of which are less developed and dependent. This is another example of the operation of the principle–stated by historical materialism – that theories of development keep pace with the evolution of social relations and conflicts. Hence, the lack of reference to 'underdevelopment' is not in principle an insurmountable objection against historical materialism being a theory of development, although it obviously poses some problems for such a theory if it is to explain new historical developments which it could not fully anticipate.

At the same time, it is true that to the extent that historical materialism is a general theory of history that seeks to construct the concepts necessary to render historical processes intelligible,[84] its scope is much larger than that of the typical theory of development. Yet historical materialism starts from a principle which is also at the centre of any theory of development, namely the fact that 'the first premise of all human history,'[85] what distinguishes human beings from animals, is the actual process whereby human beings practically produce their material conditions of life. In other words, the process of material *production* which is at the basis of any theory of economic development is also crucial for understanding history. In this sense historical materialism is both a general theory of history and a theory of development in a more narrow sense. In so far as it is a general theory of history, historical materialism seeks to understand the basic elements which explain the operation and evolution of different modes of production throughout history as the key to account for significant historical changes in concrete social formations. In so far as it is a theory of development in a more restricted sense, historical materialism concentrates on the analysis of the capitalist mode of production, the first mode of production in history which is capable of producing a sustained and systematic development of productive forces. The latter is the focus of my present analysis.

Marx's concept of development

For Marx, development in the restricted sense of capitalist creation of wealth can be described in a twofold manner. In its material content, development is about the expansion of productive forces and the increased production of commodities. In its form, development is about the accumulation of capital, that is to say, the drive of capital both to appropriate the surplus-value produced by labour and embodied in the commodities and to realize it by selling the commodities in the market, thus allowing the process to be repeated on a wider scale. This process of expansive accumulation Marx synthesized in the following formula:

$$M \longrightarrow C \overset{\overset{\displaystyle LP}{\diagup}}{\underset{\underset{\displaystyle MP}{\diagdown}}{}} \longrightarrow P \longrightarrow C' \longrightarrow M'$$

With money M the capitalist buys two kinds of commodities C in the market, labour-power LP and other means of production MP, which he or she combines and puts to work in the production process P in order to produce commodities C' which possess more value than those he or she bought in the market and which he or she now sells in the market for more money M' than the amount originally invested, and which he or she must re-invest again in order to get even more money. This is the process of capital accumulation which is entirely dependent on the fact that 'the value of labour-power, and the value which that labour-power creates, are two entirely different magnitudes; and this difference of the two values was what the capitalist had in view, when he was purchasing the labour-power.'[86]

To increase accumulation is therefore to extract more surplus-value. Given the physical limitations to prolonging the working day (absolute surplus-value), capitalists must try to reduce the value of labour-power (relative surplus-value) by increasing the productivity of labour by means of new technology and improved methods of production. There is 'immanent in capital an inclination and constant tendency, to heighten the productiveness of labour, in order to cheapen commodities, and by such cheapening to cheapen the labourer itself'.[87] This is the reason why the process of development can be described simultaneously as increased capital accumulation and as continuous growth of productive forces and of commodity production. The latter is the condition for the former.

However, the development of productiveness does not only accelerates accumulation, it also brings about a tendency for the rate of profit to fall as a result of the higher composition of capital, which is, in its turn, a necessary consequence of the falling relation of variable capital (surplus-value) and rising relation of constant capital to total capital advanced. In other words, because the technological development needed to increase relative surplus-value means that capital contains an increasingly larger portion of means of production and a progressively smaller portion of living labour, surplus-value tends to decline as compared to the value of the total capital advanced. The effect of this is that whereas the mass of capital increases, the rate of profit falls and existing capital is depreciated. Furthermore, the increased mass of capital tends to concentrate as the minimum capital required to employ labour productively rises, and the competition between capitalists grows. All this may eventually lead to a crisis of over-production of means of production and increased stocks which cannot be sold. Surplus-value cannot be realized and this results in bankruptcies and unemployment. Part of the capital is then destroyed or withdrawn, thus allowing the stronger capitalists who survived the crisis to recover their value.[88]

In this way Marx shows that the two aspects which define capitalist development end up contradicting one another:

> The contradiction, to put it in a very general way, consists in that the capitalist mode of production involves a tendency towards absolute development of the productive forces, regardless of the value and surplus-value it contains, and regardless of the social conditions under which capitalist production takes place; while, on the other hand, its aim is to preserve the value of existing capital and promote its self-expansion to the highest limit . . .[89]

Whereas for Ricardo the main barrier to capitalism was the inherent limitation of the agricultural sector, that is to say, the rate of profit was adversely affected by the law of decreasing returns in agriculture, for Marx the contradiction is in the industrial sector itself. Nevertheless, side by side with the tendency of the rate of profit to fall, counteracting influences operate which cancel or lessen these negative effects. Marx mentions several mechanisms such as increasing the intensity of exploitation, depression of wages, etc. But the problem of the mechanisms which directly seek to raise the rate of surplus-value is the fierce working-class opposition to them. This is why, among the counteracting influences, foreign trade is of particular relevance because it avoids a direct confrontation with the working class. This explains the reason why capitalism necessarily seeks to expand everywhere in the world. First, foreign trade cheapens the production of commodities, both means of production and necessities of life, thus increasing the rate of surplus-value and cutting the value of constant capital: 'Since foreign trade partly cheapens the elements of constant capital, and partly the necessities of life for which the variable capital is exchanged, it tends to raise the rate of profit by increasing the rate of surplus-value . . .'[90] Ricardo had proclaimed the benefits of foreign trade mainly because cheaper food would lower the value of labour. Marx contends that foreign trade also lowers the value of constant capital:

> Ricardo misunderstands entirely the influence of foreign trade, when it does not directly lower the price of the labourers' food. He does not see how enormously important it is for England, for example, to secure cheaper raw materials for industry, and that in this case, as I have shown previously, the *rate of profit* rises *although prices fall*, whereas in the reverse case, *with rising prices*, the rate of profit can fall.[91]

As the rate of profit is equal to $s/c + v$ (where s = surplus-value; c = constant capital and v = variable capital) and raw materials are an important part of constant capital, then 'the rate of profit . . . falls and rises inversely to the price of raw material. This shows, among other things, how important the low price of raw material is for industrial countries.'[92]

Second, foreign trade permits an expansion of the scale of production and contributes to solving the problem of realizing surplus-value by satisfying 'the innate necessity of this mode of production, its need for an ever-expanding market.'[93] Furthermore, it allows excess capital to be invested in backward and colonial countries where the rate of profit is higher. Here lies the impulse behind the colonial expansion of those countries which first began to develop under the capitalist mode of production. As Marx puts it:

> A precondition of production based on capital is therefore *the production of a constantly widening sphere of circulation* . . . the tendency to create the *world market* is directly given in the concept of capital itself.[94]

> During its first stages of development, industrial capital seeks to secure a market and markets by force, by the *colonial system* (together with the prohibition system).[95]

> . . . the colonial system ripened, like a hot-house, trade and navigation . . . the colonies secured a market for the budding manufactures, and through the monopoly of the market, an increased accumulation.[96]

2

THE EXPANSION OF CAPITALISM: COLONIALISM AND IMPERIALISM

Marx's analysis of capitalist development establishes the crucial importance of the world market and consequently of foreign trade and colonialism in at least two main respects. On the one hand the early colonial expansion of European nations was essential for the process of 'primitive accumulation' which necessarily preceded capitalist production proper. Thus Marx contends that the discovery and conquest of America led to the massive importation of precious metals into Europe which facilitated the accumulation of capital necessary for the formation of manufacturing industry.[1] This far from enlightened process is forcefully described by Marx at the end of the first volume of *Capital* :

> The discovery of gold and silver in America, the extirpation, enslavement and entombment in mines of the aboriginal population, the beginning of the conquest and looting of the East Indies, the turning of Africa into a warren for the commercial hunting of black-skins, signalised the rosy dawn of the era of capitalist production. These idyllic proceedings are the chief momenta of primitive accumulation.[2]

On the other hand, as I have already shown, after 'real' capitalist relations have been established, the continued expansion of colonization becomes crucial for getting cheap raw materials, finding new markets for industrial commodities and counteracting the tendency for the rate of profit to fall. In 1858, on the verge of a new wave of colonial conquest which was to come about in the late nineteenth century and beginnings of the twentieth century, Marx believed that this expansion was in the main practically completed:

> The specific task of bourgeois society is the establishment of a world market, at least in outline, and the production based upon this world market. As the world is round, this seem to have been completed by the colonization of California and Australia and the opening up of China and Japan.[3]

Now, it is crucial to ascertain Marx's evaluation of the results and potentialities of this colonial expansion because it has important bearings on his concept of development. Many-well known authors in development studies find in Marx's work a single but consistently complex view which, while denouncing the greedy motives and cruel excesses of colonialism, justifies its historical necessity as the only means to liberate backward societies from their millennial stagnation and to initiate them in the path of capitalist industrialization and development. This interpretation of Marx's thought is normally based on some key texts on British colonialism most of which were written before the 1860s. Thus, for instance, the following classic formulations about the British rule in India state that

> England, it is true, in causing a social revolution in Hindustan was actuated only by the vilest interests, and was stupid in her manner of enforcing them. But that is not the question. The question is, can mankind fulfil its destiny without a fundamental revolution in the social state of Asia?[4]

> England has to fulfil a double mission in India: one destructive, the other regenerating – the annihilation of old Asiatic society, and the laying of the material foundations of Western society in Asia.[5]

> I know that the English millocracy intends to endow India with railways with the exclusive view of extracting at diminishing expenses the cotton and other raw materials for their manufacturers. But when you have once introduced machinery into the locomotion of a country which possesses iron and coals, you are unable to withhold it from its fabrication . . . The railway system will therefore become, in India, truly the forerunner of modern industry.[6]

On the one hand Marx castigates the misery and destruction, the arbitrariness and sufferings imposed on India by the East India Company. But on the other hand, he refuses to idealize the Indian autochthonous village life, which had been the basis of the poverty, cruelty, massacres and barbarism which characterized oriental despotism. Painful as the destruction of a patriarchal mode of life may be and vile as the British motives may be in bringing that destruction about, the process is still necessary as a pre-condition of the capitalist regeneration which will inevitably lead to India's industrialization. Even if it is true that the Indians 'will not reap the fruits of the new elements of society scattered among them by the British' until there is a proletarian revolution in Britain or the Hindus become independent, Marx is confident that 'at all events, we may safely expect to see, at a more or less remote period, the regeneration of that great and interesting country.'[7]

These ideas can be articulated with the aforementioned passages which support a deterministic and unilinear conception of history in that colonial domination would seem to be the way in which the country which is more developed industrially can show to the less developed the image of its own future. They could also be related to Marx's dislike of protectionism in so far as free trade helps to destroy the old modes of production which keep backward countries stagnant. Thus, for instance, in a letter to Engels, Marx argues that

Carey, . . . our ultra-free-trader finally recommends *protective tariffs.* In order to escape the effects of bourgeois industry, for which he makes England responsible, he resorts like a true Yankee to hastening this development in America itself by artificial means . . . The *Tribune* is of course hard at it trumpeting Carey's book . . . Your article on Switzerland was of course an indirect smack at the leading articles in the *Tribune*, . . . and *its Carey.* I have continued this hidden warfare in my first article on India in which the destruction of the native industry by England is described as *revolutionary.*[8]

Most development specialists who accept that these views are fully representative and typical of Marx's and Engels's thought are critical of their implications, particularly because they assume that capitalism would necessarily go on to industrialize the whole world after conquering backward nations and destroying their traditional structures. Sutcliffe, for instance, argues that the British destruction of the Indian indigenous textile industry allowed the expansion of the modern textile industry in Britain, 'but also, by this fact, the same thing became less possible in the future in India because it destroyed capital stock, thus weakening accumulation, and also deprived a possible Indian national industry of its market.[9] Similarly, Barrat Brown contends that although Marx was right in believing that capitalism would expand world-wide, he was mistaken in assuming that industrialization would happen everywhere apart from a few favoured lands of Europe.[10]

Samir Amin criticizes Marx's mistake about the future industrialization of India for similar reasons but also tries to explain why Marx committed it: he did not experience the new monopolistic phase of capitalism which would entail that 'monopolies would prevent any local capitalism that might arise from competing with them.'[11] From a more general perspective, Hinkelammert sees as the crucial limitation of Marx's conception the fact that it does not include the idea of a qualitative difference between development and underdevelopment and consequently tends to identify the latter with backwardness. This presupposes a conception of the world capitalist system as a homogeneous reality where the quantitative differences that exist are those which are due to nations being at different stages of the same necessary process.[12] An important exception to this critical trend is the work of Bill Warren, whose book, suggestively entitled *Imperialism, Pioneer of Capitalism*, extensively quotes from Marx's articles on India and strongly argues in favour of going back to the original Marxian idea that capitalism is an inherently industrializing force and that imperialism is the vehicle through which it can achieve its developing and civilizing mission in the backward regions.[13] However, whether critical or not, all these authors have one thing in common: they do not seem to see any major shift in Marx's position *vis-à-vis* colonialism throughout his intellectual evolution.

I maintain that this kind of interpretation of Marx's position fails to recognize significant changes in his approach to the colonial question and that, as Marx's understanding of the way in which capitalism expanded deepened, he altered his point of view in many respects. In this I side with authors like Davis, Mori and Scaron who distinguish some evolutionary stages in Marx's thought which are indicative of a progressive change of attitude. Scaron draws the most sophisticated outline by distinguishing four stages. The first stage goes from 1847 up to 1856 and is characterized by the moral repudiation of the excesses of colonialism, coupled with the theoretical justification of its mission. Simultaneously the idea is held that some peoples are outside history and can be swept aside by historical nations. The second period covers from 1856 to 1864 and constitutes a transitional phase where denunciation is stepped up without any change in the basic theory. The third and crucial stage spans from 1864 to 1883 where the Irish question comes to the fore and the theory seems to be fundamentally changed. Colonialism is now presented as a hindrance to the industrialization of the colonies, even in the case of

India. Still the existence of peoples or nations 'without history' continues to be upheld. The final stage goes from Marx's death in 1883 to Engels's death in 1895 and is characterized by the marked eurocentrism of Engels's final years.[14]

Davis and Mori propose simpler dichotomous outlines which locate a turning point somewhere around the 1860s under the influence of the Irish and Polish questions.[15] According to Mori, the thesis of the 'double mission' of colonialism is altered after 1860 when Marx realizes that the destructive and regenerating aspects of colonialism are not necessarily two inseparable aspects of the same process: the destruction of old societies by colonialism may not give rise to the material conditions for regeneration. Details apart, these three authors agree on the substantive thesis that there is a significant shift in Marx's assessment of the impact of colonialism in the so-called backward countries. A brief review of Marx's and Engels's writings shows that their interpretation, although insufficient, is basically correct.

In effect, while in 1853 Marx argued that the railway system would necessarily lead to the industrialization of India, in 1879 his assessment of the impact of railways on backward countries is far less enthusiastic:

> the railway system . . . allowed, and even forced, states where capitalism was confined to a few summits of society, to suddenly create and enlarge their capitalistic *superstructure* in dimensions altogether disproportionate to the bulk of the social body, carrying on the great work of production in the traditional modes . . . the railways gave of course an immense impulse to the development of Foreign Commerce, but the commerce in countries which export principally *raw produce* increased the misery of the masses . . . All the changes were very useful indeed for the great landed proprietor, the usurer, the merchant, the railways, the bankers and so forth, but very dismal for the real producer![16]

Marx had argued in 1853 that in spite of the abominable features of the zemindari and the ryotwari systems forcibly introduced by the British in India, they still were forms of private property, 'the great desideratum of Asiatic Society'.[17] In 1881, on the contrary, in the context of elaborating a reply to Vera Zasulich, he maintains that the abolition of the communal ownership of land in India 'was only an act of English vandalism which pushed the indigenous people not forward but backward'.[18] If in 1853 Marx had been totally opposed to protectionism and had castigated Carey for recommending protective tariffs to the United States, in 1867 Marx seems to advocate the opposite in the case of Ireland:

What the Irish need is 1) Self-government . . . 2) An agrarian revolution .
. . 3) *Protective tariffs against England.* Between 1783 and 1801 all
branches of Irish industry flourished. The Union, by abolishing the protective
tariffs established by the Irish Parliament, destroyed all industrial life in
Ireland . . . Once the Irish are independent, necessity will turn them into
protectionists, as it did Canada, Australia, etc.[19]

Marx's early optimistic vision that colonial capitalism, even against its
avowed intentions, could not but 'create the material basis of the new
world' and that 'bourgeois industry and commerce create these material
conditions of a new world in the same way as geological revolutions have
created the surface of the earth'[20] gives way to a more cautious approach
which is aware of the possibility that imperialist countries may succeed
in keeping colonies as mere rural and backward countries. As early as
1856 Engels maintains that 'how often have the Irish started out to
achieve something, and every time they have been crushed, politically
and industrially. By consistent oppression they have been artificially
converted into an utterly impoverished nation.'[21] Marx will reiterate this
point in 1867: 'every time Ireland was about to develop industrially, she
was crushed and reconverted into a purely agricultural land.'[22] The same
idea is extended to other European states which 'also forcibly rooted out,
in their dependent countries, all industry, as *e.g.* , England did with the
Irish woollen manufacture'.[23] When Marx in *Capital* clarifies at a more
general level the relationships between industrial and backward countries
within the world market he does not even mention the 'regenerating'
mission he had spoken about before. On the contrary, his description can
be said to anticipate in all but in name the idea of a division between
centre and periphery:

By ruining handicraft production in other countries, machinery forcibly
converts them into fields for the supply of its raw material. In this way East
India was compelled to produce cotton, wool, hemp, jute, and indigo for
Great Britain . . . foreign lands . . . are thereby converted into settlements
for growing the raw material of the mother country; just as Australia, for
example was converted into a colony for growing wool. A new and
international division of labour, a division suited to the requirements of the
chief centres of modern industry springs up, and converts one part of the
globe into a chiefly agricultural field of production, for supplying the other
part which remains a chiefly industrial field.[24]

By coupling the results of this new international division of labour to the operation of the law of value Marx is able to postulate the possibility of unequal exchange among nations and, more specifically, the exploitation of agricultural nations. In principle, because profit and surplus-value are not necessarily identical (profit could be less or more than surplus-value) it follows that individual capitalists as much as nations may trade with each other, even on an expanding scale, without necessarily gaining in equal degrees. This means that 'one of the nations may continually appropriate for itself a part of the surplus labour of the other.'[25] When this is the result of international differences in the technological base and the productivity of labour, Marx goes as far as treating this process of unequal exchange as a form of exploitation:

> The relationship between labour days of different countries may be similar to that existing between skilled, complex labour and unskilled, simple labour within a country. In this case the richer country exploits the poorer one, even where the latter gains by the exchange . . .[26]

Agricultural countries tend to be exploited in this way because in international exchange they are forced 'to sell their product below its value.' Whereas in respect of industrial goods the developed nation produces greater value than the backward nation despite the fact that individual commodities are cheaper, the contrary happens in respect of agricultural products where 'the product of the more backward nation is cheaper than that of the capitalistically developed nation . . . and yet the product of the developed nation appears to be produced by much less (annual) labour than that of the backward one.'[27] This analysis is the basis of the theories of unequal exchange which the Economic Commission for Latin America, and Marxist authors like Arghiri Emmanuel and Samir Amin were to propound after the second world war.

Marx's attitude in relation to national struggles also changes. In his early years he thinks that because in England the conflict between the bourgeoisie and the proletariat is most developed, the national struggles of other countries must be subordinated to, and can succeed only through, the English class struggle. Thus he affirms that Poland 'must be freed, not in Poland, but in England'[28] and that it is possible 'to overthrow the Irish regime by English working-class ascendancy'.[29] Marx even confesses that he used to think that Ireland's independence from England was impossible.[30] In 1869, on the contrary, he argues that 'the English working class will *never accomplish anything* until it has got rid of

Ireland. The lever must be applied in Ireland.'[31] As regards to Poland he also changes his position in 1875: it is no longer the English class struggle that can liberate Poland but Poland's independence that will allow it to work for social emancipation both internally and in Europe.[32]

Both Scaron and Mori suggest that these important shifts might amount to Marx's *de facto* discovery of, and approximation to the notion of 'underdevelopment' or 'development of underdevelopment'.[33] I do not think that such a conclusion is possible, simply because in the nineteenth century these concepts did not and could not arise in so far as the reality they alluded to did not exist. It is important to remember that the concept of underdevelopment was coined after the second world war in order to refer to countries which, within the capitalist mode of production, are dependent on, and lag systematically behind, the main industrial centres of the world. Marx, on the contrary, referred mainly to backward countries whose predominant modes of production were not capitalist. Hence Marx could not have arrived at the concept of underdevelopment. His change of attitude entails only a different assessment of colonialism in certain cases.

Marx in his maturity seems to accept the fact that colonialism, instead of being the vehicle for the successful spreading of capitalist industrialization, can delay it and therefore interrupt the process of capitalist development in the periphery. But he has little doubt that once the colonized countries get their independence, a combination of self-government, protective tariffs and agrarian reform can successfully accomplish development. He does not explain though why this programme, which Canada and Australia were forced by necessity to follow and which Ireland would surely be forced to adopt in the future, was not being pursued by the already independent Latin American nation-states. Nor does he conceive of the possibility that an independent country could fail to develop in spite of adopting such a programme. Two important problems arise in this respect. The first has to do with the way in which the native industry of a backward country is dismantled and the timing of the introduction of protective tariffs. The second concerns Marx's and Engels's attitude in relation to the so-called 'peoples without history' or countries which have not been 'thrown into the historical movement'.

INDUSTRIALIZATION, PROTECTIONISM AND BACKWARDNESS

According to Marx, when machinery is introduced in the process of English capitalist development it has in the first place an important internal effect: it destroys traditional handicrafts and more jobs than it creates; 'all political economists of any standing admit that the introduction of new machinery has a baneful effect on the workmen in the old handicraft and manufactures with which the machinery first competes.'[34] Painful as this process is in human terms ('history discloses no tragedy more horrible than the gradual extinction of the English hand-loom weavers'[35]), it is the necessary pre-condition for the creation of the new technological basis of capitalist accumulation and development. Manufacture alone, by introducing a more rational division of labour, improved the productivity but did not alter the technological basis of traditional industry. Real capitalist development starts with the introduction of machinery. But there is also an international effect of this process: 'the cheapness of the articles produced by machinery, and the improved means of transport and communication furnish the weapon for conquering foreign markets. By ruining handicraft production in other countries machinery forcibly converts them into fields for the supply of its raw materials.'[36] Thus Marx describes the terrible effects of the new English cotton machinery in India.

I have already shown how in his early approach Marx thought that this process of destruction of foreign handicrafts was painful but necessary for the development of backward countries because it would lay down the conditions for industrialization. When Marx later altered his views about colonialism, he recognized that colonial powers could artificially prevent the development of industrialization in their colonies, but he continued to think that the destruction of the old traditional industry was necessary for the capitalist industrialization of the colonies. What changes in Marx's perception is the agent which should carry out that destruction: no longer the British bourgeoisie through colonialism, but a national bourgeoisie which can create a modern industry. He saw how other European nations got rid of their own handicrafts and initiated their own processes of industrialization behind customs tariffs which protected them from the English competition. British colonies had no such option. This is the reason why Marx propounds self-government and protective tariffs, so that these backward nations could repeat what other European nations had achieved in the face of British industrial competition.

The history of the British cotton industry as outlined by Marx in *Capital* clearly illustrates this process. At the beginning the first industrial centre holds a monopoly. From 1770 to 1815, thanks to the new machinery, the British cotton industry was in a monopolistic position and therefore very prosperous. Soon other countries started their own policies of industrialization behind protective tariffs and the consequence for the British cotton industry from 1815 to 1863 was that competition from Europe and USA grew stiffer and the years of prosperity began to alternate with years of stagnation.[37] But in order for these countries to be able to compete with Britain they had to become protectionist so that the destruction of their own industrial handicrafts was carried out by their own national modern industry instead of the British modern industry. As Marx put it,

> The system of protection was an artificial means of manufacturing manufactures, of expropriating independent labourers, of capitalising the national means of production and subsistence, of forcibly abbreviating the transition from the medieval to the modern mode of production.[38]

However, if other European nations and USA were able to initiate their own processes of industrialization it was not only because of their protectionist policies, but also because they were technologically prepared to copy the British inventions. In fact the very British industrial inventions could come to exist only because they could be made with the traditional technology existing in handicrafts and manufactures. Marx describes how

> the inventions of Vaucanson, Arkwright, Watt, and others, were, however, practicable, only because those inventors found, ready to hand, a considerable number of skilled mechanical workmen, placed at their disposal by the manufacturing period. Some of these workmen were independent handicraftsmen of various trades, others were grouped together in manufactures . . .[39]

It is because the first machines were made with traditional technology that they were not so difficult to copy by other countries possessing handicrafts. But this situation of dependency of modern industry on manufacture does not last for too long because, as Marx points out, 'manufacture produced the machinery, by means of which Modern Industry abolished the handicraft and manufacturing systems.'[40] After attaining a certain degree of development, machinery rooted out its own technological foundation:

> at a certain stage of its development, Modern Industry became technologically incompatible with the basis furnished for it by handicraft and Manufacture . . . Such machines as the modern hydraulic press, the modern power-loom, and the modern carding engine, could never had been furnished by Manufacture . . . Modern Industry had therefore itself to take in hand the machine, its characteristic instrument of production, and to construct machines by machines. It was not until it did this, that it built up for itself a fitting technical foundation, and stood on its own feet.[41]

An important conclusion which one can draw from this account is that once modern industry becomes incompatible with and separated from traditional industry, that is to say, once most machines are made by other machines, it is no longer possible for a country possessing traditional industry simply to copy or produce modern machinery on its own. It has to import the machinery from an already industrialized country and to do so it has to be able to export enough raw materials in order to get the necessary international currency. This proved to be an important difficulty for the industrialization processes which started after the main industrial centres had already completed the transition to modern industry. Self-government and protectionism are therefore necessary but not sufficient conditions to initiate a process of industrialization. The timing of the industrialization process and of the introduction of protective tariffs is also crucial. Marx did not reflect on this problem, probably because until the 1880s the distance between the traditional and the modern means of production was still not unbridgeable in all spheres of production.

As Hinkelammert has argued, by the end of the nineteenth century and beginnings of the twentieth century the gap between traditional and modern means of production becomes so wide that

> from now on it is not enough to have technical knowledge and the will to produce new industrial products . . . Industrialization can no longer be the result of the effort of the non-industrialized countries themselves. The importation of technical knowledge does not suffice, it is also necessary to import the machinery required to use technical knowledge. All this means a revolution in the conditions of industrialization . . . There is now an external limit to the possible volume of industrial investment because the ability to import inevitably lags behind the needs of a rapid process of transformation of society in terms of modern technology.[42]

It can be argued that colonialism, by delaying and putting obstacles to the early development of a national industry in the colonies throughout the nineteenth century and up to the second world war, made the future industrialization of such colonies not only much more difficult but, above all, entirely dependent on the already industrialized nations. Marx did not realize that a temporary delay in starting the process of industrialization could become so important as to hinder its future development in certain areas. And yet his own distinction between traditional and modern industry could have allowed him to anticipate the problem. For those colonies which became independent in the twentieth century it was certainly not enough to introduce protectionist policies and agrarian reform in order to industrialize. But one can go even further. Marx's idea that once a former colony achieves self-government, protectionism and agrarian reform are natural policies of development imposed by necessity does not historically work, even for those countries which achieved independence at the beginning of the nineteenth century. A good case in point is Latin America, where most countries became independent by 1825, some of them with a good handicraft base, and yet their dominant agrarian oligarchies chose a policy of free trade which favoured the export of raw materials and import of British consumer goods, thus postponing national industrialization.

This shows again that the process of industrial development is not the inevitable result of easily available technological progress but ultimately depends on class structures and class struggles. True, the technological gap became an important hindrance to the industrial development of many countries trying to start the process in the twentieth century. But even when the technological gap was more easily bridgeable in the nineteenth century, the formally independent Latin American countries did not go for protectionism and industrialization. Yet Marx does not analyse at all why the policies he thinks would be absolutely necessary to an independent Ireland were not pursued in independent Latin America. Nor does he provide any class analysis which may justify the policies oriented to the export of raw materials established by the new republics. This requires an explanation. One cannot say in Marx's defence that he did not know enough or was not interested in Latin America. In fact he read and wrote quite a deal about Latin America. Why then did he not analyse its situation in the same terms as he analysed the United States, India and Ireland? Or did he?

Difficult to believe as it may seem to some people, it is a fact that Marx and Engels refer rather contemptuously to certain nationalities and countries. Thus the Mexicans are said to be 'lazy', the Montenegrins are labeled as 'cattle robbers', the Bedouins are branded as a 'nation of robbers', and there is a reference to the 'hereditary stupidity' of the Chinese.[43] It is no surprise therefore that they condone their forcible subjection for the sake of progress. Thus for Engels the conquest of Algeria by the French is 'an important and fortunate fact for the progress of civilization'. One can see that this approach has many disquieting points of contact with the perspectives and prejudices of the classical political economists.

A brief survey of the writings of Marx and Engels on Latin America immediately reveals the striking absence of any class analysis or any consideration of its possible industrial future. Latin America is not treated as a reality with its own specificity, worth investigating in itself. The bulk of the writings are scattered references used for comparative purposes in order to illustrate a point in texts concerned with other problems. A few more substantial pieces tend to be journalistic or biographical accounts for European or North American political consumption. Most of the time the context is rather negative in that it tends to portray the character of Latin Americans as inherently flawed and their political processes as lacking all rationality and historical direction. This is why Engels was pleased with the North American invasion of Mexico:

> In *America* we have witnessed the conquest of Mexico, which has pleased us. It constitutes progress too that a country until the present day exclusively occupied with itself, torn apart by perpetual civil wars and prevented from all development . . . that such a country be thrown by means of violence into the historical movement. It is in the interest of its own development that Mexico will be in the future under the tutelage of the United States.[44]

It is as if Mexico were outside history and its only chance to be incorporated into it would be through the agency of the 'energetic' North Americans, a historical nation with a mission to accomplish in the rest of America. For Engels, it is rather fortunate that

> magnificent California was snatched from the lazy Mexicans, who did not know what to do with it . . . The 'independence' of a few Spanish

Californians and Texans may suffer by this, 'justice' and other moral principles may be infringed here and there; but what does that matter against such world-historical events?[45]

Even when years later Marx and Engels strongly oppose the joint intervention of England, France and Spain in Mexico as 'one of the most monstrous enterprises ever registered in the annals of international history',[46] their main concern is politically to condemn the policies of Palmerston because they suspect that such an adventure, while the North American civil war is taking place, is only a pretext to attack the United States. The fate of Mexico itself seems to be a secondary consideration, although they do say that it may slip back into anarchy. Much as Marx and Engels despise Napoleon III and celebrate the Mexican victory over general Lorencez in May 1862, they still cannot refrain from referring to the victorious Mexicans as 'les derniers des hommes'.[47] Marx's biography of Bolívar, the Venezuelan hero of Latin American independence, written for The New American Cyclopaedia in 1858, depicts him as cowardly, brutal and miserable.[48] This kind of abuse, which is excessive although it has more basis than Latin American historians normally recognize, is not in itself so regrettable as the fact that the Latin American independence process is reduced, by default, to a story of personal betrayal, envy and cowardice without any mention or analysis of the social forces which operate behind the process.

The general thrust of Marx and Engels's writings on this subject inevitably reminds one of Hegel's description of South America as 'physically and psychically powerless', inhabited by individuals whose 'inferiority' 'in all respects, even in regard to size, is very manifest' who 'live like children who limit themselves to exist, far away from all that means elevated thoughts and goals', in sum, a world outside 'the true theatre of History', where 'what has taken place is only an echo of the Old World – the expression of a foreign Life.'[49] In more general terms, Marx and Engels seem implicitly to be resorting to Hegel's notion of peoples 'without history' as an adequate category to understand Latin America. In effect, Hegel had distinguished between world-historical peoples, those capable of building a state and of contributing to the progress of world history, and peoples without history, those unable to build a strong state and with no civilizing mission to carry out in history. The latter had to submit to the former. Marx and Engels used this distinction and in particular the notion of 'peoples without history' or 'counter-revolutionary nations' to refer to certain small nations of central

Europe which stood in the way of progress and which could be rightly swept aside for the sake of the proletariat of historical nations. Thus for instance Engels referred to the Slavs who

> lack the primary historical, geographical, political and industrial condition for a viable independence. Peoples which have never had a history of their own, which come under foreign domination the moment they have achieved the first, crudest level of civilization, or are *forced onto* the first level of civilization by the yoke of the foreigner, have no capacity for survival and will never be able to attain any kind of independence.[50]

That Marx and Engels were thinking of Latin American nations in the same vein, is more than an implicit conclusion inferred from the general drift of their writings. Engels specifically applies such criteria in the aforementioned quotations about the conquest of Mexico and California, where he maintains that it is in the interest of all America, and of the development of Mexico itself, that the United States should gain predominance over the Pacific Ocean, and that in the face of such world-historical events it does not matter whether 'justice' and 'moral principles' may be infringed. Marx and Engels explicitly assimilate the situation of the Spanish *criollos* in the territory occupied by the United States to the situation of Slav peoples:

> thus were finished, for now and very probably for ever, the tentatives by the German Slavs to recover an independent national existence. Dispersed relics of many nations whose nationality and political vitality were exhausted long ago, which because of that had been forced, for almost a millenium, to follow in the tracks of a more powerful nation that had conquered them – just as the Welsh in England, the Basque in Spain, the low-Bretons in France and, more recently, the Spanish and French creoles in parts of the United States occupied by the Angloamerican race.[51]

Marx and Engels doubted the Latin American countries' ability to become historical nations not so much because they wanted to deny such a possibility in principle but because they did not detect it in practice. If Marx's account of the events in which Bolívar participated is taken as representative of his vision of Latin America, then it is clear that he regarded most processes and struggles in Latin America not as the necessary subject of a class analysis but as somewhat arbitrary and irrational occurrences, at best forms of Bonapartism supported by the absence of a clear class project. As Aricó has suggested, for Marx Latin America seem to have been

> a puzzling collection of extremely weak states, governed by restricted oligarchies lacking in national spirit, or by *caudillos*, usually from the military, unable to prevent territorial fragmentation and secure the presence of a national power except by means of ferocious dictatorships, almost always ephemeral; weak countries subject to economic domination by and political subordination to capitalist imperialism. National formations seemed to him mere state constructions erected upon an institutional vacuum and the absence of a popular will, unable to constitute themselves because of the jelly-like quality of their social fabric.[52]

On the other hand, it is not that Marx and Engels conceived of a rigid classification of nations and of their perspectives for independence that was given once and for all. Their concern with the fate of certain nations was always political and related to the advance of socialism. Their analysis of the rights of peoples and nations was always carried out from the point of view of whether they were in accordance or contradiction with the interests of social progress. As Haupt and Weill have argued, for Marx and Engels 'the national state is not an objective in itself, nor is it a supreme value, just as the right that nations have to manage themselves is not an absolute principle. They are all variables subordinated to a constant: the interest of the working class and of the socialist revolution.[53] This is compounded by what Rosdolsky has called 'an error of rhythm', that is to say, the belief of Marx and Engels that the collapse of capitalism is imminent and that therefore the socialist revolution has to be considered as the immediate practical task of their time.[54] All other considerations must be subordinated to the requirements of such a task. Thus more developed nations must prevail over backward nations inasmuch as that promotes the advance of socialism in the world.

If in the case of Ireland they take the opposite view, it is not only because they see important differences between the Irish and the Latin American nations themselves, but also because they see these countries playing different roles in relation to the prospects of revolution. Whereas in the case of Mexico they see its submission as crucial for the strengthening of the American capitalism and hence for the development of the proletariat in that area, in the case of Ireland they see its independence as crucial for the development of the English proletariat:

England, the metropolis of capital, the power which has up to now ruled the world market, is at present the most important country for the workers' revolution; and moreover it is the *only* country in which the material conditions for this revolution have reached a certain degree of maturity. It is consequently the most important object of the International Working Men's Association to hasten the social revolution in England. The sole means of hastening it is to make Ireland independent . . . the *national emancipation of Ireland* is not a question of abstract justice or humanitarian sentiment but *the first condition of their own social emancipation.*[55]

Marx's change of heart in respect of colonialism must therefore be qualified in that it does not necessarily mean that all former colonies have the chance to constitute themselves as viable and developing nations. Marx recognizes that colonialism may become an obstacle to the development and industrialization of colonies, but on the other hand he continues to accept the possibility that, even after independence, some small countries may not have the ability to sustain a national project that makes industrialization feasible and for that reason they may be rightly subordinated to the needs and wishes of historical nations. Marx does not blame other, more subtle forms of imperialism (neo-colonialism) for this situation, but rather identifies the lack of a popular will and of a strong civil society as the causes which put these nations outside history. Moreover, self-government and independence are not for Marx absolute principles, the inalienable rights of all peoples, but on the contrary, they must be subordinated to the needs of the struggle for socialism.

Ultimately, one must recognize that in important respects Marx and Engels share in a common eurocentric mentality typical of the nineteenth century. In general this perspective entails the belief that the progress brought about by the new humanistic and scientific rationality in capitalist Western Europe is inherently superior and must finally prevail in the world against opposing forces. The process can be synthesized in the antagonism between historical reason and backwardness. This basic orientation, although with many differences and nuances, is present in classical political economy, Hegel and the founding fathers of Marxism. Reason is, of course, incarnated in different historical subjects. For Hegel it is the Spirit as it manifests itself through the primacy of historical nations, for classical political economy it is the bourgeoisie as the representative of the industrial capitalist nations, for Marx and Engels it is the proletariat of the most advanced capitalist nations as the agent of the socialist transformation. Backward countries or nations have of course the prospect of development and progress, but only through the agency of, following the path of, and in so far as they do not interfere with the main European historical agents and their needs. In spite of many differences, there is a remarkable consistency in the way in which Marx and Engels, Hegel and classical political economists deal with backward societies.

THE CLASSICAL THEORY OF IMPERIALISM

In many ways Marx anticipated the main trends and features which were to characterize the age of imperialism. The concentration and centralization of capital, the creation of monopolies, the export of capital, the process of colonization and the constitution of a world market were all tendencies already at work during Marx's time and he was probably the first political economist who in his writings rigorously sought to identify and explain their logic. But obviously he did not witness the operation of these factors in their maturity nor could he see the full impact of their combined effects on the development of capitalism. The aggressive expansion of finance capital, the acceleration of the process of monopolization and the surge of imperialist annexationism brought with them new contradictions and tensions, both at the national and international levels, which required specific treatment. These were the problems at the centre of the new theories of imperialism which emerged in the first two decades of the twentieth century.

The main landmarks in the construction of the classical theory of imperialism are the works of Hobson (1902), Hilferding (1910), Luxemburg (1913 and 1915), Bukharin (1915 and 1924) and Lenin (1916).[56] Although Hobson is the only non-Marxist author of the group, his early work exercised quite a degree of influence on the others, especially on Lenin. Despite the various distinctions that one could draw among these authors, they all share many common elements which are of sufficient importance to allow one to include them together in the classical theory of imperialism. Because these theories are fairly well known and many books exist which provide systematic accounts of each of them,[57] I shall not deal with them independently but shall concentrate on a general discussion of their most salient common features and differences.

Characteristics of imperialism

Classical theory describes imperialism as a complex political, economic and ideological phenomenon. Lenin gives pride of place to its economic aspect in describing it as 'the highest stage of capitalism' where cartels and monopolies, including banks, have become 'one of the foundations of the whole of economic life'.[58] Yet he is quite aware of its political and ideological impact. In fact this is likely to be the only reason why he decided to deal with a subject which had already been extensively treated by Hilferding, Hobson and Bukharin, whose contributions he summarizes and acknowledges. His intention is to attack Kautsky, but more generally, in the wake of the collapse of the Second International, he wants to explain how it is possible that sections of the European proletariat had allowed themselves to be led by leaders who had been bought off by the bourgeoisie and how 'the imperialist ideology also penetrates the working class.'[59] His answer is that

> Imperialism, which means the partition of the world, and the exploitation of other countries besides China, which means high monopoly profits for a handful of very rich countries, creates the economic possibility of bribing the upper strata of the proletariat, and thereby fosters, gives form to, and strengthens opportunism.[60]

In summarizing the theories of Hobson, Hilferding and Bukharin, Lenin gives five basic features to imperialism. First the concentration of capital; second the emergence of finance capital, namely the merging of industrial and bank capital. Third, the export of capital; fourth the emergence of international monopolies, and fifth, the territorial division of the whole world.[61]

Hobson was the first to mention the process of concentration of capital and the creation of trusts and combines in connection with imperialism. But it was Hilferding who developed the idea within a Marxist framework by arguing that this was a new model which represented the situation of Germany and the United States rather than the situation of Great Britain. The British bourgeoisie was for free trade and for curbing the mercantilist policies of the state. In the European continent and America, on the contrary, the struggle against the predominance of British industry in the world led the bourgeoisie to accept an interventionist state and the erection of protective tariffs. It was the exclusion of foreign, especially British, competition and the lack of accumulated capital in the hands of individuals that led to the emergence of cartels and the importance of banks. The unification of industrial, commercial and bank capital, the process of concentration and centralization of capital under the direction of high finance is what he called 'finance capital'.[62] As the protective tariffs propounded by finance capital have a harmful effect on the rate of profit, the need arises to acquire new economic territories to which to export capital. This leads to the political conquest and division of the world.

Thus an imperialist ideology of a belligerent and racist nature arises which is opposed to the liberal ideology of early capitalism:

> The demand for an expansionist policy revolutionizes the whole world view of the bourgeoisie, which ceases to be peace-loving and humanitarian . . . It has no faith in the harmony of capitalist interests, and knows well that competition is becoming increasingly a political power struggle . . . The ideal now is to secure for one's own nation the domination of the world . . . Since the subjection of foreign nations takes place by force . . . it appears to the ruling nation that this domination is due to some special natural qualities, in short to its racial characteristics.[63]

The ideological and political aspects of imperialism are also highlighted by Bukharin and Luxemburg. The former argues that imperialism is mainly the policy of conquest of finance capital but that one can also speak of imperialism as an ideology.[64] The latter conceives of imperialism as an eminently political phenomenon, namely, the struggle for non-capitalist territories which is the necessary expression of the accumulation of capital.[65]

The causes of imperialism: underconsumptionism versus superprofits

In so far as the analysis of the major driving forces behind imperialism is concerned, it is possible to distinguish at least two broad lines of approach among these authors. On the one hand, Luxemburg concedes some importance to the search for cheap raw materials and labour-power but she clearly emphasizes as the main cause the inevitable capitalist over-production of commodities which cannot be sold in the metropolitan internal markets and which leads to the necessary search for new world markets to realize the surplus-value embodied in them. What is not often appreciated is that Luxemburg does not refer to an expansion to just any foreign market, for instance, other capitalist markets. Her definition of imperialism is more restricted than that: 'Imperialism is the political expression of the accumulation of capital in its competitive struggle for what remains still open of the *non-capitalist environment.*'[66]

Arguing against Struve, who thought that countries with vast territories and large populations did not need foreign markets, she maintains that 'capitalist production is by nature production on a universal scale . . . it is producing for a world market already from the word *go.*'[67] So the inevitable contradiction between the production of surplus-value and its realization, which according to Luxemburg Marx did not fully consider,[68] already takes into account, and develops within, the whole of the capitalist world market. Hence, in order to realize surplus-value, capitalism must sell its commodities to peoples and strata whose mode of production is pre-capitalist.[69] This is why the very possibility of capitalist accumulation is tied up with the existence and slow disappearance of non capitalist modes of production: 'Historically, the accumulation of capital is a kind of metabolism between capitalist economy and those pre-capitalist methods of production without which it cannot go on and which, in this light, it corrodes and assimilates.'[70]

On the relation between capitalism and its non-capitalist periphery, Luxemburg criticises Marx because the model of reproduction presented in *Capital* volume 2 assumes that the whole world is capitalist and hence imperialism cannot be explained:

> However one defines the inner economic mechanisms of imperialism, one thing is obvious and common knowledge: the expansion of the rule of capital from the old capitalist countries to new areas. . . But Marx assumes, as we have seen in the second volume of *Capital* , that the whole world is one capitalist nation, that all other forms of economy and society have already disappeared. How can one explain imperialism in a society where there is no longer any space for it?[71]

For Luxemburg therefore, imperialism is not just any kind of expansion to foreign countries and their markets. By definition imperialism makes a reference to pre-capitalist economies. This means that in a wholly capitalist world there cannot be imperialism. But it means also that the end of pre-capitalist economies and consequently of imperialist expansion signals the end of capitalism itself: surplus-value can no longer be realized, the accumulation of capital ceases, productive forces cannot advance and hence the capitalist economy collapses.

On the other hand, the rest of the authors mentioned above recognize the importance of getting cheap raw materials too, but tend to emphasize, as the primary motor force of imperial expansion, the monopolistic search for superprofits and/or the need to counteract the trend for the rate of profit to fall. Hobson is already aware that the new imperial expansion occurring at the end of the nineteenth century to mainly tropical and highly populated areas of the world is of a totally different nature from the earlier colonization of temperate and sparsely populated zones by white European settlers (United States, Australia, Canada, New Zealand). The new colonies are not given civil liberties and the political right to self-government and trade with them is poor.[72] Hobson argues that the bulk of the foreign trade of industrial nations is with other industrial nations and that the supposed inevitability of the imperialistic expansion as a necessary outlet for industrial goods is a fallacy. Were it not for the maldistribution of income and over-saving of profits, imperialist countries could absorb all the commodities they produced. The search for areas where capital can be exported and indeed the struggle among imperialist nations for profitable markets of investment is a reality, but not a necessary one.[73]

Explicitly arguing against Luxemburg, Bukharin recognizes that capitalist accumulation is inextricably linked to the non-capitalist world, but this does not mean that Marx got it wrong in *Capital* volume 2 simply because he abstracted from the non-capitalist world. Capitalist accumulation is possible in a hypothetically isolated and purely capitalist society although such a capitalist society has never existed. The real cause of capitalist expansion is not so much a constant over-production as the possibility of acquiring greater profits.[74] To support this view he quotes a passage from *Capital* where Marx says that 'if capital is sent abroad, this is not done because it absolutely could not be applied at home, but because it can be employed at a higher rate of profit in a foreign country.'[75] Furthermore, he disagrees with Luxemburg's restricted concept of imperialism because it leads to the belief that a fight for territories which have already changed to capitalism is not imperialism.[76]

For Hilferding the impulse behind the imperialistic expansion and division of the world is the export of capital. The export of capital is crucial to monopolistic capitalism as a way of canceling out the effects of the falling rate of profit and, at times, as a way for monopolies and cartels to get extra-profits.[77] As Hilferding puts it,

Export capital feels most comfortable, however, when its own state is in complete control of the new territory, for capital exports from other countries are then excluded, it enjoys a privileged position, and its profits are more or less guaranteed by the state. Thus the export of capital also encourages an imperialist policy.[78]

But this drive to control new territories necessarily leads to increasing competition and conflicts between the European states. Hilferding quite correctly anticipates the war between England and Germany.[79] But more generally, he notices that monopoly capitalism brings about a change in the relations between the bourgeoisie and the state. Hobson had already hinted at it when he argued that imperialism entailed the use of the state by private interests in order to secure for them superprofits abroad.[80] Hilferding develops this point more theoretically within Marxism. Before the emergence of finance capital the bourgeoisie had been opposed to state power, and liberal ideology had wanted to exclude the economy from the sphere of state intervention. On the contrary, finance capital makes use of the power of the state to eliminate the competition and gain a privileged position in the world markets. The ideology of imperialism is completely opposed to liberalism:

> Finance capital does not want freedom, but domination; it has no regard for the independence of the individual capitalist, but it demands its allegiance. It detests the anarchy of competition and wants organization ... But in order to achieve these ends ... it needs the state which can guarantee its domestic market through a protective tariff policy and facilitate the conquest of foreign markets.[81]

Lenin does not add anything substantial to this issue which had not already been advanced by Hobson, Bukharin or Hilferding. His work summarizes all their views. The motor force of the imperialist expansion is the search for increased profits which monopolistic firms achieve by exporting capital abroad. In the so-called 'backward' countries, which are the recipients of export capital, 'profits are usually high, for capital is scarce, the price of land is relatively low, wages are low, raw materials are cheap ... The necessity for exporting capital arises from the fact that in a few countries capitalism has become "overripe" and ... capital cannot find a field for "profitable" investment.'[82] Brewer has argued that there may be underconsumptionist overtones in Lenin's position which are due to the influence of Hobson.[83] Indeed Lenin argues that if the standard of living of the masses were to be improved and agriculture were to be developed there could not be a superabundance of capital. And he revealingly adds, 'if capitalism did these things it would not be capitalism.'[84] This might indicate that, unlike Hobson, Lenin believes that low wages are a fundamental premise of capitalism and that the ensuing lack of demand is a necessary impulse to imperialist expansion. However, the problem is not so simple because Lenin also thinks that improving salaries would mean a decline in profits. Capitalists, therefore, in any case would prefer to export capital abroad in order to expand their profits.

The consequences of imperialism for central economies

Apart from Hilferding, most of the classical theorists of imperialism conceive of this new phase as tendentially leading to the collapse of capitalism or, at least, to a dangerous corruption of its operation. Even Hobson, who is no Marxist, derives from his analysis the conclusion that imperialist nations live increasingly on 'tribute from abroad', as 'parasites':

> This is the largest, plainest instance history presents of the social parasitic process by which a moneyed interest within the State, usurping the reins of government, makes for imperial expansion in order to fasten economic suckers into foreign bodies so as to drain them of their wealth in order to support domestic luxury.[85]

The effect of parasitism is that crucial industries and agricultural activities tend to disappear from Europe. Lenin was quite influenced by this idea and elaborated it to try to show that capitalism had entered into a stage where the tendency to stagnation and decay had become established. The monopolization of the economy led to economic stagnation and the possibility of retarding technical progress. European countries lived like 'rentiers' exploiting the labour of foreign countries like parasites. However, this economic parasitism allowed the ruling class to get rich and to bribe sections of the proletariat.[86] Although Hilferding too had mentioned the problematic effects of imperialism on working class consciousness, he did not emphasize the tendency to stagnation of capitalism. On the contrary, he maintained that the export of capital

> increases domestic production, which has to supply the commodities which are exported abroad as capital. Thus it becomes a very powerful impetus to capitalist production, which enters upon a new period . . . during which it seems to be the case that the cycle of prosperity and depression has been shortened and crises have become less severe. The rapid increase in production also brings about an increased demand for labour power which is advantageous to the trade unions, and the tendencies towards pauperization

inherent in capitalism appear to be overcome in the advanced capitalist countries. The rapid rise in production inhibits a conscious awareness of the ills of capitalist society and generates an optimistic view of its viability.[87]

However, even for Hilferding, imperialism leads to an intensification of social contradictions and increased possibilities for socialism. Monopolies tend to impose great burdens on dominated classes and as the dangers of war increase and the pace of accumulation necessarily slows down because no new territories can be found to which to export capital, a socialist revolution becomes closer: 'in the violent clash of these hostile interests the dictatorship of the magnates of capital will finally be transformed into the dictatorship of the proletariat.'[88] It is interesting to note that despite the preponderance of economic analysis in Hilferding's work, he does not fall into the trap of anticipating the inevitability of the economic collapse of capitalism and stresses the political nature of the struggle for socialism.

For Rosa Luxemburg, on the contrary, the necessary economic collapse of capitalism is closely related to the exhaustion of the imperialist expansion. The moment that new pre-capitalist territories cease to be available as 'third markets' for the commodities produced in the central economies, accumulation comes to a halt because surplus value can no longer be realized: 'for capital, the standstill of accumulation means that the development of the productive forces is arrested, and the collapse of capitalism follows inevitably, as an objective historical necessity.'[89] For Luxemburg, therefore, socialism is inevitable not because the workers will bring it about in a political struggle, but because capitalism will necessarily collapse. As she puts it, 'according to Marx, the rebellion of the workers, the class struggle, is only the ideological reflex of the objective historical necessity of socialism, resulting from the objective impossibility of capitalism in a certain economic stage.'[90]

Bukharin, too, believes that 'it is a fact that imperialism means catastrophe, that we have entered into the period of the collapse of capitalism, no less.'[91] However he also asserts that Luxemburg's deterministic and over-simplistic position is theoretically and factually mistaken. It is theoretically flawed because it rests on the assumption that the realization of surplus-value is impossible in a wholly capitalist world. It is factually wrong because although it is true that capitalism has become the dominant economic form everywhere, most of the world's population are still peasants, who constitute precisely that market of 'third persons' whose existence Luxemburg considers to be essential for the survival of capitalism. There is no sign of the numbers of pre-capitalist 'third persons' declining 'and yet the whole epoch is already showing the most *acute* sharpening of contradictions, the most *acute* and general tension, the most *acute* catastrophical character. And yet capitalism is *already* beginning to "burst".'[92] Hence Bukharin attacks Luxemburg's deterministic approach to the necessary economic collapse of capitalism with the facts of a more immediate political collapse which does not have to wait for the disappearance of 'third persons'. This collapse has already started:

> Today we are able to watch the process of capitalist collapse not merely on the basis of abstract constructions and theoretical perspectives. The collapse of capitalism has started. The October revolution is the most convincing and living expression of that.[93]

The consequences of imperialism for peripheral economies

One of the most important features of the classical theory of imperialism is that despite talking about the expansion of capitalism to pre-capitalist areas, annexationism and the division of the world by imperialist countries, it pays scant attention to and hardly analyses at all the specific situation of 'backward' countries. Much as these classical theorists criticize the race to conquer foreign territories and the dangers of corruption and war that this brings about, they still feel that this process is not only inevitable but actually necessary for the development of peripheral areas. Paradoxically, it is this very process of peripheral development, which is taken for granted, that the theory of imperialism sees as the main problem for central capitalism: either the realization of surplus-value becomes impossible or investment and expansion is rechanneled to the benefit of the periphery. Imperialism is bad for Europe but ultimately good for the colonized peoples.

Hobson, for instance, accepts that 'backward' countries must be 'opened up'. He criticizes British expansion not so much because it is bad for the colonized countries as because it is a burden for and not in the interest of Britain. He argues that if it is necessary that Western industrial civilization develops foreign countries for the 'general good', then Britain has done its share, and now it is the turn of France, Germany, Japan and Russia to do theirs.[94] It is not without significance that in a chapter entitled 'Imperialism and the lower races', Hobson argues that the autonomy of backward countries is not inviolable. The reason is that the ease with which human life can be maintained in the tropics breeds indolence and torpor of character. The inhabitants of these countries are not 'progressive people'; they neither develop the arts of industry at any satisfactory pace, nor do they evolve new wants and desires, the satisfaction of which might force them to labour.[95]

Although it is not morally right to compel foreign peoples to develop their own resources, it is legitimate for advanced nations to utilize natural resources which are left undeveloped and to ensure 'the progress of the civilization of the world'. But this must not be left in the hands of private adventurers and profit seekers: 'every act of "Imperialism" consisting of forcible interference with another people can only be justified by showing that it contributes to "the civilization of the world".'[96]

Hilferding, in his turn, does not indulge in a discussion about the moral justification of acts of imperialism. As a Marxist he just verifies the fact that the export of capital accelerates the 'opening up' of foreign countries. True, one of the main obstacles to 'opening up' backward countries is the shortage of wage labour which can only be solved by forcibly expropriating the land of the natives. (Directly by the white settlers taking the land or indirectly by oppressive taxation.) These violent methods are the main task of colonialism. Yet the results of the capitalist expansion are ultimately positive for the 'nations without a history' because 'it promotes the maximum development of their productive forces', 'the old social relations are completely revolutionized', 'they are swept into the capitalist maelstrom', and 'capitalism itself gradually provides the subjected people with the ways and means for their own liberation.'[97]

The use of force, the destruction of rural industries, oppressive taxation and the expropriation of the land are also well described by Luxemburg.[98] But ultimately she too believes that the results of the imperialist phase of accumulation are

> the industrialization and capitalist emancipation of the *hinterland* where capital formerly realized its surplus value . . . Revolution is an essential for the process of capitalist emancipation. The backward communities must shed their obsolete political organizations . . . and create a modern state machinery adapted to the purposes of capitalist production.[99]

Lenin himself saw the main problems of imperialism as happening in the central advanced countries: the decay of capitalism, the arrest of development and, especially in the political arena, opportunism, the 'buying off' of the leadership of the European working classes, etc. But when it comes to assessing the effects of imperialism in the 'backward' countries, then he repeats the traditional line:

> The export of capital affects and greatly accelerates the development of capitalism in those countries to which it is exported. While, therefore, the export of capital may tend to a certain extent to arrest development in the capital exporting countries, it can only do so by expanding and deepening the further development of capitalism throughout the world.[100]

THE CRITIQUE OF THE THEORY OF IMPERIALISM

Among the many criticisms of the classical theory of imperialism that one can find in the literature, those which focus on the following three areas seem significant. The first concerns the relevance for contemporary capitalism of some of the features of imperialism given by the above-mentioned authors. The second is related to the eurocentrism of the theory; and the third has to do with the connection between imperialism and the collapse of capitalism.

Two main features of imperialism come under critical scrutiny: the primacy given by the theory to the export of capital as the main defining feature of imperialism and the predominance of banking capital over industrial capital. Barrat Brown has argued that both in the period up to 1939 and in the period since 1945 the income of the central economies from overseas investment was in excess of the outflow of capital to third world areas. Moreover, neither up to 1939 nor since 1945 has the larger part of central export capital gone to third world countries. British investment abroad before 1939 was divided into 20 per cent in British colonies, 20 per cent in Latin America, and the bulk, 60 per cent in the developed world. So he concludes that 'the widening gap between poor and rich countries' is 'the result rather of the withdrawal of capital than of the export of capital . . . the continued exercise of economic power by the advanced countries over the underdeveloped is still not explained in terms of capital exports.'[101] On the other hand Cardoso, following Baran and Sweezy, argues that the emergence of transnational corporations and multinationals which act as self-sufficient units of capital accumulation throws doubts into the notion that banking capital controls industrial capital.[102]

Cardoso's point should not be construed as a criticism of the accuracy of the original theory itself in so far as it describes the situation prevalent in the second decade of the twentieth century but rather must be taken as an invitation to rethink the theory in the context of important changes which have occurred in the development of capitalism ever since. Barrat Brown's point is less simple. The question arises as to whether the fact that the bulk of the central economies' export of capital goes to other developed countries and the fact that in the underdeveloped countries the outflow of capital is greater than the inflow of capital of themselves change the nature of imperialism. Is it of the essence of imperialism, as defined by the classical authors, that most of the export of capital should go to third world areas and that the repatriation of profits should be smaller than the export of capital? I do not think so. What would have been the point of talking about the 'parasitism' of European countries living like 'rentiers' off foreign lands if this had been the case?

Barrat Brown might counter-argue that what is obviously affected by these facts is the idea that the economic domination of the third world occurs through capital exports. First because they are relatively small as a proportion of the totality of capital exports; second because they are smaller than the repatriation of profits. But these facts are not really decisive enough to reject the impact of foreign investment on the third world. To say that the problem is the withdrawal of capital rather than the export of capital is disingenuous because the former depends on the latter. The influence and importance of foreign capital is relative to the size of the underdeveloped productive structure and must be judged in relation to factors such as state revenues, employment, access to foreign currency in order to import, etc. For instance, before the nationalization of the copper mines by Allende's government in Chile the American copper companies took more capital out by repatriating profits than the capital they originally invested in the mines. Yet for a long time they were the main source of foreign currency and of an important part of the state revenue through taxation, they allowed the development of related industries, contributed to employment in various regions of the country and developed a resource which would have been otherwise unexploited. In short, Chile was highly dependent upon that foreign investment.

However, as Warren has argued, it is rather difficult to show that the export of European capital is an exclusive feature of the imperialist stage of capitalism or that it is directly connected with the drive to annex new territories. Capital exports seem to have been a normal feature of capitalism from its inception and they do not show any dramatic increase during the imperialist phase. Besides, the peak of capital exports precede the rise of European monopolies and many imperialist countries (like

USA, Japan, Spain and Portugal) were net importers rather than exporters of capital between 1870 and 1914.[103] Warren's point is that the imperialist expansion has more to do with trade and strategic considerations than directly with capital exports. Still he acknowledges that what was called 'trade' included the acquisition and protection of areas for investment.

The second area of criticism concerns the general eurocentric perspective of the theories of imperialism. No matter how it is defined by the various authors, imperialism is mainly concerned with the processes, and analysed from the perspective, of advanced capitalism in Western Europe. The role of the periphery is in the first instance purely passive and it is considered only in so far as it is a reflection of socio-economic forces and changes occurring in the industrial world. The periphery is not deemed worthy of serious analysis, except as the recipient and sufferer of external forces it cannot resist. Its fate, and also its only chance of progress, seem to be inextricably tied up with the forcible process of being 'opened up' by colonial powers. The nineteenth-century vision of 'peoples without history', stagnant and backward, incapable of any material progress on their own and unable to present any opposition to the European expansion, lingers on in the theory of imperialism. Because the periphery is not seriously analysed in its own right, imperialism is too easily identified with colonial situations. Hinkelammert has pointed to the fact that the classical theory of imperialism fails to consider the situation of countries, like those of Latin America, which were already formally independent at the beginning of the nineteenth century and which nevertheless freely accepted British free trade, thus postponing their own industrialization and becoming dependent on industrial countries.[104]

Now it may be thought that there is little point in criticising the eurocentrism of the classical conception of imperialism since the theory was not about the moral justification of the process of imperialist expansion but about the rigorous description and explanation of the last necessary stage of capitalist development. However, in so far as the 'backward' countries are concerned, the fact that most of them were 'opened up' and their native economies disrupted does not mean that that was a strictly necessary process without which they inevitably would have remained backward. Japan was never colonized by the West and yet it was able to accomplish its own capitalist revolution. On the other hand, the early Spanish and Portuguese rule over Latin American countries can hardly be described as planting the seeds of industrial capitalism in the continent. I am not saying that if the colonization process had not taken place most 'backward' countries would have developed like Japan. But the possibility cannot be entirely excluded that at least some would and others perhaps would have been less poor.

Even if one were to concede that a different path to development would have been highly unlikely for most third world countries, such an idea would still need to be substantiated by an analysis which goes beyond the categories of 'backward peoples' or 'peoples without history'. Such categories are absolutely inadequate, ragbag concepts which cover everything that does not fit into the European pattern of development. In other words, the study of the role and consequences of imperialism, as much as of its possible alternatives, requires not just an analysis of advanced capitalism in Europe but also a more rigorous analysis of the class structures and economic processes of the periphery. This would have shown situations of dependency which were not the result of unilateral colonial impositions. But such an analysis was not carried out by the classical theory of imperialism.

As Hinkelammert has argued, the classical theory of imperialism interprets the world capitalist system as a homogeneous totality whose internal cleavages are purely quantitative and due to the fact that some countries are latecomers to capitalism.[105] The problem is not in the idea, already present in Marx, that capitalism is at that time fast expanding and penetrating the entire world. This is obviously happening and the process is forcibly accelerated by imperialism. The problem is rather twofold: on the one hand, the assumption is made that backward nations can become capitalist only through external imposition; and on the other, the development of capitalism in the 'backward areas' is too easily identified with fully fledged industrialization and expansion of productive forces. For these authors, just as much as for Marx, capitalism is inherently industrializing. They imagine that once the forces of capitalism begin to operate in the periphery, the same process of industrialization experienced by Europe will be repeated. This is why they suspect that the export of capital abroad can occur at the expense of the central economies and bring about the collapse of European capitalism. They do not have any inkling that capitalism in the central economies is not about to relinquish its control of the expansion process, let alone collapse, and that capitalism in the periphery is by no means going to produce immediately and necessarily the widespread industrialization and the qualitative expansion of productive forces which could threaten the primacy of central economies.

This brings me to the third area of criticism which is related to the idea that imperialism is a degenerate and corrupt phase of capitalism which leads to an accentuation of its inherent contradictions and to its imminent collapse. One perceives in the authors of the classical theory the same strong belief held by Marx and Engels for most of their lives that the collapse of capitalism and its replacement by socialism is not far away. They also share with Marx and Engels the idea that the revolution and the ensuing demise of capitalism will start in Europe, where capitalism is most advanced. They did not have an inkling of the fact that, as Warren puts it,

> Imperialism, far from being the product of a senile, decaying capitalism compelled to invest abroad the capital it no longer had the 'vigour' to absorb at home, was on the contrary the product of young and vigorous capitalist economies newly emerging onto the international arena to challenge their rivals in *trade*.[106]

I entirely agree with Warren on this point. There can be little doubt that the necessary linking of the imperialist stage with the collapse of capitalism was more wishful thinking than rigorous analysis. This was not because imperialism did not bring about political opportunities for revolution (in fact it brought about many, to which the Russian revolution and other failed socialist uprisings in Europe bear witness) but because (a) the analysis of the imperialist stage as economically stagnant, overripe, corrupt and decaying was clearly flawed; and (b) even when the economic conditions are propitious the political success of a revolution is never secured. The Marxist authors of the classical theory of imperialism shared the orthodox belief in the absolute necessity of socialism and thought that the economic and political contradictions of imperialism would inevitably lead to it. But this deterministic conception of historical materialism cannot be sustained, as I have tried to show elsewhere.[107]

Warren's critique goes further though. He points out that Lenin's insistence on the parasitic and decaying nature of the imperialist stage of capitalism inevitably tended to suggest the idea that colonial countries were simply being robbed and exploited and that, in spite of formally stating that imperialism greatly accelerates the development of capitalism in the colonies, the idea was implicit in his theory that imperialism was an obstacle to industrialization in the third world. [108] I do not think that this is a fair reading of Lenin's position. Warren is interpreting Lenin in the light of the subsequent evolution of the communist movement and attributing to him the paternity for changes which were introduced in the 1928 congress of the Communist International, years after his death. I do not think this attribution is accurate, first because there is no textual basis for it, and second because all the other theories of imperialism which Lenin used for his own book subscribed to the opposite view. Warren argues that Lenin completely changed Marx's position on this issue. But he makes two mistakes. First, he has a very narrow view of Marx's position as being simply and unproblematically expressed in his early writings on India. Warren entirely neglects other texts written after 1860, especially the letters on Ireland. Second, even if we take the early writings on India as genuinely representative of Marx's position, Lenin does not substantially depart from their general thrust.

THE POLITICAL READJUSTMENT OF THE THEORY OF IMPERIALISM

Brewer has argued that 'the period between the wars produced no notable innovations in the Marxist theory of imperialism.'[109] This may be true in the sense that no new theoretical contribution of importance emerged during that period but, politically, the interpretation of the classical theory of imperialism changed in the practice of the communist movement and, increasingly, imperialism began to be considered as the main obstacle to development in the third world. The change of perspective was officially sanctioned during the 6th Congress of the Third International in 1928 in the context of the discussion about the failure of the 1927 Chinese revolution. Although the disaster had been brought about by the line of collaboration with the Kuomintang imposed on the Chinese Communist party by Stalin through the Comintern, Bukharin's report managed to deflect the criticisms away from the Comintern and blamed the Chinese themselves. Naturally, the collaboration between communist parties and nationalist bourgeois movements came in for harsh criticism. This did not mean that the struggle against the 'imperialist slavery' or the 'imperialist yoke' should relent, but it meant that backward colonial peoples in their anti-imperialist struggles should look now to the Soviet Union and the revolutionary proletariat of the imperialist countries for alliances instead of following the leadership of their national bourgeoisies. This new alliance with the USSR

opens for the masses of China, India and all other colonial and semi-colonial countries the prospect of independent economic and cultural development,

avoiding the stage of capitalist domination, perhaps even the development
of capitalist relations in general . . . There is thus an objective possibility of
a non-capitalist path of development for the backward colonies . . .[110]

There is no need to trace this view back to Lenin, as Warren[111] and
Cardoso[112] do, in order to explain its emergence. The truth is simpler: the
communist movement was increasingly confronted with the plight of
colonized nations and the third world representatives in the Communist
International began to put in question the eurocentrism of its resolutions.
Even as this change of perspective is being stated, the labouring masses
of the colonies are described as 'a most powerful *auxiliary force* of the
socialist world revolution' led by advanced proletariats, especially the
Russian.[113] The theoretical shift, although important, must not be
overestimated. The Soviet Union was assigned a pre-eminent role in the
anti-imperialist struggles of the third world and the development of
colonized countries was judged to be temporarily impossible for as long
as these nations did not achieve independence. It did not declare, as
Warren alleges, that capitalism was devoid 'of positive social functions
anywhere',[114] although it did contemplate the *possibility* that capitalism
could be leapt over.[115]

In spite of envisaging the possibility of leaping over capitalism, the 6th
Congress did not state at any point that capitalist development in the
colonies was impossible or undesirable. In fact the position on the
national bourgeoisies changed again in 1935 during the 7th Congress
held against the background of Hitler's accession to power. Increasingly,
the Soviet communists subordinated all the policies and theoretical
statements of the International to the foreign policy needs of the Soviet
Union. At the 5th Congress in 1924 tactical alliances with the bourgeoisie
were encouraged which in the main rubber stamped Stalin's policy of
forcing the members of the Chinese Communist party to enrol in the
Kuomintang. In 1928, after the Chinese disaster, it was felt that any
alliances with aggressive bourgeois movements had to be curbed. In
1935, on the contrary, it was argued that Nazism could only be stopped
with the help of other European bourgeoisies and the formation of
popular fronts.

One cannot derive from these policy about-turns definite theoretical
conclusions about the chances of capitalism in the third world. It is clear
though that imperialism became a negative force for third world
development. Yet this is only a temporary obstacle for colonial countries.
Development is supposed to be able to resume its course after

independence, either in a capitalist or in a socialist way. This is why the change of perspective which occurred was hardly a major doctrinal alteration. In so far as it defined imperialism as a shortlived fetter on the development of the third world, it had been already partially anticipated at an early stage by Marx himself when he said that

> the Indians will not reap the fruits of the new elements of society scattered among them by the British bourgeoisie till in Great Britain itself the now ruling classes shall have been supplanted by the industrial proletariat, or till the Hindus themselves shall have grown strong enough to throw off the English yoke altogether. At all events, we may safely expect to see, at a more or less remote period, the regeneration of that great and interesting country.[116]

Palma has argued, on the contrary, that the 6th Congress of the Comintern in 1928 constituted a turning point which not only emphasized imperialism as a temporary obstacle to development but went further and radically doubted 'the historical progressiveness of capitalism in the backward regions of the world'.[117] This would be implicit in Kuusinen's 'Theses on the revolutionary movement in colonial and semi-colonial countries' approved in the 6th Congress, where the idea of a 'feudal-imperialist alliance' is formulated:

> Where the ruling imperialism is in need of a social support in the colonies it first allies itself with the ruling strata of the previous social structure, the feudal lords and the trading and money-lending bourgeoisie, against the majority of the people.[118]

I do not think that one can derive a radical questioning of the progressiveness of capitalism in the third world from this quotation. Palma overlooks three facts. First, further below, the theses clearly repeat the old Leninist tenet that 'the export of capital to the colonies accelerates the development of capitalist relations there. The part which is invested in production does to some extent accelerate industrial development; but this is not done in ways which promote independence.'[119] Second, the passage in question refers mainly to colonial situations and not to formally independent countries. And, third, in so far as it could be applied to independent backward countries, the feudal–imperialist alliance thesis served to justify a political and developmental strategy based on bourgeois nationalism supported by popular classes. This was in fact the basic strategy expressed by the programmes of the majority of Latin American communist parties from the late 1930s onwards. They never doubted the viability of capitalism as a developing force and this was the reason why they were taken to task by the Cuban revolutionaries and by certain 'dependency' theorists in the early 1960s.

After the second world war the theory of imperialism was readjusted once more, this time, however, in a more substantial manner. This new shift was clearly determined by the increasing importance of anti-colonial movements and by the challenge of widespread and persistent poverty all over the third world. For the first time Marxist authors are forced to look more closely to the reality of 'backward' countries and to find theoretical explanations of their backwardness which go beyond the old ideas which considered the problem to be a temporary occurrence and blamed colonial arbitrary impositions for its existence. The reality of backward independent countries comes to the fore. The effects of imperialism can no longer be identified with the colonial situation. The work of Paul Baran developed immediately after the war takes account of these new circumstances and represents an important theoretical shift within the theory of imperialism. Baran is the first author within the theory of imperialism who studies the class structures and economic processes of underdeveloped countries, but more important, he is the first Marxist author who puts in doubt the homogeneous conception of world capitalism.

In the first place, Baran does not consider backwardness to be the result of pre-capitalist structures; on the contrary, backwardness is also a product of capitalism. The main question he asks himself is 'why is it that in the backward capitalist countries there has been no advance along the lines of capitalist development that are familiar from the history of other capitalist countries, and why is it that forward movement there has been either slow or altogether absent?'[120] The question simply assumes that backward countries are fully capitalist and that capitalism in them has not developed in the same way as in the industrial world. The reason for this is sought in the fact that the economic surplus[121] produced in backward capitalist countries is not entirely available for productive investment, partly because it is drained away by imperialist countries and partly because it is squandered by the local ruling classes in luxury consumption.

Baran is probably the first author who conceives of capitalism as a heterogeneous and hierarchical international system within which some countries, the metropolises, exploit and subordinate others, the dependent countries, which in their turn exploit others and thus successively down to the colonies at the base.[122] He contrasts the old competitive phase of capitalism which was progressive and expanding with the new monopolistic phase which leads to stagnation. In the era of monopoly capital, capitalism ceases to be a developing force because monopolies are not interested in expanding output or in introducing new production techniques. Economic development everywhere (in advanced and backward capitalist countries) comes into conflict with the economic and political order of capitalism and imperialism.[123] But underdeveloped countries have an additional problem: imperialist countries are opposed to their industrialization[124] and try to maintain in power the old oligarchies which squander resources and are convenient to their interests.

This means that Marx's dictum that 'the country that is more developed industrially only shows, to the less developed, the image of its own future'[125] can be applied only to some less developed countries, namely,

> those which never fell under, or had escaped from, the domination of more developed countries ... In the rest of the capitalist world, scores of colonies, neo-colonies, and semi-colonies are doomed to remain in their degraded condition of underdevelopment and misery. For them the only road forward leads straight out of the capitalist system.[126]

In those areas like Australia, North America, etc., European settlers entered more or less complete societal vacuums and succeeded in establishing indigenous societies of their own. It was different elsewhere where they faced established societies with rich and ancient cultures. There they only extracted gain and plundered the country. This extraction of surplus jolted the entire development of these countries and affected its subsequent course: 'The removal of a large share of the affected countries' previously accumulated and currently generated surplus could not but cause a serious set-back to their primary accumulation of capital.'[127] Imperialism is no longer a temporary obstacle to development; it has lasting effects which capitalism itself cannot cure. This is why development in the third world can only be achieved through a determined struggle against the conservative forces which are propped up by imperialism, in short, it can only be achieved through socialism.[128]

Baran mentions India as an example of a country which would have developed much better had it not been for the surplus torn from it by Britain. Interestingly, although Baran agrees with Marx that one should not idealize India's pre-British past, he maintains that 'at the same time, it should not be overlooked that India, if left to herself, might have found in the course of time a shorter and surely less tortuous road towards a better and richer society.'[129] By contrast, Japan could develop because it 'escaped being turned into a colony or dependency of Western European or American capitalism'[130] and so had the chance of independent national development. There is not a word about Marx's belief that British rule was necessary for India to come out of the Asiatic mode of production. In fact Baran assimilates all pre-capitalist modes of production into the feudal mode of production and believes that despite some variations between different regions this mode of production has everywhere entered into 'a process of dissolution and decay' which has allowed capitalism to develop.

If it is true that imperialism did contribute to the creation and development of some of the pre-conditions for a capitalist system in the colonies (by destroying the rural economy, expropriating the peasants and improving communications and infrastructure), it is also true that it blocked the development of other pre-conditions, not the least, it removed the accumulated economic surplus and exposed these countries to foreign competition thus smothering their incipient industries. Development was deflected from its normal course and made to conform to the needs of imperialism.[131] The internal counterpart of this process is described thus:

> The economic surplus appropriated in lavish amounts by monopolistic concerns in backward countries is not employed for productive purposes. It is neither ploughed back into their own enterprises, nor does it serve to develop others. To the extent that it is not taken abroad by their foreign stockholders, it is used in a manner very much resembling that of the landed aristocracy. It supports luxurious living by its recipients, is spent on construction of urban and rural residences, on servants, excess consumption, and the like. The remainder is invested in the acquisition of rent-bearing land, in financing mercantile activities of all kinds, in usury and speculation. Last but not least, significant sums are removed abroad where they are held as hedges against the depreciation of the domestic currency or as nest eggs assuring their owners of suitable retreats in the case of social and political upheavals at home.[132]

The lack of dynamic growth in underdeveloped countries therefore is not so much due to the reduced size of their economic surplus as to the way it is used. Baran carries out a long analysis in which he identifies the main classes and sectors which typically appropriate the surplus and assesses the way in which it is used. Unproductive use of surplus is most expanded in the agricultural sector of the economy which, in most underdeveloped countries, produces at least half of the surplus. On the one hand the surplus produced by small peasants is drained away from them (in the form of high interests, taxes and unfavourable terms of trade), thus preventing any productive investment on their part. On the other hand the big landowners spend their surplus in luxury consumption or in buying more land. Another sizeable part of the economic surplus goes to petty traders, merchants, money lenders and all kinds of intermediaries. Individually they are relatively poor but as a whole they absorb an enormous chunk of the surplus. Being scattered, very little of such surplus goes to productive investment in industry.

As for the small industrial sector, there is little incentive to invest because of foreign competition and lack of state protection. Moreover, from the beginning the most important industrial concerns are born as monopolies which control very narrow markets and therefore do not need to invest in order to compete. This is even more accentuated in the case of foreign firms which additionally send profits back home instead of re-investing locally. Finally the state, which absorbs an important part of the surplus, apart from a few exceptions, is controlled by 'comprador bourgeoisies' which serve the interests of the foreign firms which exploit the natural resources (oil, minerals, foodstuffs). They spend the surplus in huge bureaucracies, building of roads and airports and military hardware, and very little goes to the modernization of industry or agriculture.

Baran's analysis has received many criticisms, both from orthodox Marxism and from mainstream development economics. His proposed opposition between competitive and monopoly capitalism, the former a developing force, the latter leading to stagnation, is exaggerated and a remnant of the classical Marxist view which considered imperialism as the last stage of a moribund capitalism. As Brewer has pointed out, Baran's approach takes its evidence mainly from pre-war capitalism whereas 'the "long boom" of the 1950s and 1960s suggests strongly that monopoly capitalism is not incompatible with growth.'[133] There are also doubts about his description of underdeveloped structures as being fully capitalist and about his subsuming all pre-capitalist modes of production under the term 'feudal' and assuming that their decay always led to capitalism. Baran's concept of socialism also comes under attack for inducing the belief that socialism more than a qualitative change of social relations, is a means to accelerated economic growth in poor countries. Additionally, the idea of socialism as a road to development for poor countries is also somehow contradictory to Baran's awareness that socialism in underdeveloped and backward countries tends to become an underdeveloped and backward socialism.[134]

Still, for better or for worse, Baran's analysis is extremely important in several respects. First, he definitively changed the theory of imperialism from the view that imperialism is bound to accelerate the development of backward countries to the view that imperialism necessarily hinders the process of development and irrevocably twists the working of capitalism. Second he changed the traditional Marxist views about the homogeneity of the world capitalist system and the developing qualities of capitalism. Capitalism is no longer a developing force everywhere nor do all capitalist countries go through the same historical stages. Third, Baran introduced the notion of capitalist underdevelopment as a polar type within the world capitalist system which is qualitatively different from advanced capitalism. Such a concept of underdevelopment as a different category had been totally absent from Marxist studies. Fourth, he contributed to the notion that socialism is a road to development for third world countries rather than the necessary result of advanced capitalism. Fifth, for the first time he introduced a balanced analysis which considered both the actions of imperialist powers and the internal class structures and economic processes of the underdeveloped countries.

With Baran the theory of imperialism lost its eurocentrism and at the same time was profoundly changed. As a new version it became enormously influential in the 1960s and 1970s, and constituted the articulating focus of many emerging intellectual currents, including unequal exchange, world system and dependency theory. These new theories were developed in or took the point of view of the underdeveloped world and no longer trusted the developing ability of capitalism or the leadership of the European proletariat. Baran's theory marks the transfer of the geographical axis of the theory of imperialism from Europe to the third world.

3

LATE CAPITALISM: MODERNIZATION AND THE ECONOMIC COMMISSION FOR LATIN AMERICA

INTRODUCTION

After the second world war the process of decolonization and the widespread poverty of newly developing nations became important problems for social theorists and economists. A new consciousness emerged about the plight and development needs of so many peoples, partly because of the vastness of the problem and the way it could adversely affect the developed world itself, and partly because of political considerations about the appeal of the Russian socialist experience. Just as the Marxist theory of imperialism had been confronted with these new realities after 1928 and had been finally readjusted to take account of the new situation, mainstream economics and the newly created sociology had to provide answers to the same questions. But, of course, they did so from a different perspective. The theory of imperialism had become increasingly negative in its assessment of imperialism and of the capabilities for development of capitalism. Socialism was now a concrete experience whose example the new nations could follow if they really wanted to develop their productive forces. Development economics and the sociology of development, the new topical disciplines, on the contrary, took for granted the continuity and necessity of the capitalist process of development throughout the world and wanted to show that third world nations could overcome the obstacles and develop within capitalism to reach the same levels achieved by the developed world.

In this sense the first mainstream post-war theories of development within the capitalist world were born as modernization theories, that is to say, as theories of the processes and stages through which traditional or backward societies were bound to go during their transition to modern society. These processes and stages were to be determined by looking at the history of developed societies. The assumption was that newly developing societies must repeat the same experience. However, although modernization theories believe in the continuity and unidirectionality of the transition, they do not take the process of economic development for granted nor do they abstract from the social and political variables which condition it as the neo-classical political economists did. They reintroduce what had been a concern of the classical political economists, namely the exploration and study of the institutional arrangements, values and class structures which make development possible. This time, with the birth of the sociology of development, the study of the social and political processes which favour or hinder economic development acquires a new relevance. As could be expected, modernization theories dominated the academic world while the new Marxist interpretations of imperialism remained a marginal but intellectually powerful alternative.

It was in the setting of this intellectual field that the first forms of autochthonous thought emerged in Latin America, especially within the Economic Commission for Latin America (ECLA). The Latin American economists and intellectuals working within it or under its auspices developed a distinctive approach which borrowed from both paradigms but refused to go all the way with either of them. From development economics they took some central economic concepts and categories and, especially, quantitative methods of analysis. The language of the ECLA was in this respect quite orthodox and technical. They also shared a more fundamental assumption, namely, the idea that development, at least for the Latin American nations, must take place within the capitalist system. They did not question the ability of capitalism to bring about development but refused to accept an identity of interests between developed and underdeveloped nations. From the theory of imperialism they took, without ever mentioning it directly, the idea that industrial nations take advantage and get the better of underdeveloped nations, especially through unequal exchange. Their point was to argue such a case without resorting to Marxist jargon but using the same logic, language and methodology as that accepted in the mainstream academic world.

THE THEORETICAL BASES OF MODERNIZATION THEORIES

All modernization theories start with an implicit or explicit reference to a dichotomy between two ideal types: the traditional society (which in other versions can also be called 'rural', 'backward' or 'underdeveloped') and the modern society (or 'urban', 'developed', 'industrial'). This distinction describes two ideal types of social structure which are somehow historically connected by means of a continuous evolutionary process which follows certain general laws. The idea is that all societies follow a similar historical course which gains in differentiation and complexity as it departs from one polar type and moves towards the other. Since certain societies have already industrialized, they become the basis on which the 'industrial society paradigm' and the ideal typical process of transition can be constructed. Traditional societies are supposed to follow the same pattern of change undergone earlier on by the developed nations. Modernization theories, therefore, seek to identify in the organization and/or history of industrial countries the social variables and institutional factors whose change was crucial for their process of development, in order to facilitate the process for the newly developing countries.

There are many versions of this approach and for convenience I shall group them in three categories. The most sophisticated theories of modernization emphasize the role of a wide variety of social and institutional variables and carry out a mainly sociological analysis of the transition. Other theories, although recognizing the complex interaction of many variables privilege the role of one special factor or level. Thus some theories underline economic factors, while others stress the principal role of psychological factors. I shall briefly review some examples of each of these strands.

The sociological version

The idea of a transition between two polar types of society has a long tradition within the social sciences which goes back to the nineteenth century. Rationalistic and evolutionary social theories proposed in various ways, dichotomies which made reference to two societal ideal types. The distinction made by Tönnies' between *Gemeinschaft* (community or association) and *Gesellschaft* (society or organization), Spencer's dichotomy between homogeneous and heterogeneous societies and Durkheim's opposition between mechanical solidarity and organic solidarity are examples that spring to mind. The transition between the two poles – in other words, development – was understood in terms of some stages within which key processes of specialization and differentiation occurred which increased the complexity of society. Traditional societies were supposed to be 'simple' by comparison to an industrial society. As Eisenstadt has put it, differentiation 'describes the ways through which the main social functions or the major institutional spheres of society become dissociated from one another, attached to specialized collectivities and roles, and organized in relatively specific and autonomous symbolic and organizational frameworks . . .'[1]

The theory which influenced the post-war modernization theorists the most was probably Max Weber's, especially through Parson's interpretation and reworking of it. Without proposing a specific evolutionary scheme or simple dichotomy between two types of society, Weber's systematic analytical distinctions, elaborated to classify and account for a variety of historical societies and social institutions, showed at different levels the contours of a process of rationalization and disenchantment of nature which affected increasingly wider aspects of social life and which implicitly pointed to the same polarity. Thus, to give an example, by following Weber's classifications it is not difficult to construct an ideal type of a traditional society, where one can find for instance the predominance of a traditional type of action (action determined by a well-rooted custom) and a traditional type of authority (whose domination is based on 'the belief in the everyday routine as an inviolable norm of conduct'[2]). Similarly it is also possible to construct the ideal type of a modern or rational society where there is a predominance of goal-oriented rational actions and a legal authority based on impersonal norms, whose purest type is the bureaucratic rule, and so on.

Parsons systematized, elaborated and extended this kind of approach by arguing that social relations and roles can be determined in terms of five dimensions which present polar alternatives. These are the 'pattern variables'[3] which help to describe the ideal typical social structure of 'traditional' and 'modern' societies. The first is affectivity versus affective neutrality. Some roles are affectively rewarding and others are neutral; or rather, a role can have immediate gratification in the very performance of its expected activities or these activities are affectively neutral and purely instrumental for an ulterior goal. The second is ascription versus achievement. Some roles accrue to actors and provide status according to their physical and non-achievable social attributes (class, sex, age, family, and so on); others are accessible and provide status according to and depending on performance.

A third pattern variable opposes diffusion to specificity. Some relations are functionally diffuse in that they cover a series of unspecified dimensions (friendship, family roles, say). Others are functionally specific in that their content is clearly definable and delimited (bureaucratic roles). Fourth, there is particularism versus universalism. Role expectations can be defined for specific actors in terms of their particular situation, which cannot be transferred (friendship, family relations). Other role expectations can be defined for a number of persons according to objective criteria (salesman–client relation). Finally, in fifth place, orientation towards collective interests versus orientation towards private interests. Some roles are exclusively oriented towards the collective interest (public servant) some others entail the pursuit of private interest (entrepreneurs).

Parsons claims that in traditional societies roles tend to be ascriptive, diffuse, particularistic and affective. In industrial societies, on the contrary, roles which are performance orientated, universalistic, affectively neutral and specific tend to predominate.[4] He leaves out the last pattern variable, probably because of some difficulties in making a clear-cut argument in either direction. On the one hand, it could be said that actors in primitive societies would tend to be oriented exclusively towards collective interests whereas actors in more individualistic industrial societies would tend to seek their private interest. On the other hand, the opposite argument has been made that

> in economically less advanced societies there predominates an attitude of self-orientation with relation to economic goods, at least on the part of those actors who occupy positions in national or group elites, whereas in more highly advanced economies attitudes of collectivity-orientation predominate, or at least are highly valued.[5]

These two positions are not commensurable because they use a different rationale. The former focuses on the very character of social relations (classless society versus class society); the latter, quoted from Hoselitz, focuses on the different orientation of ruling classes within class societies. Both have possible weaknesses. The former because according to the liberal ideology, even in a class society, actors in seeking their private interest are supposed to secure the collective interest (remember Adam Smith's invisible hand). The latter because it is not at all clear that elites and ruling classes in developed countries are willingly much more orientated towards collective interests. Welfare state and other collective values conceded by them could be only a price to be paid to secure the stability of their private interests.

The social structure of a traditional society Parsons calls 'ascriptive particularistic' while the social structure of industrial society is called 'acquisitive universalistic'. The transition from traditional society to industrial society supposes, in general, a progressive expansion of the sphere of application of roles of the latter type and a contraction of the sphere of application of roles of the former type. But specific parts of the social structure will continue to require specific arrangements of roles which may be at variance with the general trend. For instance, family and kinship, even in industrial societies, will continue to be characterized by ascription, particularism, diffusion, affectivity and orientation to collective interests.

Many authors have followed Parsons's elaborations in their studies of modernization. Hoselitz, for instance, applies Parsons's pattern variables with some alterations, namely, he discards the couplet of affectivity and affective neutrality as without relevance[6] and revalues the discriminating ability of the alternative 'orientation towards collective or private interests', as I have just shown above. As for the process of transition and its mechanisms, Hoselitz resorts to the theory of social deviance, borrowing from Park and Schumpeter: the innovating entrepreneur, a 'marginal man', is the prototype of the social deviant, the person most suited to make innovations and 'creative adjustments in situations of change'.[7] He is the dynamic force behind the process of transition to modernity.

Perhaps the most detailed and complete sociological theory of modernization in the Parsonian tradition is that of Gino Germani.[8] For him what is typical of the transition (also called secularization) is the fact that the process of change is asynchronic, that is to say, social institutions, groups, values and attitudes do not change in a congruent manner, but they do so at different speeds with the result that social forms which belong to different epochs and stages of the transition coexist in society. Some parts of society remain fairly traditional and backward and coexist with others which have already become modern. This is why the process of transition causes conflict and is lived as a crisis which divides groups and institutions and even individual consciousness. Germani describes the two polar ideal types in terms of changes occurring in three main areas of the social structure: the type of social action, the attitude towards change and the degree of institutional specialization. As a result of these changes:

I. The type of *social action* is modified. From a predominance of *prescriptive* actions to a (relative) emphasis on *elective* actions (mainly of a 'rational' type).

II. From the *institutionalization* of the *traditional* to the *institutionalization* of change.

III. From a *conjunction of relatively undifferentiated institutions* to their increasing *differentiation and specialization*.[9]

In proposing the dichotomy between prescriptive action and elective action, Germani replaces the Weberian distinction between traditional and rational action. Unlike in Weber, the rationale of Germani's distinction is the normative framework: prescriptive action takes place within a very rigid normative framework which fixes the course of action whereas elective action takes place within a normative framework which is less rigid and determines a choice instead of a preordained course.[10] Germani's thesis is that in pre-industrial societies most actions are prescriptive whereas in industrial societies there is a predominance of elective actions. As for the second dichotomy, Germani proposes that in traditional societies change tends to be a violation of traditional norms and is therefore abnormal and rare. In a modern society, on the contrary, change becomes a normal phenomenon which the normative framework promotes and regulates. Finally, traditional societies possess an undifferentiated structure with few institutions performing many functions. In industrial societies each function tends to be performed by a specialized institution which results in a differentiated structure.

These changes entail in their turn other modifications. For instance, industrial societies suppose a shift from the predominance of 'primary' close relations and 'primary' groups to the predominance of 'secondary' impersonal relations and 'secondary' groups. More generally, in a process of secularization or transition, roles and social relations alter in the sense of Parsons's pattern variables: from diffusion to specificity, from ascription to achievement, and so on. But there are also changes in the types of personality required. In traditional societies a kind of personality predominates which is suited to the internalization of prescriptive norms whereas in industrial societies there is an emphasis on the kind of personality which internalizes elective norms, that is to say, personalities able to choose between various courses of action. Still, even societies that are highly secularized need a minimum of normative integration which secures the existence of some criteria of choice and of change.

The three main changes of the transition process must also occur in the sphere of knowledge, science and technology. Instrumental rationality, separation from theology and philosophy and increasing specialization must guide the production and development of knowledge. In the sphere of the economy, new specific and autonomous institutions must appear, operating according to principles of rationality and efficiency and with bureaucratic forms of organization. Social stratification must change from a close ascriptive system to an open system which works according to norms of achievement, performance and acquisition. This entails a shift from low levels of social mobility to high levels of social mobility. The state must be organized according to rational and bureaucratic norms and there must be an increase in the political participation of popular strata. Local communities must be integrated into the nation.

Kinship and family structures also suffer changes in the process of secularization. Primary relations must be restricted to a minimum and therefore the extended family tends to disappear and to be replaced by the nuclear family.[11] But even primary relations within the family tend to change and become more egalitarian and participative. Education tends to become universal and with a heavy emphasis on scientific aspects. Furthermore, the traditional society is characterized by a 'high demographic potential' (high birth and mortality rates). During the first part of the transition mortality rates fall rather dramatically with the introduction of modern medicine and sanitation and only later does the birth rate begin to decline. In a more advanced stage of the transition, denominated 'low demographic potentiality', mortality rates stay low while birth rates stabilize at a low rate with the introduction of choice, birth control and family planning.

All these changes occur asynchronically. Germani distinguishes several types of asynchrony: geographical (the very notions of underdevelopment and periphery emerge from this type of asynchrony), institutional, intergroup and motivational. Regions, institutions, social groups and values change at different speeds and therefore coexist with one another in traditional and modern forms. Two important phenomena accompany the process of asynchronic change: demonstration effect and fusion effect. The former refers to a situation where some people, knowing the level of consumption and standard of living of other people, develop similar aspirations. This affects the pattern of consumption and savings and may in itself constitute an incentive to change. The fusion effect, on the other hand, consists in the fact that

> when ideologies and attitudes which are an expression of advanced development processes, arrive at areas and groups which are characterized by traditional features, they are not interpreted in terms of their original context, but may reinforce those very traditional features, which now seem to acquire a new credibility, not in the name of the old structure, but as 'advanced products'.[12]

Demonstration and fusion effects are responsible for a variety of problems in underdeveloped countries. For instance, popular classes develop economic aspirations similar to those of the working classes of developed countries. Since the production structure is underdeveloped, those aspirations cannot be satisfied. Middle classes, on the other hand, may develop consumption patterns typical of highly industrialized nations and hence these patterns and corresponding attitudes may be fused with the conspicuous consumption pattern of traditional elites. Germani's point is that in underdeveloped countries consumption attitudes typical of developed economies coexist with underdeveloped production structures. Similarly, popular classes develop egalitarian political aspirations which arose in the developed world arose only after the economy had diversified and modernized. In general, Germani's idea is that due to asynchronic change and, particularly, the demonstration and fusion effects, contemporary developing countries suffer from many cleavages and problems which did not exist in those countries which developed earlier. So even within an evolutive theory of modernization Germani is able to establish the fact that the situation of underdeveloped countries 'is radically different from that which existed in advanced nations in the first stages of their development'.[13] Still, he does not lose faith in the inevitability of the process of transition and argues that despite many problems it is taking place at a quicker pace than in the past.

Germani distinguishes some stages in the Latin American process of transition. In the context of the analysis which I have just summarized he mentions six stages which characterize some well-demarcated political periods of this region in general and Argentina in particular: (1) wars of independence; (2) anarchy and civil wars; (3) unifying autocracies; (4) oligarchies or representative democracies with limited participation; (5) representative democracy with wide participation; and (6) representative democracy with total participation or national popular revolutions.[14] Later, however, in a new book, Germani proposes a different scheme of four stages which correspond to the influence of external factors: traditional society (Spanish and Portuguese colonization); the beginnings of the collapse of the traditional society (French and American revolutions); expansion towards the outside or dual society (British industrial revolution and liberal ideology); and the era of mass social mobilization (the 1930s depression, the second world war, and also the cold war and the predominance of the USA).[15] According to Germani, the important role of exogenous factors in triggering processes which are similar to each other in countries at different stages cannot but accentuate the asynchronic character of the transition.

The psychological version

Psychological versions emphasize psychological motives and other 'internal factors' which are supposed to be the motor forces of economic growth. I am going to concentrate on McClelland's version. Although he does not deny the importance of 'external factors' and objective conditions in the process of development, he is interested 'in the values and motives men have that lead them to exploit opportunities, to take advantage of favourable trade conditions; in short, to shape their own destiny.'[16] McClelland devised a method of content analysis whereby, by counting the frequencies with which certain themes appeared in individuals' written fantasies (including children's stories), he was able to isolate some of the motives which informed the behaviour of those individuals. Among them he discovered the 'need for achievement' (*n* achievement) which is defined as 'a desire to do well, not so much for the sake of social recognition or prestige, but to attain an inner feeling of personal accomplishment'[17] Starting from Weber's connection between the Protestant ethic and the spirit of capitalism, McClelland arrived at the conclusion that what Weber called the 'spirit of capitalism' must have been this special desire to do well and that therefore Protestant business entrepreneurs must have had a high level of *n* achievement. Hence the connection between rapid economic development and high concentrations of *n* achievement in European Protestant countries.

With this hypothesis in mind McClelland set about gathering evidence to show that this relationship is a general one, which holds good not only for the European industrial revolution but also for modern Japan or ancient Greece. He found, for instance, 'that the level of *n* Achievement was highest during the period of growth prior to the climax of economic development in Athenian Greece' and that 'that high level had fallen off by the time of maximum prosperity, thus foreshadowing subsequent economic decline.'[18] He found similar correlations in the case of Spain in the sixteenth century, England in the late sixteenth century and 1800, and even in contemporary primitive societies. The problem as to how to measure economic development in these cultures was solved by estimating the numbers of 'business entrepreneurs' to be found, defining them as 'anyone who exercises control over the means of production and produces more than he can consume in order to sell it for individual or household income.'[19]

The *n* achievement of some 40 contemporary societies was also measured in 1925 and 1950 through children's stories and correlated with the amount of electricity produced, which was used as an indicator of economic growth. He found again a very high statistical correlation. Among the countries with high *n* achievement whose growth performed better than expected are not only the United States and Russia but also Turkey, India, Pakistan, Bulgaria, Portugal and Greece. Among those countries with low *n* achievement whose growth performed worse than expected are New Zealand, Norway, Sweden, Italy, Denmark, Belgium, the Netherlands and Japan.[20]

In agreement with Hoselitz and Schumpeter, McClelland puts forward the idea that the link between a high concentration of need for achievement and economic development is the business entrepreneur. What distinguishes the entrepreneur from other persons is that he is prepared to take moderate risks and innovate although he does not behave as a gambler because his decisions are well informed and rationally taken. As to the question why *n* achievement exists in some societies and not in others, McClelland argues that this motivation to do well is not hereditary or innate but that children acquire it early in life. He finds that those children educated for self-reliance and achievement develop the motivation to do well. Authoritarian and interfering parents produce the opposite result. This means that *n* achievement can be raised in a country by means of education so that more children acquire the 'entrepreneurial drive'.

The economic version

The economic version emphasizes the economic factors in the process of transition. W.W. Rostow with his stages of economic growth[21] is the main representative of this version. Again, it is not that Rostow proposes a purely economic interpretation of the transition process. At the very outset he clarifies the point that economic changes are just as much the result of political and social forces as of economic forces.[22] Rostow thinks that he is departing from and proposing an alternative to Marx's theory of history. He proposes that all societies pass through five stages: traditional society, preconditions for take-off, take-off, road to maturity and the age of high mass consumption. The traditional society is characterized by being mainly agricultural, with low productivity and a pre-Newtonian attitude in respect of the physical world. This does not mean that there is no growth, but it means that there is a ceiling to growth determined by the lack of technology. Power is in the hands of the landowners and the value system is fatalistic.

With the second stage, preconditions for take-off, the process of transition begins. England was the first country which developed these pre-conditions, followed by Western Europe. But in most countries this stage was externally induced by advanced countries which accelerated the destruction of those traditional societies. Many economic changes, are introduced, such as the expansion of trade, increase in the rate of investment, setting up of financial institutions, etc., but the decisive element is the political constitution of a national state. The take-off is the moment when growth becomes a permanent feature of society. The rate of investment goes up to 10 per cent or more and new industries expand rapidly. New techniques are introduced in industry and agriculture which secure constant growth. What promotes the process of transition is, at the end of the day, a simple economic mechanism:

> the essence of the transition can be described legitimately as a rise in the rate of investment to a level which regularly, substantially and perceptibly outstrips population growth; although, when this is said, it carries no implication that the rise in the investment-rate is an ultimate cause.[23]

The road to maturity is a long period where every aspect of the economy is modernized and makes use of new technology. Imports are substituted and exports expand. All the first industries which promoted the take-off are now replaced by more sophisticated ones, and an important process of industrial diversification takes place. Finally the stage of high mass consumption is characterized by an orientation of the economy to consumer durables and services. *Per capita* incomes have increased so much that consumption expands beyond basic needs. Welfare and social security become important goals which compete for resources. Military expenditure also increases, reflecting a new search for influence and power in the international arena.

Rostow's thesis about the relationship between the stages of economic growth and the situation of the newly developing countries fits exactly the premises of modernization theories. He typically argues that

> it is useful, as well as roughly accurate, to regard the process of development now going forward in Asia, the Middle East, Africa, and Latin America as analogous to the stages of preconditions and take-off of other societies, in the late eighteenth, nineteenth and early twentieth centuries.[24]

It is not that Rostow does not recognize the existence of some historical differences between the situation of these two types of countries. His point is rather that although some differences may hinder the contemporary process of take-off, the most crucial of them tend to facilitate it. The biggest difficulty is provoked by the greatest advantage: access to modern technology, including medicine, lowers mortality rates and increases population thus creating problems of chronic unemployment and poverty which require bigger investment and growth rates just in order to avoid them getting worse. Another difficulty is the cold war in so far as developing countries are sucked into this conflict and are obliged to distract time and resources from development tasks. Still, Rostow argues that there are two major advantages which nations that took off first did not have: on the one hand the existence of an already developed modern technology which is available to underdeveloped countries; and, on the other hand, international aid and technical assistance provided by developed countries.

Rostow's theory of stages was never thought out as a purely academic exercise. As a scholar at the Massachusetts Institute of Technology and later Director of Policy and Planning in the US State Department during the Kennedy administration and chief adviser on Vietnam to President Johnson, he was from the very beginning concerned with the international and political context of the process of transition, especially from the point of view of the strategic interests of the USA and the policies to contain communism. For Rostow communism is a disease of the process of transition, which takes advantage of the conflicts and problems which developing nations confront at the stage of the preconditions for take-off in order to seize power. This is why he sees it as essential that the United States should commit itself to support, aid and protect the modernization processes occurring in Latin America, Africa, Asia and the Middle East.

It is in this context that Kennedy's 'development decade' and the 'Alliance for Progress' (the aid programme for Latin American countries) must be understood. Rostow's idea is that once the societies in transition pass from the preconditions for take-off, the natural difficulties and problems of the modernization process begin to ease off and more stable democracies can be secured within the 'free world'.

For Rostow the security of the United States depends on the process of modernization being conducted in such a way that no developing nation goes communist:

> What do we seek? What is the national interest of the United States? Why do we expend our resources and risk modern war in this world-wide struggle? For Americans the reward of victory will be simply this: to allow our society to continue to develop according to the old human lines which hark back to our birth as a nation . . . We struggle to keep in the world scenario an environment which allows an open society like ours to survive and flourish.[25]

THE CRITIQUE OF MODERNIZATION THEORIES

Modernization theories, and in particular the authors I have mentioned, have been widely criticized. A. G. Frank's trenchant and well-known critique,[26] for instance, takes these theories apart by attacking their theoretical adequacy, their empirical validity and their policy effectiveness. Other critiques are more general or assess only certain authors.[27] I shall confine myself to a few important theoretical points.

I said above that modernization theories reintroduced the concern for the institutional framework and the social aspects which condition the process of development. However, they do this in an abstract and ahistorical manner. They define in general and taxonomic terms a series of dichotomic variables which by aggregation and juxtaposition constitute abstract models of a developed society or underdeveloped society. There is hardly any theoretical analysis of the connection between these factors and the productive system. The economy is just one more variable and even when it is emphasized, as in the case of Rostow, it remains theoretically disconnected from the others. There is no real analysis of society in terms of a complex set of social relations which determines a type of domination, a production structure and a class system which correspond with each other.

The process of transition is supposed to happen by successive changes in a number of variables, and the more variables are affected, the more rapid is the process of modernization. When modernization theorists identify the entrepreneur as the motor force of change they do it rather arbitrarily, not as a result of an analysis of social relations and in the context of other groups and classes which struggle in pursuit of other interests, but as an abstract definition, the embodiment of many variables. The entrepreneur is the agent of development because he is in theory an innovator, achiever, deviant, universalist, hardworking, rational, willing to take risks, etc., not because he is a member of a class which within certain conditions, has historically succeeded in imposing its interests on society. Hence these analyses assume a prescriptive character; instead of studying historically the structural context and the development of the bourgeois class, with its specific features, they only seek to establish whether the ideal model of an entrepreneur is present or absent in Latin America. Modernization theories reduce the study of socio-historical processes to the construction of abstract models of universal applicability.

This is most noticeable in McClelland's psychological approach. Development is ultimately reduced to the existence of a certain motivation, the need for achievement, the desire to do well. No wonder then that McClelland is quite happy to compare Athenian Greece with England in the late sixteenth century and with contemporary preliterate cultures. In all of them he finds a way to measure 'economic development' and n achievement. In the case of some 50 primitive societies, for instance, he estimates the numbers of 'business entrepreneurs' existing in them as an indicator of economic development. Of course, the concepts of 'economic development' and 'business entrepreneur' must be defined in such general terms as to lose any significance. What sense is there in speaking of a 'business entrepreneur' in the context of a preliterate culture? Historical differences are totally neglected for the sake of a general theory.

But even when McClelland keeps the analysis within the context of modern nations, some of his results seem questionable. In his measurements of n achievement levels in 1950, countries like India, Portugal, Pakistan, Bulgaria and Greece appear with high n achievement whereas Japan, Denmark, Sweden, Holland, Norway and Belgium appear with low n achievement. The latter perform economically below expectation whereas the former perform better than expected. This is an effect of the regression equation which predicts, starting from the initial level of development of each country, its average expected growth. But, obviously, the initial level of development varies widely, and the lower it is, the easier it is to improve on it. At any rate, it seems very difficult to square these results with the absolute levels of development of these countries today. In fact Leon and Recacoechea correlated the same McClelland figures for the *n* achievement measured in 1950 with economic growth during two alternative periods: 1954–6 and 1960–6 (McClelland had correlated them with growth during 1952–8). They found that in both cases the correlation was not significant and negative, that is to say it pointed in the opposite direction to McClelland's thesis.[28]

The very notion of 'traditional society' as the original situation before the transition to modernity is inadequate. It is so general and abstract that it cannot properly account for the variety of situations which are to be found in Latin America, Asia and Africa. Within such a concept one can encompass a tribe in the Amazon and a Latin American or African independent country, an old feudal or slave society and a contemporary capitalist underdeveloped society. The problem of development in the twentieth century cannot be equated with the problems of traditional societies, agrarian societies or preliterate cultures. This specificity is what the concept of underdevelopment tries to capture and convey. But this means that underdevelopment cannot be considered as a universal original situation, as lack of development in general, as a stage which all developed countries experienced. The concept of underdevelopment makes sense as the specific way in which certain contemporary societies relate to the developed world.

Implicit in all the theories of modernization is the idea that contemporary developing countries should go through the same stages and processes as developed countries went through once. Even when they recognize the existence of some historical differences (Germani and Rostow acknowledge them) they refuse to accept that they could essentially alter the pattern of change. History can be repeated, developing countries can industrialize in the same way as the old industrial countries and in some respects they have even more advantages in doing so. There is hardly any discussion of the international order as a system dominated and manipulated by certain industrial countries in their own interest. Modernization theories assume that the process of modernization and industrialization is inevitable and that newly developing countries have the same if not better opportunities to industrialize. As Hoogvelt has put it, they have 'turned the abstracted, generalized history of European development into *logic*.'[29]

Modernization theories are caught in a theoretical dilemma. On the one hand they want to argue that developing countries must follow the same path as the first industrial countries. The implication of this thesis is, surely, that the transition to modernity must be the result of basically endogenous forces, because that was the way it happened in Europe and North America. On the other hand, in order to explain internal processes of change in underdeveloped countries, they are forced to acknowledge that their situation is different; they usually resort to mechanisms such as the diffusion of values, norms and patterns of consumption from advanced nations (through demonstration and fusion effects) and, in general, they rate highly the role of developed countries, international trade and other external factors as agencies which generate change. Changes must happen internally, but they are induced from abroad. In this sense modernization theories violate their own premise that the road to development is analogous for all countries.

Even if one keeps the analysis within the Latin American continent there is an important ambiguity between two simultaneous assertions. In his analysis of the four Latin American stages of transition, Germani seems to affirm that the same stages of the transition apply to all Latin American countries; but that, on the other hand, there are different roads which lead to the same result. This is confusing. As Solari, Franco and Jutkowitz have put it

> If the different roads are compatible with the same stages and the same end, it is because their differences are minor . . . Conversely, if they are really different, it is difficult to understand why they do not articulate themselves in different stages and arrive at different ends.[30]

On the other hand, their explanation of social change in underdeveloped countries, in so far as it emphasizes the causal role of external factors, is extrinsicist and does not take sufficiently into account the role of internal forces. Germani's linking of the four stages of the Latin American transition to external factors which accentuate 'the homogeneity amongst nations and also the discontinuities within themselves'[31] is an example of this. According to him 'these factors generate in each country – without taking into account the degree of modernization achieved by each of them – a series of processes which are essentially similar in all of them.'[32] The problem is not that he considers external factors as having a role. They obviously have one. The problem is the causal manner in which he conceives of their influence: external factors seem to produce

similar internal effects in all Latin American nations, directly and almost
without any internal mediation. The motor forces of change are therefore
transferred away from the societies which are undergoing change even
if they are formally independent.

THE THOUGHT OF THE ECONOMIC COMMISSION FOR LATIN AMERICA

The Economic Commission for Latin America was created in 1948 as a
regional body of the United Nations. The importance of ECLA's thought
both in the context of Latin American development studies and as a
theoretical contribution of wider influence cannot be underestimated.
The production of a distinctive and coherent approach to the development
problems of Latin America was, to a great extent, the achievement of its
director, the Argentinian economist Raul Prebisch, who by 1949 had
already written a substantial and influential report.[33] This was just the
time when modernization theories were arguing in favour of the diffusion
of modernizing values through increased international contacts and
trade, and development economics was reaffirming the advantages of the
existing international division of labour which determined that Latin
American nations should participate in the international market by
specializing in the export of primary products.

The focus of ECLA's analysis was the existence of a centre–periphery
world system which favoured the central industrial countries. Prebisch
argued that, although the two world wars and the depression of the 1930s
had forced Latin American nations to begin the diversification of their
economies by means of import-substituting industrialization, the
predominant forms of economic thought were still in favour of the old
ideas: specialization and international exchange were supposed to be the
best mechanisms to eliminate international differences between countries.
Even though the traditional theory of international exchange was
theoretically unobjectionable, in practice it was contradicted by facts:
inequalities between centre and periphery were growing. This is why the
traditional theory had to be criticized so that Latin American countries
were not tempted to relapse into its mistaken assumptions at a time of
booming international trade.[34]

The premises of the traditional position were two. First, the fruits of
technical progress tended to be evenly shared in the international
community. Non-industrial countries benefited from technical advances
in the developed world because the prices of industrial products tended

to go down. Second, the demand for raw materials was going to increase in the industrial centres, thus putting up their prices. Hence the price relation had to move in favour of non-industrial countries: by exporting the same amount of raw materials, peripheral nations would be able to import an increased amount of industrial goods. ECLA's first report of 1949 and Prebisch in 1950 argued, on the contrary, that the industrialized countries kept for themselves the benefits of technical progress: instead of transferring away these benefits by lowering the prices of industrial products they increased their incomes. Industrial monopolies were interested in defending the rate of profit and trade unions wanted to maintain the level of salaries. So the real sharing of the advantages of technical progress occurred in the industrial centres between entrepreneurs and workers. Those advantages did not get to the periphery. As Prebisch put it, the problem of the first premise is that 'it attributes general character to what of itself is very circumscribed.'[35]

Another reason for this was the existence of a relative surplus of economically active population in the periphery and a relative scarcity of workers in the industrial centres. In effect, in peripheral countries there was a higher rate of population growth which was compounded by labour-saving new technologies. The extra supply of badly organized and weak labour pushed down salaries and the prices of primary products. In the developed world there was a relative scarcity of labour and workers were well organized in strong trade unions which were very successful in defending the level of salaries. This helped to keep industrial prices high. Nonetheless, ECLA argued, if there had been perfect international mobility of productive factors – and this was one of the presuppositions of the traditional theory – the surplus population of the third world could have been absorbed by the industrial centres and the pressure on salaries and prices of raw materials would have eased. But in fact industrial centres restricted to a minimum the entry of foreign workers.

On the other hand, while the demand for industrial goods grew very rapidly, the demand for raw materials was found to be oscillating and to grow very slowly. This was due to several factors: new products developed in the centres were increasingly substituting for them; technical progress determined that primary products were a decreasing proportion of the aggregated value of final goods; and, finally, developed countries exploited their own primary resources and followed protectionist policies.[36] Consequently, the terms of trade were adverse to the peripheral world, that is to say, with the exportation of the same amount of primary products it was able to import progressively fewer industrial goods. If the orthodox theory of international trade had been right, then the prices of raw materials should have grown faster than the prices of the manufactured products. ECLA found that, on the contrary, the prices of primary products had deteriorated in relation to the prices of industrial goods. This meant that the periphery was transferring to the developed world part of the benefits of its own technical progress. For instance, say that

> the primary producers obtain 20 per cent less in industrial goods for the same amount of primary products; but if in order to produce the same amount they need only half the hours of work, they could buy 60 per cent more of industrial goods with one hour's work, instead of 100 per cent more, which would have occurred had they been able to take full advantage of their own technical progress . . .[37]

The conclusion of ECLA's analysis was that those countries specialized in the production of industrial goods would grow faster than those specialized in the production of raw materials and that therefore the gap between central and peripheral economies would increasingly widen. Industry had a dynamic effect that primary production did not possess: industrial growth promoted raw material extraction, but conversely primary production did not necessarily stimulate industrial activity. Additionally, industry could absorb surplus active population being shed by primary activities. So what Latin American nations had to do was to deepen their processes of industrialization in order to lessen their dependency on the external demand for raw materials and substitute for it the expansion of the internal demand. This meant for ECLA a change from a model of development 'towards the outside' to a model of development 'towards the inside'. At the centre of the latter model is the process of industrial diversification which is considered to be crucial to any process of development. This process appears in the Latin American context as an 'import-substituting industrialization' because it replaces those imports which these nations cannot afford with the available hard currency.

However, in order to embark on a process of import substituting industrialization some preconditions and policy decisions were required. In all of them the state had to play a crucial role. According to ECLA, protectionist tariffs were indispensable given the differences in productivity between developed and underdeveloped countries. This recommendation went beyond the traditional economic views which accepted protection only for isolated industries which were just beginning and until they were strong enough to face foreign competition. For ECLA the totality of the industry of a developing country needed protection for as long as its productivity remained lower than that of developed countries. ECLA was aware that the differences in productivity could be alternatively compensated by a reduction of the level of salaries in the less developed country. But this was judged to be undesirable not just for political and social reasons but also because such a policy would lower the level of prices of exports and would cause the terms of trade to deteriorate even further.[38]

Another recommendation had to do with state intervention and planning. ECLA contended that, given the many difficulties which a process of industrialization had to face, it was crucial that the state took the initiative of organizing, promoting and supervising all the industrializing efforts in order to guarantee the continuity of the process. Industrial development had to be carefully planned, both globally and by sectors, and the state had an especially important responsibility in the fields of energy, transport and some essential industries. However, ECLA was careful to emphasize that planning should not be confused with regimentation of the economy by the state. In fact in order to avoid any identification with socialist planning, ECLA spoke of 'programming'. A development programme should not supersede private initiative but should guide it and orientate it in particular directions by means of fiscal policies which provide incentives and disincentives. The 'programme' had to establish some development goals, and determine the necessary rate of investment and the areas where it should be located in order to secure a regular pattern of growth.[39]

In order to be able to get a higher rate of growth, ECLA also recommended the assistance of foreign capital. Additional resources were necessary because a process of industrialization increased the need to import equipment and technology from abroad and the relatively deteriorating price of primary exports did not allow the developing countries to keep pace with the expansion of necessary imports. Foreign capital was also deemed necessary to supplement internal savings and increase the rate of investment without having to restrict consumption too much. Additionally, ECLA thought that foreign capital would serve as an agent for the transfer of technology and new organizational techniques required by industry.[40] ECLA conceived of the role of foreign capital as a temporary one until the very process of development allowed internal savings to take over. It was also aware of possible problems created by foreign indebtedness and so it established some conditions which had to be met for foreign capital to be acceptable: although private foreign investment was not to be discarded, preference had to be given to low interest public loans by developed countries and international financial organizations; there had to be continuity in the flow of resources; a regional (Latin American) policy had to be implemented; and new international financial institutions had to be created.[41]

Finally, ECLA proposed regional integration as a long-term goal which would allow an expansion of national markets and would increase the opportunities for the import-substituting industrialization. The model of development 'towards the inside' would work better if the markets were extended and Latin American countries could specialize in certain areas, thus expanding regional trade and avoiding having to substitute for all imports separately. On their own, Latin American countries could not compete with developed nations. By joining in a common market, Latin American nations would take advantage of the enormous natural resources of the region, of a growing market of more than 250 million people and in general the process of development would be enhanced.[42] ECLA was aware that a policy of import substitution helped by foreign capital could lead, as it actually did, to serious balance of payments problems for Latin American nations, which resulted, among other things, in a limited capacity to import and inflationary processes. Regional integration was part of the answer to these problems inasmuch as it provided opportunities for additional exports and trade, expanded markets, a more efficient use of regional resources and bigger and technologically sophisticated industries able to take advantage of the economies of scale of mass production.[43]

It is less well known that ECLA complemented its economic analyses with some sociological approaches which sought to clarify the 'social aspects' of economic development. Thus for instance ECLA argued that economic development entailed (a) the adaptation of society to new functions; (b) the creation of new forms of life; and (c) the formation of a new social stratification.[44] The first point included modernization of some activities and new types of occupations: entrepreneurial, professional and technically skilled. The second point referred to new lifestyles, consumption patterns, forms of entertainment, and so on. The third aspect presented a change from a heterogeneous stratification which combined traditional and primitive strata with new classes without clear forms of integration, to a more homogeneous and well-integrated stratification system where a modern class, the 'new middle class', is expanding.[45] Another focus of attention for ECLA's social analyses was the process of urbanization and more generally the opposition between rural and urban patterns of life.[46] Again, the role of the middle classes in the process of development was emphasized and it was contended that 'the middle classes of Latin America are performing in their countries the role which the middle classes performed in other nations which are today completely industrialized.'[47]

A CRITICAL APPRAISAL OF ECLA'S ANALYSIS

It can be appreciated that ECLA's position is a mixture of modernization theory, a belief in capitalist development and foreign investment and a perception that, nevertheless, the capitalist world is divided into centre and periphery, that the latter has had a raw deal in the international markets and that many economic analyses about developing countries elaborated in the industrial centres are inadequate. ECLA shared with modernization theories both the optimism about the viability of development and the faith in the capitalist road to development. But, on the other hand, its views about the centre–periphery division of the world coincided with some of the tenets of the refurbished theory of imperialism about the opposition of interests between industrial and underdeveloped countries. In fact in many conservative quarters ECLA's views were seen as suspiciously close to the anti-imperialist Marxist tenets which spoke against a feudal–imperialist alliance and in favour of industrialization.

ECLA's radicalism could be seen in three directions. First, they doubted the universal beneficial effects of international trade and, methodologically, they introduced explanations, based on structural factors such as the role of monopolies and trade unions in the developed world, which went beyond the mechanism of the market. Second, they were able to show that the underdeveloped countries of the periphery were transferring part of the value they produced to the industrial centres, mainly through a mechanism of unequal exchange. ECLA was unwittingly pioneering what would later become the basis of new Marxist analyses of imperialism. Third, as Hirschman has pointed out, ECLA articulated and gave expression to feelings which were diffuse 'among important intellectual and middle-class circles in Latin America: first to various resentments against the United States . . . and, second, to the idea that the cure for society's ills lies in empowering the state to deal with them.'[48]

The most radical and heterodox aspects of ECLA's analyses were criticized by orthodox liberal economists as deeply flawed and verging on a socialist strategy. ECLA's scepticism about the primacy and equalizing results of the market forces and its recommendations in favour of protectionism, state intervention and planning were considered to be not only politically dangerous but also economically disastrous. Such policies could only lead to corrupting subsidies and an inefficient use of resources. ECLA's identification of development with industrialization was considered to be misplaced, especially if some countries had comparative advantages in other forms of production. The idea that the prices of primary products were always and inherently deteriorating in relation to the prices of manufactured goods was challenged as inaccurate. On the other hand, ECLA was also criticised from the left because it did not carry out a class analysis of Latin America and its disagreements with the international theory of trade did not alter its faith in a capitalist road of development. For all its radical and critical assessment of the centre–periphery system ECLA failed to analyse capitalism itself in the periphery as a structure of domination and class exploitation. As Cardoso has put it, 'the vision of CEPAL was treated as if it were a way to put blinkers on the consciousness of the peoples, showing them just a straight path ahead towards a prosperous future through industrialization and the strengthening of the State.'[49]

But perhaps the most hotly disputed aspect of ECLA's analyses is the question of the deterioration of the terms of trade for primary producers. This was crucial to the whole vision and was substantiated by UN statistics on price relations which covered almost 75 years since 1876. The statistics showed a trend towards deterioration of primary prices relative to industrial prices. However, this interpretation was challenged by Harberler who argued that, apart from some statistical deficiencies, the extent of the problem had been exaggerated, that if it had been possible to detect a deterioration of cyclical terms of trade it was because in times of depression the relative prices of raw materials did tend to worsen, but that in times of prosperity they tended to improve and that, because of this, it was impossible to predict future regularities.[50]

Still, Harberler did not deny that a form of historical generalization in the sense proposed by ECLA was possible. But his point was that 'the mere historical proposition that the terms of trade have deteriorated in a certain way does not prove anything.'[51] Ultimately, Haberler's argument seems to boil down to the not very impressive suggestion that whatever secular trend can be detected in the past, the future may be different. True, but hardly constructive or enlightening. Nevertheless, as Cardoso points out, Harberler's critique highlights a weakness in ECLA's analysis: 'the lack of a more detailed analysis of the role and nature of economic cycles, and the distinction between such cycles and tendencies towards constant deterioration.'[52] It is in this that Cardoso sees the seeds of future negative elaborations which will end up in a kind of catastrophism. Some of ECLA's followers and left-wing critics began increasingly to confuse the effects of recessions with irreversible tendencies and hence the idea emerged that underdevelopment necessarily meant stagnation.

According to Cardoso the originality of ECLA's contribution was not purely its critique of the theory of international trade but resided 'in its effort to convert this interpretation into the matrix of a whole set of policies to promote industrialization'.[53] Not surprisingly it was this aspect which came in for the heaviest criticism especially in the early 1960s. A wave of pessimism became prevalent at the time due to the poor performance of important economic indicators. The 'easy' phase of the import-substituting industrialization was coming to an end and Latin American countries were not succeeding in going on to the more 'difficult' phase of substituting for capital goods. The hopes that dependency on primary exports was going to be diminished were dashed by the fact that the import requirements of the industrialization process were even more substantial than before and this resulted in balance of payment deficits and renewed dependence on primary exports. That, in its turn, meant a renewed lease of economic and political life for the more traditional primary producers (mainly landowners) who had began to be displaced as the ruling class by the process of industrialization.

Additionally, the industry that was growing behind protectionist barriers was inefficient, expensive and catered for privileged minority groups with high incomes. Industrial growth was no longer keeping pace with the expansion of the active population and the migration from rural areas to the cities, and so unemployment and poverty were growing and income distribution was becoming more unequal. On the other hand, ECLA's expectations that industrialization would bring about a transference of the decision making processes from the centres to the periphery, thus contributing to the increasing autonomy of Latin American economic development, were also hindered by the fact that an increasing number of the most dynamic industries, especially those in monopoly positions, were being taken over or formed by foreign capital. As Cardoso and other 'dependentistas' remarked later, industrialization was no longer in contradiction with imperialism but was the new vehicle of foreign penetration.[54] This foreign control of industry did not necessarily mean the influx of fresh capital because international firms made use of local savings and local profits in order to re-invest and expand their industries. Consequently, it was pointed out, underdeveloped countries were exporting capital to the centres (repatriation of profits, royalties and licences) and not the other way about.

All these facts and considerations led many authors to think that ECLA's strategy of autonomous industrialization had failed[55] and that Latin America was stagnating. Others did not accept the idea of permanent stagnation, but rejected the notion that a national or autonomous form of development was possible any more. ECLA itself initiated a process of reformulation of its thought which underlined the obstacles to development. The process of import-substituting industrialization and its protection was critically examined even by Prebisch himself:

> An industrial structure virtually isolated from the outside world thus grew up in our countries . . . The criterion by which the choice was determined was based not on considerations of economic expediency, but on immediate feasibility, whatever the cost of production . . . tariffs have been carried to such a pitch that they are undoubtedly – on an average – the highest in the world. It is not uncommon to find tariff duties of over 500 per cent. As is well known, the proliferation of industries of every kind in a closed market has deprived Latin American countries of the advantages of specialization and economies of scale, and owing to the protection afforded by excessive tariff duties and restrictions, a healthy form of internal competition has failed to develop, to the detriment of efficient production.[56]

Out of these radical critiques and reformulations of ECLA's thought and out of the widespread pessimism concerning the Latin American chances of independent development a new vision began to emerge in the 1960s which emphasized the dependent character of Latin American economies. These new approaches, normally known by the name 'dependency theory', are the subject of the next two chapters. But it is important to stress here that although these new theories of dependency were critical of ECLA's thought they were also deeply influenced by it and that at least a part of the new dependentist vision was developed by scholars closely connected with or working for ECLA. It is in this sense as well that the intellectual environment created by ECLA proved to be seminal and stimulating.

4

DEPENDENCY, UNEQUAL EXCHANGE AND UNDERDEVELOPMENT

INTRODUCTION

The decline of modernization theories and of ECLA's approach in the 1960s coincided with the end of the almost uninterrupted expansion of post-war capitalism. A new phase opened up world-wide, the slowing down of economic growth, a falling rate of profit and more frequent recessions and trade crises. The economic situation of Latin American countries in particular took a turn for the worse: terms of trade deteriorated for primary products and the import-substituting industrialization process lost its dynamism. Hence the new wave of pessimism which led to trenchant criticisms of modernization theories and ECLA's policies. These critiques were at the centre of the new dependency theories which emerged in the mid-sixties as a radical challenge to the optimism of the old established theories. However, as I pointed out at the end of the last chapter, the first versions were developed within ECLA itself as part of an internal process of reformulation of its thought.

Two main features of the beginnings of dependency theory must be highlighted.[1] First it had an eminently critical and tentative character, that is to say, in its inception it did not presume to be a totally new and fully fledged methodology or theory with alternative explanations of the Latin American development process. Dependency theory was certainly critical but it also wanted to keep a line of continuity with previous analyses. In this sense ECLA's studies of the centre–periphery relationship and its asymmetries were the crucial starting point. Second, its interpretation emphasized the dialectical integration of sociological and political aspects of the process of economic development and tried to break with the unilateral emphases or the mere juxtaposition of variables of many analyses of modernization. A non-vulgar and historical form of Marxism was instrumental in achieving these goals by integrating the determination of economic structures with the agency, projects and strategies of domination of class subjects.

However, not all theories which are widely considered to be quintessentially 'dependentist' necessarily shared these two characteristics. In effect, these two features were above all to be found in the Latin American authors who first developed this critical approach. But they were not its sole representatives. Some North American Marxists, including Baran, Sweezy and Frank, were identified in one way or another with this current, especially by commentators in the United States and Europe. In fact A.G. Frank, quickly became the most important and well-known representative of dependency theory in the developed world. But his approach in particular, heavily influenced by Baran, was quite different from the original dependentist views developed by Sunkel, Cardoso, Faletto and other Latin Americans. This is why it is very difficult to speak of 'dependency theory' as if it were a single coherent and fully worked-out theoretical paradigm. Perhaps the only thing in common which all dependency analyses share is their interest in studying the situation of peripheral capitalist countries from the point of view of the conditioning effects which external forces and structures produce on the internal structures of these countries.[2] But here the similarity stops, because the way in which the interplay of internal and external factors is conceived varies widely.

Palma has proposed a very useful classification of three intellectual tendencies within dependency approaches.[3] First he distinguishes a tendency which seeks to construct a 'theory of underdevelopment' whose principal tenets are that underdevelopment is directly caused by dependency on central economies and that capitalism itself in the periphery is unable to bring about a process of development. Here Palma locates the work of A.G. Frank, followed in Chile by dos Santos, Caputo, Pizarro, Marini and others. A second tendency, represented by Sunkel and Furtado, seeks to reformulate ECLA's analyses and emphasizes the obstacles to national development stemming from external conditions. But they stop short of any generalization which may either put in doubt the developing capabilities of capitalism or seek to outline a general theory of underdevelopment. Finally, there is a tendency which seeks to study 'concrete situations of dependency' and stresses the internal processes of class struggle which necessarily mediate the influence of external factors. This approach rejects the formal and abstract attempts to construct a general theory which applies like a blanket to all underdeveloped countries and simply pins on external factors all the blame for their underdevelopment. This tendency is represented by the work of Cardoso and Faletto and is favoured by Palma himself.

Although this classification is very useful, it is still a bit restricted in that it leaves out some theories which, if not fully dependentist in the strict and formal sense, are very closely and substantively related to dependency studies. Palma's classification focuses mainly on the Latin American versions, or, rather, on those versions (including Frank's) which were developed in the Latin American context and refer to the Latin American reality. But above all, the problem of this classification is that the characterization of the distinction between Frank and Cardoso as an alternative between an attempt to construct a general-abstract theory of underdevelopment and an analysis of concrete situations of dependency may induce the mistaken belief that Cardoso's advantage over Frank is the fact that he is an anti-theoretical empiricist concerned only with the uniqueness of each case whereas Frank is a theoretical thinker totally detached from reality because he is concerned with abstract conceptual elaborations and generalizations.

If Cardoso's position is more convincing than Frank's, and I agree it is, it is not because it is less theoretical but because it seeks to illuminate and understand historical processes with the help of an appropriate theory, that is to say, by using a particular system of interrelated concepts and categories which are necessarily abstract in order to understand the Latin American reality. Theories are necessarily abstract not in the sense of being detached from the observational level, but in the sense of a system of mental constructs, often without a direct empirical referent, which are developed in a relationship with the observational level in order to render intelligible empirical and historical realities. The problem of Frank's approach is neither the abstraction or generality of the theory he applies nor the lack of empirical analysis. All theories are abstract and general and Frank does provide abundant historical and empirical analysis. The problem is that (a) the theory of capitalism on which he bases his analysis is simply wrong and tautological, as I will show further below, and (b) his object of analysis, dependent societies, is treated as an object in general, abstracted from specific historical determinations. Frank reduces dependent societies to a general category. As I pointed out elsewhere, 'the consequence of such a reduction is the mistaken attempt to derive the particular concrete from the general abstract and to substitute a suprahistorical logical account for historical analysis.'[4]

Therefore, I would like to propose a more general classification which will, nevertheless, keep Palma's distinctions but on a different basis. The criterion of distinction is the conception of capitalism. On the one hand, we have a group of theories which emphasize two aspects: first, capitalism is conceived as a world system characterized by an inherent duality, a centre–periphery dichotomy which determines two radically different developmental potentialities; and second, these differential potentialities are caused by transfers of resources through mechanisms of unequal exchange in the international market. This means that some countries develop because others underdevelop, and that the latter underdevelop because the former develop. Here we can locate Frank's theory which is genuinely dependentist, but also Wallerstein's world system approach, and Emmanuel's and Amin's unequal exchange theories.

On the other hand, we have a second group of approaches which, although accepting the conditioning influence of the capitalist world system, focus on capitalism as a mode of production or as an economic system which must be specifically and historically analysed within concrete social formations and national boundaries. They tend not to emphasize international market relations and transfer of resources through trade as the decisive basis of exploitation but look instead into the internal relations of production and class conflicts as the crucial elements which determine how external influences operate and are internally redefined. Here one can locate Palma's two last strands plus Hinkelammert's theory as three different versions.

First, the structuralists like Pinto, Sunkel and Furtado emphasize the obstacles to national development and adhere to a rather humanitarian and moral conception which distinguishes a genuine process of development from a mere process of economic growth. Second, Hinkelammert's theory of unbalanced peripheries rejects the confusion of peripheral situations with situations of underdevelopment and emphasizes technological dependence by drawing on Marxism and theories of economic space. Third, the Marxist-inspired approach of Cardoso and Faletto distinguishes concrete situations of dependency and various historical phases of it which depend on the integrated analysis of international conjunctures and internal class struggles of particular dependent countries or groups of countries. For these authors, dependency and development are not incompatible and can go together in a process which they call 'associated dependent development'.

THE DEVELOPMENT OF UNDERDEVELOPMENT AND THE WORLD
SYSTEM

As I said in chapter 2, the work of Paul Baran can be considered a very important landmark in the refurbishing of the theory of imperialism after the second world war. He introduced such crucial changes to it that it is possible to argue that his contribution is the hinge which joins or articulates the theory of imperialism with, and marks the beginning of, dependency theory. I shall not repeat the outline of his approach here, but I shall briefly reiterate a few points which directly lead to dependency theory, especially of the first 'Frankian' group. First of all, Baran develops a new interest in the analysis of the underdeveloped world itself, something that the theory of imperialism had been lacking. Second, he no longer identifies backwardness with the colonial situation but considers the case of backward independent countries. Third, he abandons the idea that backwardness is the result of pre-capitalist structures or modes of production and proposes the idea that it is the product of a certain type of capitalist development. So, in fourth place, capitalism, as a world system, is no longer considered to be homogeneous but it constitutes an hierarchical international system where more developed countries exploit the less developed ones.

Fifth, the exploitation of the less developed countries consists in the transfer of a part of their economic surplus to the developed world and the squandering of another part of it in luxury consumption by backward local oligarchies. It is because of the loss and misuse of their economic surplus that backward countries become underdeveloped. Sixth, imperialism is opposed to the industrial development of backward countries and therefore seeks to prop up and make alliances with the local 'comprador' bourgeoisies. Seventh, capitalism in its new monopolistic phase is no longer an expanding and dynamic force but leads to stagnation, particularly in less developed countries. Consequently, the only chance for these countries is to abandon capitalism and adopt a socialist road to development.

Despite their significance, Baran's theses, elaborated soon after the second world war, remained marginal to the academic world for quite a while. It was A. G. Frank who in the late 1960s expanded on and popularized Baran's views and adapted them to the analysis of the Latin American situation. Frank's historical analyses and theoretical conclusions quickly became well known all over the academic world and gave intellectual currency to dependency theory. Frank starts from the idea that capitalism expanded from Europe and managed to incorporate the whole world in a single international system. This world system is divided into 'a whole chain of metropolises and satellites, which runs from the world metropolis down to the hacienda or rural merchant who are satellites of the local commercial metropolitan center but who in their turn have peasants as their satellites.'[5]

The whole system has a monopolistic structure which entails the misuse and squandering of resources all over the system. A particularly important form of misuse is 'the expropriation and appropriation of a large part or even all of and more than the economic surplus or surplus value of the satellite by its local, regional, national or international metropolis.'[6] Ultimately, it is the main imperialist power that appropriates the resources extracted all along the metropolis–satellite chain. Thus for instance Frank shows that in the case of Brazil between 1947 and 1960 there is a net outflow of capital to the United States of $1,667 million[7] and that something similar can be affirmed for the rest of Latin America and the whole of the underdeveloped world.[8] Two consequences stem from this. First, the same historical process of capitalist expansion generates the continuous development of the metropolises and the continuous underdevelopment of the satellites. Second, the development of the metropolis necessitates the underdevelopment of the satellite, or, as Frank puts it, 'development and underdevelopment each cause and are caused by the other in the total development of capitalism.'[9]

The relations between metropolises and satellites entail the following aspects. First, the economic, social and political structures of the satellite are closely connected with those of its metropolis. Second, a national metropolis which is at the same time an international satellite cannot have autonomous development. Third, the weaker the ties between metropolis and satellite, the more possibility there is of local autonomous development. Fourth, the stronger the ties between metropolis and satellite the more there will be underdevelopment in the satellite. Therefore, satellites can never develop properly. They can only underdevelop in various degrees. Hence, underdevelopment is not a phase which predates development nor can it be confused with lack of development. Underdevelopment 'developed right along with economic development – and it is still doing so.'[10] This is what Frank calls the 'development of underdevelopment', a thesis which he tries to illustrate with his historical analyses of Chile and Brazil. Basically, Frank seeks to show that these two countries, like the rest of Latin America, became peripheral satellites of the Iberian and European metropolis from the sixteenth century and that, therefore, as fully capitalist economies, they have underdeveloped since the day they were colonized.

Frank strongly rejects the thesis that the agricultural sector or indeed any other part of Latin America can be considered 'feudal' or pre-capitalist. He also rejects the idea that in Latin America 'dual societies' exist which mix modern capitalist structures with traditional, 'closed', pre-capitalist sectors. For Frank these ideas are derived from a confusion of the system with its various features and, most significantly, from a confusion about the real nature of the feudal system. Frank castigates those authors who diagnose feudal relations by referring to 'types of relation between owners and workers' because this and other similar features do not refer to what is really central in the system. Analysing the case of Brazil he argues that

> Whatever the types of personal relations in a feudal system, the crucial thing about it for our purposes is that it is a *closed* system, or one only weakly linked with the world beyond. A closed feudal system would not be inconsistent with though it need not follow from – the supposition that Brazil and other countries have a 'dual society.' But this closure – and the duality as well – is wholly inconsistent with the reality of Brazil, past or present. No part of Brazil, certainly no populous part, forms a closed, or even an historically isolated, system. None of it can therefore in the most essential respect be feudal.[11]

So, what appear to be feudal or pre-capitalist features are in reality the consequences of underdeveloped capitalism. Even in the case of the Latin American Indian populations the problem for Frank cannot be defined in terms of economic isolation or lack of cultural integration. For him 'the expansion and development of capitalism incorporated the Indian population into its exploitative monopoly structure immediately upon conquest.'[12] So the 'Indian problem' is no different from the general problem of underdevelopment and the metropolis–satellite chain. Frank mentions slavery and the *encomienda*[13] as the first systems of exploitation of the Indians introduced by the Spaniards, but refuses to see anything pre-capitalist in them mainly because all the relationships of the Indians with other groups and classes are determined, from the very beginning, by the cash nexus and the metropolis–satellite structure of capitalism. Indian populations became just the last of the satellites in the capitalist exploitative chain which started in the European metropolises.

In more recent works Frank pays more detailed attention to the different modes of production (*encomienda*, yeoman farming, slave plantations, etc.) created in the various colonies, but still insists that their analysis 'must begin with an examination of the historical process of capital accumulation on a world scale since that was the driving force of the various processes in the New World.'[14] A subtle change in the model seems to have occurred. It now appears as if these various modes of production, instead of being dissolved into the world capitalist system, can keep their identity and be simultaneously a part of the capitalist process of accumulation:

> There is a variety of modes or, at least, of relations of production and of combination among them and between them and the capitalist mode of production. Many of them are preserved or even created by the incorporation into the capitalist process of capital accumulation of the production that is organized through this variety of 'noncapitalist' relations or modes of production.[15]

In describing this process of capitalist accumulation Frank also introduces the idea that it is partly 'based on a superexploitation of labour power through excess–surplus value, which . . . denies the labourer even the minimum necessary for subsistence . . . this less-than-subsistence superexploitation occurs both through wage labour and through other relations of production . . .'[16] This notion is to become crucial for some of Frank's followers such as Marini[17] who maintains that the hyper-exploitation of workers is intrinsic to dependent capitalism and crucial to the process of accumulation in central countries: the superexploitation of workers in dependent countries cheapens the exports of foodstuffs thus allowing a lowering of the cost of reproduction of labour in central countries. Because superexploitation means that the local working class is practically excluded from the consumption of manufactured products, a double sphere of consumption is created: luxury consumption for the few members of the ruling classes and subsistence consumption for the majority of the workers.

Frank's approach to pre-capitalist modes of production has important political consequences because the struggle for development cannot be based on the erroneous strategy of abolishing pre-capitalist structures or feudalism, a system which either does not exist (first version) or exists as a part of the capitalist process of accumulation (second version). If underdevelopment is in any case the result of capitalism, then it is capitalism that needs to be abolished. So Frank declares himself in fundamental opposition to bourgeois authors who want the same course of development to be followed as in European countries, but also to 'the Communist parties in Brazil and elsewhere in Latin America, which establish their programs and alliances with the bourgeoisie on the premise that the bourgeois revolution has yet to be made.'[18] In fact, in the preface to his first book he argues that a most important conclusion of his studies is that 'national capitalism and the national bourgeoisie do not and cannot offer any way out of underdevelopment in Latin America.'[19]

In practical political terms this means, first, that development is possible only under socialism; second, that because of that, the United States is inevitably opposed to the development efforts of underdeveloped countries;[20] third, that the immediate enemy of development is tactically the native Latin American bourgeoisies, but the principal enemy is strategically the United States;[21] and fourth, that the destruction of both the neo-colonial dependence and the resulting internal class structure 'cannot be done through reform but requires a revolution'.[22] Frank argues that a revolutionary process entails two necessary aspects: on the one hand an internal transfer of power and expansion of popular participation, and on the other, the achievement of external independence by means of a process of delinking.[23] According to Frank neither of these two aspects can on its own produce good results:

> to try neither delinking nor popular participation gets you nowhere. To try only external delinking without internal participation also gets you nowhere and leads back to rapid relinking. To try only internal participation without external delinking is extremely dangerous, very difficult to do, and likely to lead to disaster. External delinking and internal participation, social and political mobilization, reinforce each other and are necessary in order to be able to pursue rapid structural change to a threshold from which one would not immediately slide backward.[24]

If the development of the third world is only possible under socialism, if the United States is opposed to socialism, and so 'external delinking' coupled with internal revolution are the only solutions, how does Frank account for the more or less continuous process of industrialization and economic expansion which occurred in Korea, Taiwan, Singapore, Hong Kong, Brazil and Mexico, precisely under the influence of the United States? For Frank this phenomenon must be studied in the context of the growing economic crisis of the capitalist world system in the 1970s, which in order to reduce costs of production has brought about the emergence of a new international division of labour which relocates some agricultural, mining and manufacturing processes in the third world.

According to Frank this process is 'fueled and oiled' by the international financial system, especially through the agency of the International Monetary Fund, and leads to the promotion of 'export-led growth'. In this new international division of labour, what the third world countries have to offer is, 'first and foremost, cheap labour', and so the 'political consequences of all these economic policies are that it is necessary to repress the labour force in order to keep wages low or to reduce wages.'[25] In the face of this crisis and transformation of the capitalist world system, two alternative responses are possible. One is a model of rejection which leads to delinking and a possible internal socialist revolution (Angola, Nicaragua, Vietnam, etc.). The other is a model of acceptance which leads to the export-led growth of the newly industrializing countries ('NICs' – Singapore, Brazil, Hong Kong, Taiwan, etc.).[26]

Hence, for Frank, the case of the NICs must be understood as one possible policy response to the crisis and transformation of the capitalist world system. First of all he argues that these are exceptional cases which cannot be generalized to or followed by other third world countries. If the experience of these countries is really miraculous, as is often portrayed, then it 'can hardly serve as a model for the remainder of the third world, which would be hard put to duplicate the same circumstances and experience.'[27] Export-led growth by a few small countries is possible 'as one of the processes *of* the world system itself', but it should not be perceived as an autonomous process 'taking place in particular countries'.[28] In the case of the four Asian countries there are 'particular *political* reasons for their establishment and survival':

> South Korea and Taiwan clearly were created as 'independent' entities as a result of the Cold War against China and the Soviet Union and have been politically supported and economically subsidized as strategic pawns against them. Hong Kong emerged from history to a similarly peculiar position, and Singapore became a state because of the preponderance of overseas Chinese population on the Malay Peninsula.[29]

Furthermore, Frank questions the implications and consequences of 'export-led growth'. It leads to very low wages for labour, balance of payments crises and international indebtedness; it generates unemployment and creates fewer jobs than are needed for the labour it attracts into the cities. The NICs experience only questionable technological development as these countries are usually 'allocated the least remunerative and technologically obsolete contributions and the corresponding meagre benefits'.[30] For Frank there is very little difference between this model and the old raw material export-led model which underdeveloped the third world. Finally the political costs of the export-led growth are patent: authoritarianism, political repression and suppression of human rights.

Frank's ideas about the world system and especially his conviction that the development of the metropolises has been sustained by the underdevelopment of the satellites (through a process of surplus transfer) have been supported and further elaborated by the work of Wallerstein. For him a capitalist world economy was created in the sixteenth century with the expansion of European capitalism. This expansion involved

> unequal development and therefore differential rewards, and unequal development in a multilayered format of layers within layers, each one polarized in terms of a bimodal distributions of rewards . . . there was the differential of the core of the European world-economy versus its peripheral areas, within the European core between states, within states between regions and strata, . . .[31]

This differentiated world economy subsumes a variety of kinds of workers, from slaves working in plantations and serfs working on large domains to wage labourers working in factories. The different modes of organizing and controlling labour are in operation because each of them 'is best suited for particular types of production'.[32] But, and this is the crucial thing, they do not constitute the base of different modes of production coexisting with some articulation between them, because, unlike the old pre-capitalist modes which produced for the local economy, they produce for and are integrated into a capitalist world economy, hence they are all equally 'capitalist':

> it is *not* the case that two forms of social organization, capitalist and feudal, existed side by side, or could ever so exist. The world-economy has one form or the other. Once it is capitalist, relationships that bear certain formal resemblances to feudal relationships are necessarily redefined in terms of the governing principles of a capitalist system.[33]

To the objection that if, in different parts of the world, you have predominantly slave or servile forms of labour then that must necessarily be the result of local slave or feudal modes of production, Wallerstein answers with a question about the unit of analysis: 'is England, or Mexico or the West Indies a unit of analysis? Or is the unit (for the sixteenth–eighteenth centuries) the European world-economy including England *and* Mexico, in which case, what was the mode of production of this world economy?. . .'[34] On the one hand, there is a change of the unit of analysis, from specific social formations to international economic relations. On the other hand, just as in Frank, what becomes the decisive defining element of a mode of production is not the specific system of production relations, but the orientation to the market and the profit motivation. If slave production is oriented to the market in order to make a profit, then it becomes a form of capitalism. Or, as Wallerstein puts it, 'not all these capitalist "forms" were based on "free" labour – only those in the core of the economy. But the motivations of landlord and labourer in the non-"free" sector were as capitalist as those in the core.'[35]

Although Wallerstein seeks to generalize the Frankian model, he also introduces some modifications which tend to make it slightly more flexible. Instead of keeping the metropolis–satellite dichotomy, Wallerstein distinguishes three structural zones of the world economy which are the core, the semi-periphery and the periphery.[36] What is important about them is that they are by no means fixed once and for all because the economic activities of some areas progress while in other places they deteriorate. However,

> the fact that particular states change their position in the world-economy, from semi-periphery to core say, or vice versa, does not in itself change the nature of the system. These shifts will be registered for individual states as 'development' or 'regression'. The key factor to note is that within a capitalist world-economy, all states cannot 'develop' simultaneously *by definition*, since the system functions by virtue of having unequal core and peripheral regions.[37]

The relationships between core and periphery are understood, as in Frank, as relations of exploitation whereby the core appropriates the surplus produced by the periphery. This is the reason why 'by definition' not all states can develop. Wallerstein argues that all empires in the past were mechanisms for collecting tribute and that the modern world economy with its purely economic mechanisms offers 'an alternative and more lucrative source of surplus appropriation':

It is the social achievement of the modern world, if you will, to have invented the technology that makes it possible to increase the flow of the surplus from the lower strata to the upper strata, from the periphery to the center, from the majority to the minority, by eliminating the 'waste' of too cumbersome a political superstructure.[38]

The flow of surplus from the periphery to the core is secured both through the international division of labour and political power. The core gets a concentration of the 'tasks requiring higher levels of skill and greater capitalization'[39] and consequently the increased rewards for it. Additionally, the core develops 'a strong state machinery' which serves 'as a mechanism to protect disparities that have arisen within the world-system'.[40] The natural consequence of the transfer of surplus from the periphery to the core is the underdevelopment of the former and the development of the latter. As in Frank, development and under-development mutually cause each other and are the necessary result of the operation of the same capitalist system.

Wallerstein's and Frank's emphasis on the world economy as the basis of capitalism inevitably affects the role of class struggle in their theories. To be sure, both take class struggle into account, but Frank is more concerned than Wallerstein in establishing its centrality. However, given the general nature of the world economy and the primacy of trade in its formation, the role of class struggle cannot keep the centrality it had in Marxist analyses. In fact there is a tendency in Wallerstein to subsume its existence under the more general form of struggle 'between the small group of great beneficiaries of the system and the large group of its victims'.[41] This generic form of struggle manifests itself in various ways. Class struggle between capital and labour is one of them. But, Wallerstein goes on to say – implicitly alluding to Emmanuel's theses – that this conflict 'has been often softened by long-term, larger-scale considerations. Both the particular accumulator of capital and his work-force shared interests against other pairings elsewhere in the system.'[42] Wallerstein further argues that one should not pay attention only to class struggle because one would lose from view other forms of political struggle which are at least as important within capitalism.

A frequent criticism of Frank's and Wallerstein's positions avers that they have displaced class relations from the centre of their analyses of economic development and underdevelopment.'[43] Frank himself acknowledges the fact that class has not been the focus of his analysis:

The attempt to spell out the metropolis–satellite colonial structure and development of capitalism has led me to devote very little specific attention to its class structure and development. This does not mean that this colonial analysis is intended as a substitute for class analysis. On the contrary the colonial analysis is meant to complement class analysis and to discover and emphasize aspects of the class structure in these underdeveloped countries which have often remained unclear.[44]

One such aspect which Frank finds crucial is his conclusion that the Latin American national bourgeoisies have no positive role to play in the Latin American process of development. However, further below, and also in a more recent book,[45] he presents a different and more theoretical argument which instead of construing his approach as a complement to class analysis proposes an explanation of the role of classes which has strong structuralist overtones and which one can find in other deterministic forms of Marxism. In effect, in the context of a discussion about the main interest groups of the ruling class in Chile and their role in Chilean underdevelopment, Frank argues that it is not enough to say that these various groups of landowners, mineowners, merchants and industrialists hindered Chilean development because of the pursuit of their particular interests. The question is why this combination of interests did not lead to underdevelopment in England, Japan or the United States. His answer is that the interests and actions of classes are determined in particular ways by the underlying structures of the world capitalist system:

My thesis holds that the group interests which led to the continued underdevelopment of Chile and the economic development of some other countries were themselves created by the same economic structure which encompassed all these groups: the world capitalist system . . . It was in the nature of the structure of this system to produce interests leading to underdevelopment . . . The most powerful interest groups of the Chilean metropolis were interested in policies producing underdevelopment at home because their metropolis was at the same time a satellite.[46]

A similar thesis is developed with more historical detail for Latin America as a whole in his book *Lumpenbourgeoisie: Lumpendevelopment*. Here a sequential three-fold process is described in the following terms. The starting and founding event is the subordination of Latin America to the world capitalist system by means of the Hispanic conquest and colonization. The second and sequential occurrence is the formation of the class structure and culture of Latin America as an effect of the colonial relationship. In third place, the colonial and class structures determine the class interests of the bourgeoisie's ruling fractions which thus follow various policies that generate underdevelopment. The first event alludes to the basic and determining structure of dependency, the second aspect defines the class structure and normative values in terms of the necessary primacy of the *lumpenbourgeoisie*, and the third aspect determines the policy of underdevelopment or *lumpendevelopment*.[47] The causal sequence goes rather mechanically from the world system to the political activities of Latin American bourgeoisies.

Surprisingly enough, Frank does not seem fully to realize the implications of his theoretical position. When confronted with the criticisms of Cabral et al. and dos Santos that class exploitation is absent from or not easy to combine with his colonial analysis, he apologetically answers with a *mea culpa*[48] and a renewed effort to incorporate 'the active "internal" class participation in the determination of the historical process'.[49] Instead of defending his theoretical position by using, for instance, the traditional arguments of the Marxist orthodoxy[50] in the sense that class interests and activities are determined and pre-ordained by the economic structures (of the capitalist world system, in this case), he apologizes for lacking historical depth in his class analyses and for not making himself clear. Instead of exploring the concept of exploitation and trying theoretically to articulate regional exploitation with class exploitation, as one of his followers, Gonzalez Casanova[51] does, he is content with expanding on the historical evidence as if the sheer accumulation of historical data could restore a theoretical imbalance.

So, on the one hand Frank wants to reorient his analysis by emphasizing class participation in the determination of the historical process, but on the other he continues to maintain that class political practices are determined by Latin American dependency on the imperialist metropolis. But of course, he cannot have it both ways. Despite his willingness to make amendments, the main thrust of Frank's work is ultimately mechanistic and deterministic. Hence, the true problem of Frank's approach is not the self-confessed lack of clarity and historical depth in its class analysis, but the rigidity and determinism of his formal model, which applies in the same way to all class structures and practices of the underdeveloped world since colonial times, whatever their differences. This is the reason why his historical analyses of underdeveloped countries are bound to try to 'fit' the model and seek to show empirically what has already been theoretically pre-established as a premise. Frank's empirical class analyses always support his model, or, to put it in other words, the external relations always and everywhere produce the same internal relations. The problem here is the tautological nature of the theory he uses which leads to the reduction of the object of analysis to a general category devoid of historical determinations.

Wallerstein's theory is also deterministic but, unlike Frank's, it is not at pains to maintain the centrality of class struggle against heavy theoretical odds. Historical capitalism and the world economy it creates manifest themselves in a variety of conflicts and struggles of which the class struggle between capital and labour is only one possible form. Here the problem is not so much the reduction of all class conflicts to the same pattern everywhere in the third world, but the insufficient consideration of the capital–labour contradiction as the basis of capitalist development. As Brenner puts it, for Wallerstein 'the rise of distinctively capitalist class relations of production is no longer seen as the *basis* for capitalist development, but as its *result*.'[52] Instead of new class relations determining the capitalist development of productive forces, it is the already capitalist development of trade, the market-oriented constitution of the world economy, which determines the transition to the new class structure and to a variety of other patterns of conflict. The centrality of class disappears from the conception of capitalism.

Despite his efforts to reassert the centrality of class relations Frank's theory shares this problem and gives a very clear formulation to the idea that class relations are not constitutive but a consequence of capitalism:

> the owner–worker relationship, far from being the starting point of the chain of determination – or the fundamental contradiction, to use Marxist terms – is only an extension and manifestation of the determinant economic structure and relation. That structure is monopoly capitalism . . .[53]

But of course, this raise the question as to what then is capitalism. This leads me to the serious flaws in Frank's and Wallerstein's conceptions of capitalism and feudalism. Laclau, one of the best and most convincing of their critics, has rightly pointed out that Frank, just as much as Wallerstein, totally ignores the relations of production in trying to characterize these modes of production.[54] In effect, capitalism appears as a system of production oriented to the market whereas feudalism, as the above quotation about Brazil confirms, appears as a 'closed' system only weakly connected with the outside world. The orientation to the market and the maximization of profits become the decisive factors. Given this conceptualization, it is not surprising that Frank should affirm that Latin

America has been capitalist since its colonial days because the Spanish exploitation of its resources was carried out with a view to making profits by selling to the European markets.

The mistake is, of course, that the orientation to the market is not an exclusive characteristic of capitalism; other modes of production, including feudalism and slavery, have also historically sold at least part of their produce in the world market. Thus, for instance, Brenner shows how in the sixteenth and seventeenth centuries the export of grains from Eastern Europe to the West European markets, far from making East European economies more capitalist, determined the re-feudalization of their production relations.[55] Equally, Laclau shows how in the semi-feudal *haciendas* in Chile during the seventeenth and nineteenth centuries, increased servile exactions were imposed on the *inquilinos* [56]as the world market demand for grains increased and the landowners sought to maximize the exportable surplus.[57] So, pre-capitalist modes of production are not only perfectly compatible with the expansion of the world market but their inherent system of extra-economic coercion can even be enhanced by such expansion. Again, Frank's problem is that however much he wants to incorporate into his analysis the variety of modes of production existing in colonial Latin America,[58] he is ultimately bound to dissolve them all into the capitalist world system. Or is he?

My criticism perfectly fits Frank's early version of the incorporation model developed in *Capitalism and Underdevelopment in Latin America*, where he conceives of a single world capitalist system which, in the words of Banaji, 'instantly reconstructs relations of production through incorporation into the world market'.[59] However, in *Dependent Accumulation and Underdevelopment* and in *World Accumulation, 1492–1789*, as I showed above, Frank introduces another version whereby incorporation into the world capitalist system does not necessarily dissolve the pre-capitalist modes of production. According to this new version, then, the same process of world capitalist accumulation includes both capitalist and non-capitalist relations of production. Which means (a) that there would be a non-capitalist accumulation of capital, and (b) that capitalist accumulation would reproduce non-capitalist modes of production. Both these propositions seem manifestly absurd and do not represent an improvement on the first version.

Wallerstein has tried to come to the rescue of Frank's earlier incorporation model by saying that although Laclau's critique is right in terms of the letter of Marx's position, it is not in terms of its spirit.[60] It is not very clear what he means by the spirit in this case. But obviously he refuses to accept that the feudalism Laclau is talking about in the Latin American context is the same as the European feudalism of the Middle Ages. The reasons he adduces are that in the Latin American form of feudalism most of the surplus is destined for the market (as against only a part), the orientation is to the world market (as against the local market) and the exploiting class seeks to maximize and partially re-invest profits (as against spending them). All these differences would justify the dissolution of the so-called feudalism in Latin America into capitalism.

However, even if one recognizes the existence of these differences, the point is, really, that they do not discriminate between modes of production because they do not focus on the relations of production. To which Wallerstein retorts that 'the point is that the "relations of production" that define a system are the "relations of production" of the whole system, and the system at this point in time is the European world economy.'[61] But here, of course, Wallerstein confuses the world economy with a mode of production. There is little sense in talking about the relations of production of the world-economy, especially when even Wallerstein himself accepts that within the world-economy there is free labour in the core and coerced labour in the periphery. Which of them will represent the production relations of the whole system and why?

In fact Brenner has shown that there would be a very good case for maintaining that the early European world economy, to the extent that 'it was defined by the interconnected systems of production based on coerced cash crop labour in the periphery and based on free labour in the core', 'remained fundamentally "pre-capitalist": a sort of renewed feudalism, with a somewhat wider scope'.[62] The reason for this is, according to Brenner, that most of Europe after the abolition of serfdom was dominated by an economy based on peasant freeholders and therefore lacked the indispensable class structure which, by securing technical progress and the continuous advance of productive forces, characterizes capitalism, namely, that which is based on free wage-earners. This is why the early European world economy could not provide the bases for continuous industrial growth in most of Europe any better than could the Middle Ages. But of course Wallerstein cannot see this point because he ignores the connection between the specific class system of capitalism and the progress of productive forces. He simply has a different concept of capitalism which instead of focusing on production relations emphasizes the profit motive and the orientation to the world market. Thus for Wallerstein the technical progress characteristic of capitalism is not the result of a particular structure of class relations of free wage labour, but the result of competition in the market and the impulse to profit maximization.

Frank and Marini's thesis of the superexploitation of labour in dependent capitalist societies also deserves some critical comments. Frank's approach is cautious in that he describes capitalist accumulation as 'partly' based on superexploitation. For Marini, on the contrary, superexploitation seems to be a more essential feature of dependent capitalism. Whatever the extension of this phenomenon, there is a problem in its conceptualization and utilization by Frank and Marini. If they mean to use the Marxist concept, superexploitation entails the paying of wages which do not represent the total value of the means required by the workers to reproduce themselves, that is to say, the denial of the workers' minimum needs for subsistence. This cannot therefore constitute a permanent situation because it would lead to the physical extinction of the workers. If what Marini and Frank mean is that the value of labour is cut to the real minimum by extending the day's work and increasing the physical exertion as much as possible, but the workers can still reproduce themselves, then this is not superexploitation but simple exploitation.[63]

Besides, the idea that the workers of dependent countries are totally excluded from the consumption of manufactured products is simply false. Even if their consumption is very limited, they still need and buy clothes, building materials, food, medicines and increasingly radios and television sets. In spite of a widespread belief which has its source in the early works of ECLA, Latin American industrial production is far from being limited to luxury goods.[64] On the other hand, the idea that dependent capitalism is characterized by the extraction of absolute surplus-value totally neglects the fact that the increasing use of modern technology by both national and international industries determines the extraction of relative surplus-value in all but the most backward sectors. This does not mean to deny the existence of widespread poverty and unemployment and the fact that wages are extremely low. The point is that this happens not because capitalism does not work, but precisely because it is working in the specific historical conditions of peripheral countries.

Palma has maintained that the only part of Frank's analysis which is valuable is his critique of the theories which stress the supposedly dual character of Latin American societies.[65] This assessment does not seem very generous but it is true to say (a) that dualism, in so far as it propounds the idea of a lack of connection between the modern and traditional sectors of the economy, is a mistaken interpretation; and (b) that around this issue Frank makes a valuable contribution by showing, historically, how even the poorest and most remote parts of Latin America were linked to the world economy and how this connection did not necessarily bring economic development to them. However, even in this context Frank makes two serious mistakes. First, he seems to affirm that to accept the feudal nature of the agricultural relations of production in Latin America is necessarily to accept a form of dualism. But obviously this is not so because as we have seen above, the very *connections* with the world market may accentuate the servile nature of the social relations. Second, instead of cautiously restricting his theory to claiming that the international links do not necessarily bring about development to colonized areas, he goes further and claims, rather mechanically and without foundation, that the insertion in the capitalist world system necessarily precludes development and causes underdevelopment.

In a perverse kind of way, Frank's mistake mirrors that of the modernization theories which he so fiercely attacks. They affirm rather mechanically and in deterministic fashion that capitalist modernization necessarily brings about development in the third world; Frank counterargues, also mechanically and in a deterministic manner, that capitalism cannot produce development at all in peripheral areas. As Cardoso has pointed out, Frank's pessimistic formulation confuses 'the socialist criticism of capitalism with its non-viability'.[66] Marx was a strong critic of capitalism but it never occurred to him to deny that capitalism could produce economic development. True, he may have insufficiently emphasized the fact that capitalism does not necessarily bring about development everywhere in the same way, but he certainly never underpinned his hope for socialism on capitalism's supposed inability to develop productive forces.

At any rate, Frank's and Wallerstein's very conception of capitalism makes it more difficult to understand why socialism should be the cure to dependent underdevelopment. If capitalist underdevelopment is defined in terms of the incorporation to the world economy, then severing the links with the world market must produce development. Would this separation of itself bring about the destruction of capitalism in a socialist manner? It does not seem to follow necessarily that this should be so. As Brenner rightly remarks, if the world economy of itself breeds underdevelopment, 'the logical antidote to capitalist underdevelopment is not socialism, but autarky.'[67] True, Frank has made the point that a genuine revolutionary process must couple external delinking with internal participation and mobilization. But apart from a brief review of some historical failures and disasters (Allende's Chile, Ghana of N'krumah, Nasser's Egypt, Sukarno's Indonesia, etc.), which according to him show the need to have both aspects together, there does not seem to be an internal logic which unite them. In fact he even detects a worrying tendency to reintegration and relinking of socialist countries into the capitalist world system.[68]

It is the logic implicit in the Frankian model that makes Warren suspicious about the nature of the socialism it proposes. He argues that rather than fighting for socialism

> the effects of such theories on the working-class and socialist movement has been to subordinate them to ideologies of nationalist, anti-imperialist unity, to prevent their independent political development, and to induce them to bow to undemocratic regimes.[69]

Equally Banaji points out that

> The whole theory of dependency is still today fundamentally a petty-bourgeois theory which is inherently incapable of breaking loose from the platform of national capitalism . . . it has become fashionable to advocate 'disengagement from world capitalism'. But this is tantamount to a program of isolationist state capitalism, and has nothing at all to do with the revolutionary interests of the working class, which *at all stages* are bound up with the *world* market and its further development . . .[70]

These criticisms may well be too harsh, but there is an interesting point in what they say. Latin American countries have known quite a few seemingly left-wing political movements of a populist nature whose radical nationalistic and anti-imperialist rhetoric conceals their true capitalist and anti-socialist orientation. Warren is also correct – but only in so far as Frank's theory of dependency is concerned – when he accuses dependency theory of being static, of assuming that imperialism is a monolithic structure and of minimizing the wide range of options open to Latin American countries.[71] He does not realize though that his own position mirrors the rigidity of Frank's – in a manner not dissimilar to the theories of modernization – in so far as for him imperialism is monolithically everywhere the pioneer of capitalist development. Against both Frank and Warren, Cardoso rightly emphasizes that 'in specific situations it is possible to expect *development* and *dependency*' and that 'it would be wrong to generalize these processes to the entire third world.'[72]

This is why Frank is right in believing that the 'export-led growth' of Taiwan, South Korea, Hong Kong and Singapore cannot be generalized as a model for the rest of the third world; but he is wrong in dismissing it as if it was not a true process of development. For a start, the process of economic expansion in these Asian countries began before the crisis of the capitalist world system and the emergence of a new international division of labour in the 1970s. As Hamilton points out,

> Rapid industrial growth escalated in the second half of the sixties, although the process had been gathering momentum from the early fifties in Hong Kong and early sixties in Taiwan. Each of Taiwan, Korea, Singapore and Hong Kong achieved annual average growth rates of real GDP of around 9% in the sixties . . . These rates of growth of the Four were sustained and increased in the early seventies . . .[73]

Furthermore, the fact that these processes of industrial expansion are highly dependent both politically and economically on the United States, and have highly contradictory and authoritarian internal features, cannot eliminate their character as processes of capitalist development. As is often repeated, Frank forgets that all processes of capitalist development are inherently contradictory and do not lose their developmental character for that reason. On the other hand, although North American political and strategic considerations did play an important role in securing aid, foreign investment and markets for these countries, one should not disregard internal factors, such as for instance the fact that both Taiwan and South Korea had important processes of land reform in the early 1950s which weakened the landlord class and made the distribution of land more equitable. As Corbridge rightly points out, 'Frank quite ignores the internal economic and political histories of his "Gang of Four."'[74] Moreover, as Corbridge argues in true Cardosian vein, not even the very NICs should be lumped together, for if, for instance, one compares Taiwan with Brazil, the latter is burdened by a large landless peasantry whereas Taiwan's 'class structure and its past history have ensured a far more benign integration into an evolving international division of labour than could ever be the case in its Latin American counterpart.'[75]

Unequal exchange

In its origins the problematic of dependency – certainly at least the approach developed by Frank – was closely connected with the work of ECLA and the Latin American situation.[76] However, in the 1970s the notion of a world capitalist system which ECLA had outlined and Frank, following ECLA and Baran, had initially elaborated in order to understand Latin America's underdevelopment was further developed in a more general context by Wallerstein, Emmanuel and Amin. But whereas Wallerstein remained at a high level of generality, both Emmanuel and Amin, Marxist economists, went back to the specific problem of underdevelopment from a perspective which (a) started from the idea of an internally polarized capitalist world system, (b) incorporated ECLA's problematic of unequal international trade, and (c) simultaneously redrew its tenets in order to produce a new Marxist approach to imperialism. These are the so-called theories of unequal exchange. Although they implicitly share Frank's and Wallerstein's conception of the capitalist world economy, they – particularly Emmanuel's approach – advance much further in the analysis and refinement of the mechanisms of surplus transfer from the periphery to the core, which had been left rather vague by Frank and Wallerstein.

Just like ECLA 20 years earlier, Emmanuel starts his analysis with a critique of Ricardo's theory of comparative advantages. However, Emmanuel wants to sustain his critique on arguments which do not coincide with ECLA's pioneering analysis. According to Ricardo's well-known paradigm, it is advantageous for all countries participating in international trade to specialize in commodities for whose production they have comparative advantages. Within this framework it is possible for certain countries to benefit more than others, but all necessarily gain. ECLA and many economists like Singer and Prebisch attacked that conclusion. By using United Nations statistics they showed that there had been a systematic deterioration of the terms of trade of primary products which were predominantly exported by underdeveloped countries and provided explanations for that deterioration which I have summarized in chapter 3. However, according to Emmanuel, they failed properly to explain the statistical tendencies because 'there is no such tendency characteristic of certain products or certain categories of products. The "worsening of the terms of trade for primary products" is an optical illusion.'[77] Emmanuel tries to show that the problem lies elsewhere and that there is 'a certain category of countries that, whatever they undertake and whatever the produce, always exchange a larger amount of their national labour for a smaller amount of foreign labour . . .[78]

Emmanuel thus suggests that certain countries are exploited at the level of exchange. The problem stems from the fact that whereas there is an international mobility of commodities and capital, there is immobility of labour. This means that while there is a tendency for the equalization of profits throughout the world, the remuneration of labour varies from one country to another according to historical conditions. In fact, Emmanuel detects a tendency towards an increasing international differentiation whereby the wages of central economies are 20 to 40 times higher than those of Asia, Africa or Latin America. If one allows for the intensity of labour, which is about 50 per cent higher in the developed world, the average wage in the developed countries is about 15 times the average in the backward countries. This is the root cause of unequal exchange which entails the transfer of surplus-value from backward countries to developed countries thus negatively affecting the possibilities of development of the former.

However, not all types of unequal exchange are necessarily due to wage differentials. Emmanuel distinguishes a first type of non-equivalence between two countries when, in spite of having equal rates of surplus-value and the same level of wages, they specialize in branches of production having different organic compositions.[79] The country exchanging goods with a lower organic composition transfers part of its surplus-value to the country specializing in goods with a higher organic composition. Emmanuel does not regard this type of exchange between two countries as unequal because (a) it is a kind of non-equivalence due to technical reasons which occurs in every exchange between regions or branches of production within the same capitalist society and so there is nothing specific that international trade adds to it; and (b) the differences in organic composition are inevitable even in a model of perfect competition whereas wage differentials are due to imperfect competition in the international labour market due to political frontiers.[80]

A second type of non-equivalence between countries, for Emmanuel unequal exchange in the strict sense, is when the exchanging countries start from different levels of salaries and have different rates of surplus-value. (The country with the lower level of wages has the higher rate of surplus-value and vice versa.) In this case the country with the higher level of wages gets part of the surplus-value produced in the country with the lower level of wages, even if the total capital invested is the same in both countries and there is a higher organic composition in the backward country: 'it thus becomes clear that inequality of wages as such, all other things being equal, is alone the cause of the inequality of exchange.'[81] This is why Emmanuel maintains that wages are the 'independent variable'[82] of the system. The necessary consequence of the drain of surplus from the countries whose level of wages is comparatively low is the reduction of their rate of capital accumulation. Unequal exchange thus leads to unequal development:

> Even if we agree that unequal exchange is only one of the mechanisms whereby value is transferred from one group of countries to another, and that its *direct* effects account for only part of the difference in standards of living, I think it is possible to state that unequal exchange is the *elementary* transfer mechanism, and that, as such, it enables the advanced countries to begin and regularly to give new impetus to that *unevenness of development* that sets in motion all other mechanisms of exploitation . . .[83]

ECLA had also mentioned the relatively lower wages in the Latin American countries as compared with European wages, but it did not seem to consider wages as an independent variable. On the contrary, low wages were rather a consequence of the lower demand for and the lower prices of raw materials as much as of the poor organization of the working class and the excess supply of labour. For Emmanuel, on the contrary, the problem does not lie in a particular kind of product with poor demand and low price. It is the low level of wages that determines the low price of whatever product is exchanged. This is why he proposes that it is no use to underdeveloped countries to specialize in those dynamic branches of industry which provide superprofits to industrial countries. One must not lose sight of the fact, Emmanuel argues, 'that they are only "dynamic" because they belong to the high-wage countries and would cease to be so the moment they crossed over to the underdeveloped countries, as happened with the textile industry.'[84]

Without justifying his position, but obviously for practical reasons, Emmanuel rules out a solution consisting in a sudden levelling up of the wage levels of underdeveloped countries to the level of advanced countries.[85] Hence the choice for underdeveloped countries seems to be a difficult one: either unequal exchange or autarky. As in the case of Frank, the true logic of Emmanuel's analysis is autarky, but he is too experienced to believe that total autarky is a practical possibility either, so he suggests diversification and perhaps a sort of common market of backward countries. The idea is that a substantial reduction of exports and imports and the diversification of the economy by transferring resources from the traditional export branches to branches whose products can substitute for imports would be beneficial for underdeveloped countries.[86] At least in the latter aspect, Emmanuel's suggestion does not seem to differ a great deal from ECLA's policies of import-substituting industrialization. The problem is, as the experience of Latin America shows, that a policy of internal diversification causes more not less dependency on imports, and consequently on exports. So when Emmanuel says that 'the policy of diversification and autarky has more inherent logic than that which consists in choosing the branches that political economy has recently described as dynamic,'[87] he may be right in that particular comparison but he is wrong in believing that diversification and autarky are entirely compatible in practice.

Emmanuel's analysis specifically considers the consequences of unequal exchange for the international solidarity of working people. The classical theory of imperialism had been aware of the fact that class struggles in Europe had been weakened through some reforms which the European bourgeoisies had implemented by using the superprofits provided by imperialism. It was in this context that Lenin and Bukharin had spoken of the labour aristocracies and of their opportunistic deception of the working-class movement. But, Emmanuel says, they restricted this phenomenon to the upper stratum of the proletariat and thought that it was a transitory problem which the masses would soon reverse. However, the long process of integration of the working class into the system did not go away and consequently 'to explain a historical fact that has endured for nearly a century by the corruption of the leaders and the deception of the masses is, to say the least, hardly in conformity with the method of historical materialism.'[88]

The fact is, Emmanuel goes on, that the antagonism between classes in Europe has been progressively displaced by the antagonism between rich and poor nations, and that this is what explains the lack of revolutionary consciousness in the masses:

> It is not the conservatism of the leaders that has held back the revolutionary élan of the masses . . . it is the slow but steady growth in awareness by the masses that they belong to privileged exploiting nations that has obliged the leaders of their parties to revise their ideologies so as not to lose their clientele.[89]

Class antagonisms in the developed world have not disappeared, but have become secondary. Emmanuel's model starts from the premise that the rate of surplus-value extraction (rate of exploitation we may call it) is several times lower in the centre than it is in the periphery. The workers of the developed world have become conscious of this fact. So, from their point of view, the increase of the national income provided by the exploitation of third world countries has become more important than the internal struggle for improving their relative share of the cake. As Emmanuel puts it, 'a de facto united front of the workers and capitalists of the well-to-do countries, directed against the poor nations, coexists with an internal trade-union struggle over the sharing of the loot.'[90]

Not surprisingly, Emmanuel has been seriously criticized, especially by Marxist authors who distrust any analysis simply based on exchange in the market and not directly on the relations of production, and who consequently also disapprove of Frank and Wallerstein. Perhaps the most articulate of them is Bettelheim. He does not necessarily reject the existence of unequal exchange but disputes the basic premise of Emmanuel's explanation of it, namely the idea that wages can be taken as the 'independent variable' of the system able to determine changes in other spheres of society. The logical consequence of such a premise is that if underdeveloped countries were to raise the level of wages, they could avoid unequal exchange and underdevelopment.[91] True, Emmanuel does say that moving the level of wages upward is not a practical possibility in a capitalist economy, but he cannot deny that, theoretically, this is a correct logical inference from his approach. The point Bettelheim makes, on the contrary, questions the very logic as a mistake. Although he accepts that wages are not entirely determined by the economy and that historical and moral elements peculiar to each society play an important role in their determination, they are in no way independent or the ultimate explanation of phenomena such as unequal exchange:

> when we do not treat wages as an 'independent variable', we are led to *relate* the low wages in the poor countries both to the low level of development of their *productive forces* and to the *production relations* that have hindered and continue to hinder the growth of these forces . . . To achieve a lasting escape from 'unequal exchange', there is no other means than *the transforming of this objective basis* and thus the removal of those production relations that 'hinder the development of productive forces.'[92]

It is also the level of productive forces that determines the organic composition of capital so that the more advanced the productive forces the higher the organic composition of capital. So, in Bettelheim's view there is no reason to dismiss unequal exchange in the 'broad sense' just because it is not based on wage differentials. In fact both wages and the organic composition of capital depend on the level of productive forces and it is ultimately the poverty of the latter that is the source of international inequalities. As Bettelheim puts it, 'the poverty of the "poor countries" and the wealth of "rich countries", that is, their economic inequality, is "prior" to exchange between them and to what is called the "inequality" of this exchange.'[93] Furthermore, Bettelheim criticizes Emmanuel's equilibrium model and his assumption of perfect competition because they may distort some results of wage differentials which are the opposite to the postulated ones: low-wage countries can achieve surplus profits by combining low wages with advanced techniques. This is in fact the complaint which many industries in the developed world have against the 'unfair' competition from Hong Kong, Singapore, Taiwan and South Korea.

Bettelheim also objects to the notion that underdeveloped countries are 'exploited'. Exploitation entails the extraction and appropriation of surplus-value by a ruling class. Relations between countries cannot be conceived as class relations even if there is a transfer of value between them. Otherwise the working class of the developed countries appears to be the exploiter of the poor countries. In fact, Bettelheim argues, technically speaking the workers of developed countries are more exploited than their counterparts in poor countries because their higher productivity and intensity of labour results in a relatively higher surplus-value extraction, even if their wages provide them with a better standard of living. This criticism can also be extended to Frank's idea of surperexploitation which entails the denial of the minimum necessary for the subsistence of the worker. If the rate of exploitation depends on the proportion of surplus labour to necessary labour, it is possible, though admittedly somehow paradoxical, that a worker of a poor country where productivity is very low may starve and yet be less exploited (because of the small amount of surplus labour he performs) than a relatively highly paid worker in a country with high productivity.

This is the reason, goes on Bettelheim, why there is such a concentration of capital investment in the central countries. As Brewer has also pointed out, if exploitation is higher in the periphery 'why should the high-wage, high-price products go on being produced in the high-wage countries? *Given the free mobility of capital between countries why should any investment go to the high-wage countries at all?*'[94] As in the case of Frank and Wallerstein, the nationalistic interpretations and the ideological mystifications which Emmanuel's theory can unwittingly engender worry Bettelheim. The national bourgeoisies of underdeveloped countries

> are always trying to convince the working masses of their countries that their poverty is due not to the class exploitation of which they are victims, and the existence of production relations that block the development of the productive forces, but to the national 'exploitation' of which rich and poor, capitalists, peasants, and workers are said to be *all alike victims*, and which could and should be reduced through a sufficient alteration in the terms of trade.[95]

Amin, in his attempt to construct a theory of accumulation on a world scale, starts by addressing the problem raised by the controversy between Emmanuel and Bettelheim. Amin basically accepts Emmanuel's theory of unequal exchange and praises him for having discovered the 'preeminence of international values', the fact that the world is no longer a juxtaposition of nations which relate externally, but a single world capitalist system.[96] However, Amin wants to introduce some modifications which stem from his own theory and which also take into account Bettelheim's criticisms. For a start he says that Emmanuel made an empiricist and mechanistic mistake in calling wages the 'independent variable'. There are no independent variables or unilateral causalities in the capitalist mode of production, but, agreeing with Bettelheim, there is a close relationship between wages and the level of productive forces. So 'the level of wages is determined through the class struggle (the subjective element) which takes place within a context governed by the conditions of accumulation (the objective element).'[97]

Amin also insists that in order to improve Emmanuel's conception of unequal exchange one must take into account the fact that most of the exporting sectors of the third world use the same advanced techniques as similar sectors in the developed world and yet pay less to their workers. By introducing the notion of productivity Amin arrives to what he labels a 'superior' and correct definition of unequal exchange: 'the exchange of products whose production involves wage differentials greater than those of productivity.'[98] Amin adds that not all exports from the third world are produced within a capitalist mode of production but that this does not affect unequal exchange. There is unequal exchange, whatever the modes of production of the exchanging partners, when the wage differentials are bigger than the differentials in productivity.[99]

To the question as to whether Emmanuel's analysis necessarily leads to an exploitative alliance of bourgeoisie and proletariat in the centres and to an anti-imperialist solidarity between bourgeoisie and proletariat in the periphery he answers that this is not so. But he accepts that Emmanuel has wrongly suggested that the class contradiction has been replaced by a contradiction between rich and poor countries. Nevertheless, he rejects Bettelheim's argument that the workers in the industrial centres are more exploited than the workers of underdeveloped countries. Amin points out, once more, that Bettelheim forgets that three-quarters of the third world's exports come from high productivity sectors, which nevertheless pay their workers much less than their equivalents in the centres.[100] However, the fact that the third world worker is more exploited than the central worker and that this results in a transfer of surplus to the centre does not mean that the central workers benefit from that transfer. High wages in the centre are due to the high level of productive forces and not to international transfers.[101] How then to transcend the controversy? By displacing the issue of class struggle from its (pre-Leninist) national context to the context of the world system: the contradiction is now between the world bourgeoisie and the world proletariat. Who is the world bourgeoisie? Mainly the bourgeoisie at the centre, as the most powerful. Who is the world proletariat? Mainly the proletariat of the periphery. Why not the central proletariat as Marx thought? Because the peripheral proletariat is more exploited than the central proletariat.[102]

According to Amin, in spite of its path-breaking contribution, which for the first time formulates the problem of international values, Emmanuel's theory stops short of an analysis of the real problem, which has to do with 'the specific nature of the peripheral capitalist mode with respect to the central one'.[103] The world capitalist system is not homogeneous and there is a fundamental difference between the model of capital accumulation and of economic and social development in the central economies and the model characteristic of third world countries. The former is called 'self-centred system' and the latter is labeled 'peripheral system'. Their difference can be shown by distinguishing four sectors in the economic system: exports, consumption of luxury goods, 'mass' consumption and capital goods.[104]

A self-centred system is characterized by an articulation of the production of capital goods with the production of mass consumption goods. This is the typical capitalist mode of production as defined by Marx in *Capital* and it has characterized the historical development of capitalism in Europe, the United States and Japan. In this model international exchange can be left out not because historically the central economies developed in autarky, but because external relations are not essential for the model to work. The model works in the following way: the rate of surplus-value determined by the level of productive forces determines in its turn the distribution of the national income between wages and profits. Wages constitute the main source of demand for mass consumption goods whereas profits are the main source of savings and new investments. Increases in the rate of surplus-value tend to depress demand whereas a reduction of the rate of surplus-value negatively affects the level of investment and therefore the level of employment. Thus cycles of depression and expansion alternate which the system has been able to moderate.

In the context of an increasing monopolization of capital and of the creation of a strong trade union movement, a sort of 'social contract' is achieved between capital and labour whereby increases in real wages are related to increases in productivity, and in this way a state of permanent quasi-full employment results. This 'social contract' is expressed in social democratic ideologies which integrate the workers into the system. As the productive forces develop so does the demand coming from the expansion of wages. If at the beginning the demand was mainly aimed at essentials like food, clothing and housing, with the expansion of the economy and the wages the demand is now aimed at consumer durables like cars and electrical appliances. But the historical progression from one type of demand to the other is important because it is the initial strong demand for essentials that allows the development of agriculture and the mass consumption industry.[105]

Amin draws three conclusions from this analysis. First, self-centred accumulation is compatible with a regular rise in wages. The immanent tendency of the system is to keep the same level of wages but the working class can get improvements by means of trade union struggles. Should the level of wages remain static, the process of accumulation demands an expansion of the external markets in compensation. For Amin this was historically the case during the nineteenth century where the lack of sufficient wage rises in the centre led to an expansion abroad. Second, self-centred accumulation tends to destroy pre-capitalist modes of production. Third, self-centred accumulation causes a falling rate of profit which again is compensated by imperialism and the exploitation of the periphery.[106]

Peripheral systems, on the contrary, have a totally different model of accumulation, which is dependent on the centre–periphery relation. It is characterized by an emphasis on the export sector which eventually sustains the development of a production oriented to luxury consumption.

The economic activity of peripheral countries was initiated by the central countries developing in them an export sector which could secure (a) better returns for their capital, and (b) cheap raw materials and foodstuffs. Hence the relationship between the level of productive forces and wages disappears. Because the condition for developing certain exports is that the wages of the peripheral workers should be lower than those at the centre, and this is secured by the pre-capitalist modes of production which provide cheap labour power, wages are necessarily low and lead to unequal exchange along the lines described by Emmanuel. This means a drain of surplus which, although marginal for the internal accumulation process of the centre, crucially debilitates the accumulation process of the periphery. On the other hand, the level of productive forces is heterogeneous: high in the export sector, very low in the rest of the economy. This is what secures cheap labour power for the export sector.

Consequently, in peripheral systems a large part of the population is excluded from the capitalist exporting sector and the domestic market is dominated by pre-capitalist modes of production. Internal demand is not therefore based on the expanding wages of the workers and is restricted to a very limited number of mass consumption goods. When an internal market eventually develops, it is mainly based on the demand by parasitic ruling classes for luxury goods. Given the extent of the marginalization and unemployment suffered by the majority of the active population, it is only the elites that can influence the development of a market for consumer durables. This is why the import-substitution industrialization begins with the production of sophisticated goods instead of attempting the production of mass consumption goods. The lack of demand for these goods explains the backwardness of the agricultural sector. Hence the peripheral or 'extraverted' model of accumulation articulates an export sector with the production of luxury goods and leads to the impoverishment and marginalization of the majority of the population.[107]

Hence, in comparison with the self-centred model, the peripheral-dependent model presents opposite characteristics. If in the self-centred model there is a relation between the level of productivity and the level of wages, in the peripheral system that link does not exist and wages can therefore 'be frozen at very low levels without extraverted development being hindered'.[108] If the self-centred system has a 'vocation to exclusiveness, that is to say, to the destruction of all precapitalist modes',[109] the peripheral model accepts a plurality of modes of production because so far as the capitalist mode of production is concerned, 'extraversion blocks its development and so prevents it from becoming exclusive.'[110] Finally,

> in the self-centred economy there is an organic relation between the two terms of the social contradiction: bourgeoisie and proletariat, . . . each of them is integrated into the same reality which is the nation . . . on the contrary, in an extraverted economy one cannot understand the unity of these opposites at the national level but only at the world level.[111]

In political terms this has two consequences. First, the problem of class struggle must be located at the world level and no longer at the national level: it is the central bourgeoisie that exploits the peripheral proletariat. Second, the main nucleus of the forces of socialism has been displaced from the centre to the periphery.[112] Amin shares with Frank the idea that capitalism can no longer develop the periphery, but unlike Frank and Wallerstein, he accepts that there is an articulation of capitalism with other pre-capitalist modes of production in the periphery. Still, he does not fully endorse 'the articulation of the modes of production theory' which maintains that it is not capitalism that fails, but the pre-capitalist modes in the periphery that are more resilient than feudalism and which are able to resist the dissolving action of capitalism for longer.[113] For Amin, on the contrary, the 'extravert' character of the capitalist accumulation process in the periphery explains the failure of the capitalist mode of production itself and its accommodation to other modes.

There is no doubt that Amin improves Emmanuel's theory of unequal exchange by introducing the variable of productivity into the equation and showing that unequal exchange will exist when the wage differentials exceed the differences in productivity. Amin's analysis of the political consequences of unequal exchange is also more cautious, in that it avoids any blank condemnation of the central proletariat as an exploiter of peripheral workers. However, he insists on the fact that the latter are more exploited because their wages are lower even in the case where there is similar productivity and intensity of work. But improving Emmanuel's argument again, Amin denies that wages are an independent variable and links them with the level of productive forces.

An aspect which presents difficulties is Amin's attempt at transcending national boundaries in his analysis of accumulation on a world scale. On the one hand, he emphasizes the need to analyse all phenomena at this new world level and he seems to be successful when referring to peripheral economies. On the other hand, when studying the self-centred system, the analysis is made without a necessary reference to the periphery. This has, of course, advantages because it avoids Frank's and Wallerstein's mistaken assumption that central development is totally dependent on the exploitation of the third world. Yet this violates the need to analyse all sectors from the global perspective. In a way Amin wants to have it both ways: there is a world system which is supposed to explain all sectorial processes but one sector, the centre, can be explained without a reference to the world system, precisely because it is autocentric. If central proletariats and bourgeoisies are integrated in single nations while there is no such national integration for peripheral countries, how can one speak of an integrated single world system which transcends national systems?

True, Amin has argued that 'unity has never been synonymous with homogeneity; diversity and inequality exist within the unity of the world.'[114] But the point is a different one. Even if one accepts diversity, all sectors, in their very diversity, must be explained by a reference to the world system. But the self-centred system can still be explained in terms of 'nations' and in terms of internal variables which could essentially work without a reference to the periphery. In fact it is the lack of this self-centredness that constitutes the problem of underdeveloped countries. Hence the combination of pessimism and nationalism which many critics see as the hallmark of Amin, Frank and Emmanuel. Kitching compares them with the Russian populists:

> Pessimism about the possibilities of indigenous capitalist development, hostility to free trade and a certainty that it leads to national exploitation, demands for state-led 'national' industrialization, sometimes socialist and sometimes capitalist in form, are all hallmarks of modern underdevelopment theory, through which runs a pervasive nationalism. Baran, Frank, Amin, Emmanuel are much more the heirs of Flerovsky, Vorontsov, Danielson and other Russian populists, than they are of the Marxist tradition with which most of them consciously identify.[115]

Amin also shares some of the problems and ambiguities which Frank and Wallerstein have in defining the capitalist mode of production and in establishing its relation to other modes. Amin proposes that 'there is no juxtaposition of the capitalist mode and the precapitalist modes. The crux of the problem is to understand the meaning of the domination by the capitalist mode over the other modes, the domination being the basis of this unity.'[116] The crucial word here seems to be 'domination'. There is no juxtaposition, but there is a form of articulation by domination. If the peripheral social formations contain 'dominated' pre-capitalist modes this means that the world capitalist system can articulate within itself pre-capitalist modes which keep some identity even if they are dominated. But then, perhaps realizing the dualist consequences of this formulation, Amin rephrases it further below by saying that the process of domination 'has radically altered the noncapitalist modes and has reduced them to a simple form, a "shell" whose content has since become a relation of the sale of labour power.'[117] Ultimately, therefore, he seems to opt for Frank's early solution of dissolving other modes into the capitalist system.

S. Smith has criticized Amin for sharing with other dependency theories the idea that 'the world system is such that the development of part of the system occurs at the expense of other parts.'[118] To prove this assertion she quotes Amin when he says that

> The accentuation of the features of underdevelopment in proportion as the economic growth of the periphery – in other words the development of underdevelopment – necessarily results in the blocking of growth, in other words, the impossibility ... of going over to autonomous and self-sustained growth, to development in the true sense.[119]

I fail to see in which logical way this quotation proves Amin's adherence to Frank's 'two-sides-of-the-coin' tenet. In fact, as I have shown above, Amin is quite clear in dissociating himself from such a view. However, what the quotation does show is that Amin has uncritically accepted the Frankian idea of a 'development of underdevelopment' and the notions that in the periphery growth is blocked and there is an impossibility of development 'in the true sense'. I have already criticized the mechanistic and deterministic errors of such a position. At points Amin seems even to be keen on a distinction between growth and development in order to convey the idea that peripheral countries may grow but never have development. But this distinction is fraught with problems and pitfalls, not the least of which is the fact that it may induce the mistaken belief that capitalism in the centre has finally overcome all its contradictions and that it is only in the peripheral systems that contradictions, and the possibilities of socialism, can be found.

5

DEPENDENCY, INDUSTRIALIZATION AND DEVELOPMENT

INTRODUCTION

I have distinguished two main groups of theories within the problematic of dependency. The first group which I have already discussed in chapter 4 proposes a totalizing vision according to which there is a single integrated world capitalist system which is polarized into centre and periphery. The incorporation of the periphery into the world capitalist system occurs by means of trade and this is at the same time the source of its exploitation through unequal exchange. The transfer of surplus from the periphery to the centre explains the underdevelopment of the former and, except for Amin, the development of the latter. Hence these theories tend to be stagnationist and do not conceive of any possibility of real development occurring in the periphery. All that could exist is the development of underdevelopment. The situation of being peripheral is synonymous with poverty and backwardness. Dependency, through unequal exchange, is in itself a sufficient explanation of under-development.

The second group of theories, which is my concern in this chapter, conceives of dependency in a different way; not as a sufficient explanation of underdevelopment but as a conditioning situation which is mediated and altered in its effects by internal economic and social processes. Although these theories accept the conditioning influence of the world capitalist system they focus their analysis on the internal Latin American processes and their variability. They could be stagnationist (Sunkel, Furtado, Hinkelammert) or allow for development (Cardoso, Faletto, Pinto), they could be Marxist (Cardoso, Faletto, Hinkelammert) or non-

Marxist (Pinto, Sunkel, Furtado), but in any case the obstacles to or possibilities of development are studied in relation to internal processes and class struggles and not solely in relation to external factors, however important they may be. Furthermore, these theories tend not to give too much importance to unequal exchange and the transfer of surplus as a major cause of underdevelopment, although most of them recognize its existence. Above all, these theories do not confuse dependency with necessary underdevelopment. I shall distinguish three currents within this group of dependency theories. The 'structuralist' (Pinto, Sunkel, Furtado), the theory of unbalanced peripheries (Hinkelammert) and the theory of 'associated dependent development' (Cardoso, Faletto).

Structural Obstacles to National Development

The thought of Pinto, Sunkel and Furtado was formed within ECLA's intellectual tradition but towards the mid-1960s initiated a process of reformulation of ECLA's tenets in the context of a growing pessimism about the Latin American prospects of development. These authors did not want to draw any general conclusions about the viability of capitalism in the third world but empirically investigated the obstacles which they thought led to the stagnation or frustration of national development in Latin America. The titles of some of their publications during this time are symptomatic. Pinto, for instance, in *Chile, a Case of Frustrated Development* tries to show the structural causes which have hindered the process of development in Chile from 1830 to 1953.[1] Furtado does the same for Latin America in general and Brazil in particular in *Underdevelopment and Stagnation*.[2] He analyses both external obstacles and structural factors hindering development. Sunkel, in his turn, in 'Social change and frustration in Chile'[3] argues that a rapid process of social change in Chile has not led to the expected social results. The reason lies in certain basic structures of Chilean society. Hence the label 'structuralist' which these authors usually receive.

One of the first analyses to start this tendency was Pinto's pioneering study of Chile. His basic thesis throughout is the existence of a cleavage or contradiction between a rapid social and political expansion and a sluggish economic development. Using a metaphor Pinto argues that Chile 'stands out for an almost deformed development of its head, meaning by that its institutionality, its political organization, its structure of social relations, which seem to stand on a rickety body, or at least, a body of an age which does not correspond'.[4] According to Pinto, before the crisis of 1930 Chile presented the most favourable conditions for developing according to the classical pattern envisaged by liberalism: the expansion and modernization of primary production for export would release human and material resources which eventually would bring about internal diversification and development of other economic activities. But this did not happen. The reasons are multiple. Some of them have to do with external dependence; others, equally important, relate to internal factors, both structural and political. Among the dependency factors, Pinto mentions the fact that from the very beginning Chile lost national control over the nitrate and copper mines and foreign companies had an inordinately high participation in the Chilean total investment. This was aggravated by a systematic deterioration of the terms of trade and the so-called 'demonstration effect' which promoted foreign patterns of consumption and hindered internal saving and investment. Pinto goes so far as to speak of the lack of 'national character', such was the rush to imitate foreign institutions and values.[5] Internal structural factors compounded the problem: the basis of the Chilean export economy was too narrow and dependent on copper and nitrate alone. The traditional property structure (hacienda) and general backwardness of the agricultural sector was also a major negative determinant of the Chilean possibilities of development. It supported a class who did not reinvest the revenues of international trade but squandered them in conspicuous consumption. This in its turn put pressure on imports and resulted in the narrowness of the Chilean internal market.[6]

After the 1930's crisis and in the context of the process of import-substituting industrialization, the situation does not markedly improve and new frustrations are added to the development process. Pinto argues again that they are the result of a variety of factors. First there is the lack of clear and consistent policies and of sufficient investment. Second, and most important, is high inflation, which is partly due to failures in monetary policies and partly due to structural factors. Among the latter Pinto mentions Chile's dependency on external trade, low agricultural productivity, low incomes, transfer of surplus abroad in terms of repatriation of profits, etc. But, above all, inflation 'reflects the struggle of the different socio-economic groups and sectors to modify or keep a determined income distribution'.[7] Third, agrarian backwardness. Fourth, dependency on a narrow structure of exports. Fifth, expansion of services in detriment to the production of mass consumption goods. Sixth, bureaucratic inefficiency; and seventh, a very regressive pattern of income distribution.

Writing in 1965, Sunkel is equally pessimistic in respect of the process of Chilean industrialization which was supposed to create a dynamic and self-sustained economy. In reality, he says, the Chilean economy has been practically stagnant since 1954.[8] The most important factor which explains the 'frustration' of social change and development in Chile is the excessive concentration of income and wealth in the hands of a minority. While industrial capital is highly concentrated, the traditional concentration of agrarian property has not been altered. The media are controlled almost in their entirety by big economic interests and the education system is highly discriminatory in favour of the wealthy elites.[9] In the case of Brazil, presented as a typical case of development through import substitution, Furtado argues that

> the dynamic factors responsible for the substituting industrialization tend to get exhausted when they operate within the Latin American institutional framework. Brazil does not constitute an exception, because that weakening occurred before the national economic system could reach the degree of diversification which secures self-sustained development.[10]

What happens is that a pre-capitalist sector coexists with an industrial sector, which uses capital intensive technology thus originating a highly concentrated pattern of income distribution which determines an application of economic resources in a less efficient manner. This leads to economic stagnation in general, but more particularly to unemployment and serious social problems in the urban zones which also make growth impossible.[11] Without explicitly adhering to a stagnationist point of view, Pinto has analysed the socio-economic results of the Latin American import-substituting industrialization as leading to 'structural heterogeneity'. By this he means that the Latin American productive structure can be divided into three strata: a 'primitive' pole with a very low income and productivity, similar to colonial or pre-Columbian levels; a 'modern' pole with income and productivity similar to those of the developed world; and an 'intermediate' pole which corresponds to the national productivity average.[12]

'Structural heterogeneity' is not the same as 'dualism' because the three strata are not separate compartments but are inserted in a common context. Internal relations between these sectors are described in terms of 'internal colonialism' and exploitation: terms of trade, exchange rates, public investment and transfer of resources favour the modern pole in detriment to the 'internal periphery'.[13] While in the developed world there is a tendency to a relative homogeneity among the various economic sectors, in Latin America there are important discontinuities. Between 35 and 40 per cent of the Latin American active population work in the 'primitive' pole, and produce only an 8 per cent of the national product, whereas only 13 per cent of the population work in the modern sector.

Pinto maintains that ECLA's hopes that the process of industrialization would play a 'homogenizing' role did not materialize. On the contrary, the pace of development has not accelerated nor has it become self-sustained, external dependency has expanded, most of the population in Latin America has been 'marginalized' from the modern pole and 'there has been a *threefold concentration of the "fruits of technical progress"*: at the social level, at the level of economic strata, and at the regional level.'[14] According to Pinto there is no indication that this tendency will be spontaneously reversed. Pinto concludes with a hint that one should distinguish between growth and development:

> In so far as Latin America is concerned, the first thing one must take into account is that after so many decades of growth 'towards the outside' and 'towards the inside', between 40 and 50 per cent of the Latin American population continue to be marginalized from the benefits of development and have average incomes similar to those of the countries of Asia and Africa.[15]

In fact this distinction between growth and development is one of the main characteristics of this group of authors. Furtado, for instance, argues that in a situation of underdevelopment it is possible for the industrial sector to grow and even for the *per capita* income of the whole population to grow and yet the proportion of the population which benefits from the process of development remains reduced and the occupational structure stays basically pre-capitalist.[16] Sunkel in his turn defines development as a process of change which ultimately seeks the equalization of the social, political and economic opportunities both nationally and internationally.[17] He accepts that this position entails an *a priori* conception of what 'ought to be', but suggests that one can keep 'scientific objectivity' by recognizing the value premises from which one starts. Perhaps the clearest formulation of this position can be found in Seers. According to him, the concept of development is inevitably normative and the basic values which allow its measurement are those which allow the fulfilment of human potential, namely, an income which provides enough for food, clothing and shelter, employment and equality in income distribution:

> the questions to ask about a country's development are therefore: What has been happening to poverty? What has been happening to unemployment? What has been happening to inequality? If all three of these have become less severe, then beyond doubt this has been a period of development for the country concerned. If one or two of these central problems have been growing worse, especially if all three have, it would be strange to call the result 'development', even if *per capita* income had soared.[18]

Another point which is particularly emphasized by this group of authors has to do with national control over the process of development and over the political, social and cultural life of the nation. For Sunkel one of the basic objectives of a policy of development – together with the aspiration to a better material welfare – is the affirmation of the nation, the aspiration to overcome dependency.[19] Seers too sees economic and political national independence, coupled with adequate educational levels, as necessary requirements for the realization of the potential of the human being.[20] Furtado in his turn argues that 'the struggle to overcome underdevelopment and to preserve a national character with self-determination are dialectically integrated in political action.'[21] This is why, he says, the most advanced ideologies of development have emerged out of the process of decolonization. I have already shown that Pinto criticizes the lack or loss of a Chilean national 'character', but more generally he makes the point that those Latin American economies with the highest relative growth in the region are precisely those where the process of denationalization through direct foreign private investment is most advanced.[22] In general, there is a heavy emphasis on the national character which development must assume and which this new kind of dependency on multinational corporations hinders.[23]

In case this is not already clear, the 'new character' of dependency consists in the fact that whereas, before, industrialization was supposed to be the way to beat dependency and become self-sufficient, now it is increasingly seen that industrialization has turned out to be a new vehicle of dependency through direct investment and control by foreign capital, especially the capital controlled by transnational corporations. As Furtado puts it, participation by foreign groups in Latin America's recent development is far less a phenomenon of financial co-operation than one of control over productive activities by groups that have already been supplying the market with exports. Since they controlled trademarks that had become familiar on the local markets and could more easily mobilise technical resources and domestic and foreign credit, these groups occupied privileged positions on the markets where there was a wave of import substitutions. Moreover, foreign enterprises could nearly always count on the exceptional facilities extended by Latin American governments.[24]

For Pinto the appearance of multinational corporations means that the relative hegemonic weight of the USA has decreased and that there has been a 'diversification' of the centres. This has, on the one hand, increased the periphery's room for manoeuvre but, on the other, the centres have also become increasingly integrated, controlling and absorbing most of the trade and investment, producing their own raw materials and food and thus increasingly marginalizing the third world.[25] But whereas Pinto accepts that all this does not necessarily mean stagnation and lack of growth (it only means a 'perverse' style of development), Furtado and Sunkel seem more pessimistic.

Furtado underlines that the role of the United States is crucial for Latin America and maintains that, under the guise of safeguarding its safety and of keeping a strategic nuclear equilibrium, the United States has forced Latin America into its 'sphere of influence', which is nothing else than a way of securing its own economic domination. The North American hegemony is, for Furtado, a serious obstacle for the development of Latin America.[26] Sunkel goes further but in a different direction. For him transnational capitalism through the agency of transnational corporations causes a process of cultural and national disintegration in Latin America. At the global level, certain activities, social classes and regions from different countries are closely integrated and constitute the developed pole of the international system. Other sectors, groups and regions are excluded from the developed pole and have no relations with similar sectors in other countries. Underdeveloped countries are those in which the latter sectors, groups and regions predominate, that is to say, the sectors and groups which are marginalized and excluded from modernity. And yet, this segmented social structure

derives an important part of its dynamism from the influence which the internationalized segment of our countries receives from the central countries . . . this influence manifests itself at the level of the production structure, by the massive penetration . . . of the transnational conglomerate . . .; at the technical level, by the large-scale introduction of capital-intensive and labour-saving techniques; at the cultural and ideological level, by an overwhelming and systematic publicity for the model of consumerist civilization . . .; and at the concrete level of policies and strategies of development, by the pressure of the national, foreign and international interests, private and public, associated with the internationalized segment, in favour of policies which promote a development of this nature.[27]

Although Pinto does not exclude growth and Furtado and Sunkel tend to stress stagnation, the three of them are pessimistic about the prospects of true development in Latin America. This does not mean that they propose, as the first group of dependency theories did, that capitalism in itself has lost its dynamic qualities and necessarily underdevelops the periphery. Sunkel in the last article quoted comes close to that conception, but in general they all abstain from drawing such a conclusion. In this they continue to show the caution of ECLA's analysis which, while criticizing the centre–periphery dichotomy, saw in capitalist industrialization a way out. As industrialization becomes a new agency of dependency, even that hope is dashed. So one finds in these authors an unmitigated pessimism and, by default, a nostalgia for a 'national' and 'integrating' (as against 'marginalizing') kind of capitalist development which they do not really know how to bring about.

Cardoso has pointed out that these authors did not take into account the cyclical nature of capitalism and confused 'reformist ideals' with 'specific analysis of capitalism. The incompatibility between this latter and the desired reforms gave rise to frustrations.'[28] For my part I can add that the humanitarian distinction between growth and development is bound to present at least one of two main problems. Either it implicitly erects the capitalist system in the centres as an ideal paradigm and refuses to see its own contradictions. Or, if one were to apply the distinction in a rigorous way (for instance using Seers's four indicators), one could easily conclude that no country in the world is really developed, least of all the United States and other European countries with high unemployment rates and important elements of racial discrimination. Hence the very concept of development risks being dissolved in a way which does not seem very helpful.

UNBALANCED PERIPHERIES

Although the analysis developed by Hinkelammert is less well known internationally, it certainly occupies a special place among the dependency theories of the second group. It is theoretically sophisticated and draws part of its premises from a conception about the economic space and from an intelligent reading of Marx. Unlike the other analyses in this group it does not tackle the problems of underdevelopment and dependency by means of empirical and historical analyses of Latin America but keeps a higher level of abstraction and refers to Latin America only as a general background. Hinkelammert shows some sympathy for the authors of the first group of dependency theories, particularly Frank, but struggles against their mechanistic determinism and strongly disagrees with their emphasis on trade and the transfer of surplus as the main mechanism of dependency and underdevelopment. In so far as the 'structuralists' and their conception of self-sustained growth are concerned, Hinkelammert criticizes their confusion of peripheral situations with underdevelopment and their inability to understand that there could also exist 'reflected' or dependent growth.[29]

Palma locates Hinkelammert among the followers of Frank,[30] perhaps because his approach has stagnationist overtones and also because of his radical critique of the failure of capitalism in underdeveloped areas. Yet I find the differences between Hinkelammert and Frank more relevant than their similarities. It is true that Hinkelammert maintains that, in a situation of underdevelopment, the capitalist system does not work in the sense of 'functionalizing' society for growth. But his explanation is different from Frank's idea that the problem is in the profit-oriented incorporation of backward countries into the international market and the subsequent loss of surplus. For Hinkelammert, capitalism 'functionalizes' society for growth by means of a particular class structure, not just by the profit and market orientation. However, according to Hinkelammert the existence of capitalist relations of production may be a necessary, but by no means a sufficient, condition for growth. Here he introduces a series of distinctions which take into account various categories of economic space.

First of all it is necessary to distinguish between centre and periphery and explain why the tendency of the first industrial centre to transform the rest of the world into periphery of its own industrialization was successful in some cases and failed in others. Then it is necessary to distinguish 'balanced peripheries' from 'unbalanced peripheries', something which is totally absent in Frank and other dependency authors. Central economies and 'balanced peripheries' have the conditions to develop. So underdevelopment must not be simply identified with a peripheral situation. It is in the 'unbalanced peripheries' that some conditions for growth fail. What is interesting is that for Hinkelammert, again unlike Frank, the condition which may falter in unbalanced peripheries is neither external (transfer of surplus) nor, initially, necessary. At the beginning the problem is a class contingent political decision which could be reversed, later that original class decision becomes irreversible due to the historical emergence of a qualitative technological gap.

In effect, according to Hinkelammert, there was an inherent tendency of English capitalism to transform all other countries into peripheries of its own industrialization, that is to say, to transform them into buyers of manufactured products and providers of raw materials. Certain West European countries, particularly France and Germany, resisted and fought against their transformation into peripheries mainly by introducing protective barriers. Their own bourgeoisies, fighting against the British ideology of free trade (hence Frederik List's campaign in Germany in favour of protectionism), reserved the right to destroy traditional forms of production in order to replace them with an autochthonous modern industry. The destructive and regenerating tasks were not left to the competition of British goods but were assumed by national bourgeoisies. This allowed the emergence of new industrial centres.

Other countries, on the contrary, chose not to oppose the British penetration (or did not have a chance to oppose it as in the case of the British colonies). These countries were transformed into peripheries and specialized in particular productions necessary for British industry. Notice that the constitution of a peripheral country is not the same as colonization. For Hinkelammert a region can be transformed into periphery by its own autochthonous ruling classes, simply by accepting free trade and the penetration of British goods, as in the case of Latin America. However, not all peripheries became underdeveloped. Countries like Australia, New Zealand, Canada, Denmark and Holland developed as 'balanced peripheries' inasmuch as by producing mainly raw materials or foodstuffs they secured full employment of their labour force at a technological level comparable with that of the centre and with a similar level of salaries.[31]

What determines an unbalanced periphery is (a) chronic unemployment or underemployment of the labour force; (b) use of traditional or backward technology; and (c) lack of those skills appropriate to the use of advanced technology.[32] These conditions are more likely to occur in densely populated areas which come in contact with an industrial centre. Yet so far as Hinkelammert is concerned there is nothing inevitable about this situation. During the nineteenth century it was still possible to resist the transformation into periphery, just as Germany and Japan did. Of course, this was not possible for a colony, but Latin American countries had achieved independence since the beginning of the century and they could have tried. Two conditions would have been required: (a) protectionist barriers against British goods; and (b) a bourgeois revolution which transformed the internal pre-capitalist relations of production into fully capitalist ones.

Neither of these two requisites were ultimately met by Latin American countries basically because their traditional ruling classes imposed a model of peripheral development which was favourable to their exporting interests.[33] And yet the conditions for a bourgeois revolution had been present in Latin America, especially in Brazil, Chile and Paraguay during the first half of the nineteenth century. In fact these countries started their independent life with protectionist policies which allowed a promissory early development of their metallurgical industry. The Paraguayan process was destroyed by a war whereas in the case of Brazil and Chile it was the triumph of the exporting ruling classes and their free-trade ideology during the second half of the nineteenth century which frustrated the process. It goes without saying that the interests of these traditional classes coincided with and were supported by the interests of the British bourgeoisie.

When at the beginning of the twentieth century the Latin American export-oriented economic model entered a crisis and new ruling class alliances tried to initiate or re-initiate a process of industrialization in order to rescue their countries from the situation of unbalanced periphery, it was found that the conditions for the process of industrialization had radically changed. What had been a 'delay' became then entrenched underdevelopment. This was caused by 'a true revolution in the technological conditions of industrialization'[34] which broke the close relationship that had existed between traditional and modern means of production. Drawing on Marx's analysis of the different technological basis of manufacture and modern industry,[35] Hinkelammert introduces a distinction between traditional and modern means of production. During the nineteenth century any country with traditional technology could initiate a process of industrialization because, with its traditional means of production, it could copy foreign models and produce modern means of production. In other words, the technological gap between modern and traditional means was not too big and could be easily bridged. However, the continuous and accelerated progress of technology introduced an increased distance between traditional and modern means of production. By the end of the nineteenth century and beginning of the twentieth century, the relationship between traditional and modern means is finally broken:

> From now on the modern means of production of new industrialization processes cannot come from the transformation of a basic traditional structure into a modern industrial production structure. From now on it is no longer sufficient to have the technical knowledge and the will to produce in order to get the production of new industrial goods. More and more the modern means of production can be produced only by other pre-existing modern means of production. The consequence of this process is clear: industrialization can no longer be the result of the non-industrialized country's own productive effort. It is not enough to import technical knowledge, but it is necessary at the same time to import the machinery to use that technical knowledge.[36]

The importation of means of production, which in the past had been only a supplement to an autonomous effort, became the only basis of possible new industrialization processes. There is now an important limitation to any new industrialization: the capacity to import which is inevitably smaller than the requirements of the process. Japan was for Hinkelammert the last country which could industrialize at the end of the nineteenth century under the old conditions. Other countries which went into the twentieth century as unbalanced peripheries had that situation made irreversible and became underdeveloped. This is the reason why the import-substituting industrialization attempted by many Latin American countries could not succeed. An expanded capability to import capital goods could not be satisfactorily achieved and this led to chronic deficits in the balance of payments and huge indebtedness. Industry may still grow but 'without an expansive effect over the global economic system'. The industrial sector becomes an 'enclave' with little impact on the creation of more employment or on the technological progress of other sectors. This is what Hinkelammert calls a situation of 'dynamic stagnation'.[37]

There are many valuable insights in Hinkelammert's contribution. His approach is both less mechanistic and less pessimistic than the theories of dependency of the first group in that it explicitly contemplates the case of developed peripheries (thus avoiding the confusion of development with industrialization)[38] and gives more weight to internal processes of class struggles even in the case of unbalanced peripheries. Hinkelammert explicitly rejects the explanation of underdevelopment by dependency. However, one may ask whether he has not really changed one sort of determinism for another. True, not all peripheries are underdeveloped, not all development requires industrialization and formally independent unbalanced peripheries could have chosen to industrialize. But is it not the case that once unbalanced peripheries chose to accept their peripheral status they forfeited for ever their right to industrialize because of the technological gap which developed in the twentieth century? Is it not the case, then, that a class choice became irreversible by the role of technological factors? Are we not in the presence of another form of technological determinism? This seems to be a fair assessment of the import of Hinkelammert's theory. And yet he explicitly rejects it:

> we equally reject the explanation of underdevelopment by facts occurred on the technological plane. The gap between the traditional and modern means of production by no means can be treated as the very cause of underdevelopment. A thesis of this kind would result in a total fatalism in relation to the problem of development: as the technological gap is not reversible, underdevelopment itself would be irreversible ... the importance of the technological gap resides in another problem. It rather changes the historical situation within which the capitalist criterion of rationality operates . . . This originates the problem that a theory of socialist accumulation must resolve. It has to demonstrate that there are other criteria of rationality, capable of promoting a process of industrialization and development of unbalanced peripheries. . .[39]

The paradox now becomes clear. It is not the technological gap *per se* which makes underdevelopment irreversible, it is the technological gap within the capitalist mode of production that does so. Socialism is the only way to overcome underdevelopment. This is, of course, a point Hinkelammert shares with Frank: in the twentieth century capitalism has totally lost its ability to bring development to unbalanced peripheries. But the explanation is entirely different from Frank's: not external dependency, not the the drain of surplus, but an internal blockage made up of technological backwardness and the inability to import. Hinkelammert forgets that the limited capacity to import can be circumvented by borrowing and the direct investment of multinational corporations (the so-called 'new character' of dependency). In ruling out all possibilities for a capitalist development of underdeveloped countries, Hinkelammert has really plunged into the determinism and fatalism he had tried so hard to avoid in many other ways. He has only substituted internal reasons for Frank's dependency in order to show that capitalism cannot work.

In the end, Hinkelammert falls into the temptation of (a) identifying underdevelopment with a form of stagnation, albeit 'dynamic'; and (b) denying all possibility of fully-fledged capitalist industrialization to unbalanced peripheries in the twentieth century. With Hinkelammert's theory it is difficult to explain the rapid industrialization processes of Brazil, South Korea, Taiwan, Hong Kong and Singapore. He may counterargue by saying that his theory does not exclude industrial growth and that it only emphasizes the fact that it is the growth of an 'enclave', incapable of transforming the totality of those economies. A good example would be the case of Brazil where the enormous industrial expansion around Sao Paulo coexists with the backwardness, misery and starvation of the north east. Although one can see his point, one can also ask whether it is not the case that practically all industrial nations have pockets of backwardness and poverty within them. When is a growing industrial sector an enclave and when is it not? Even if the pockets of backwardness and poverty are far more extended and accentuated in underdeveloped countries, can one really rule out all possibility of capitalist development? These are the questions to which only Cardoso and Faletto's theory of dependency provide a different answer.

ASSOCIATED DEPENDENT DEVELOPMENT

Although less well known than the theories of the first group (Frank, Wallerstein, Emmanuel, Amin), Cardoso and Faletto's approach is by far the most cogent, balanced and complete analysis of dependency that has appeared so far. It is also the analysis which best combines the new categories expressing the novelty of the situation of underdevelopment and dependency in Latin America with the old concepts used by classical Marxism in its analysis of capitalist societies. This is no small achievement since for many Marxists the very category of dependency is irreconcilable with, and constitutes a 'nationalistic' theoretical alternative to Marxist analysis.[40] It is no wonder that they should think so for the best-known theories of dependency do treat dependency as the external cause of underdevelopment thus necessarily neglecting the crucial role of the internal relations of production. Cardoso and Faletto start by rejecting the conception of dependency as an external cause and follow with an analysis which, although taking into account the general conditioning role of dependency, emphasizes 'the historical transformation of structures by conflict, social movements, and class struggles'.[41] Dependency is not an 'external' factor which causes necessary internal effects but a general condition which can only express itself through internal class conflicts.

Hence the changes occurring in the capitalist world system do not produce similar automatic changes all over the periphery, but find a concrete expression through local interests, state policies and class struggles.[42] This is why there are different forms of dependency. As Cardoso and Faletto put it:

> The very existence of an economic 'periphery' cannot be understood without reference to the economic drive of advanced capitalist economies, which were responsible for the formation of a capitalist periphery ... Yet, the expansion of capitalism in Bolivia and Venezuela, in Mexico or Peru, in Brazil and Argentina, in spite of having been submitted to the same global dynamic of international capitalism, did not have the same history of consequences. The differences are rooted not only in the diversity of natural resources, nor just in the different periods in which these economies have been incorporated into the international system ... Their explanation must also lie in the different moments at which sectors of local classes allied or clashed with foreign interests, organized different forms of state, sustained distinct ideologies, or tried to implement various policies or defined alternative strategies to cope with imperialist challenges in diverse moments of history.[43]

So careful are Cardoso and Faletto in trying to avoid an abstract and totalizing concept which may substitute for real historical class analysis that they prefer to speak of 'situations of dependency' rather than of the 'theory of dependency'. They argue that, in a strict sense, one can have a theory of capitalism and of classes but not a 'theory of dependency'.[44] The very concept of dependency 'is defined within the theoretical field of the Marxist theory of capitalism' because it cannot be thought of 'without the concepts of surplus-value, expropriation, accumulation, etc.'[45] A situation of dependency is nothing more than the particular way in which the impact of the international capitalist system whose dynamic centres are not in the third world is received, that is to say, negotiated, accepted, modified, adapted or rejected, through the internal political and class system of a specific peripheral country or region. To the objection that all countries including the centres are necessarily 'interdependent' because they are inserted in the same world system and have to negotiate internally the same international impact, Cardoso and Faletto respond that the point is to assess the form that inderdependency assumes. If one does that, it is possible to find important asymmetries:

> Of course, bankers need clients, as much as clients need bankers. But the 'interrelationship' between the two is qualitatively distinct because of the position held by each partner in the structure of the relationship. The same is true for the analysis of 'interdependent' economies in world markets. Capitalism is a world system. But some of its parts have more than their share of leadership and an almost exclusive possession of sectors crucial to production and capital accumulation, such as the technological or financial sectors.[46]

Cardoso and Faletto share with other *dependentistas* the idea that a dependent economy is characterized by the fact that to a large extent its capital accumulation cannot be sustained by internal dynamic forces. This means that even when peripheral economies go beyond the production of raw materials, 'sector I (the production of means of production) – the strategic part of the reproductive scheme – is virtually non-existent in dependent economies.'[47] That is to say, the 'capital-goods production sectors are not strong enough to ensure continuous advance of the system, in financial as well as in technological and organizational terms.'[48] This means that the circuit of capital accumulation in the periphery cannot be fully realized locally, but needs the technology and the capital goods sectors of the main industrial centres.

But whereas for most of the dependency authors this fact is enough to preclude all possibility of development, for Cardoso and Faletto a real process of capitalist dependent development is perfectly possible and does exist in specific situations in Latin America.[49] This is what, in the context of Brazil, Cardoso has called 'associated-dependent development'.[50] It is a form of development which is sustained by foreign investment (especially by multinational corporations) in association with internal capital through the import of technology and which cyclically produces, as in any other process of capitalist development, increased wealth and the progress of productive forces but also increased proletarianization, marginalization and poverty. So when Cardoso and Faletto speak of this kind of dependent development they do not mean necessary progress toward a fair, egalitarian and just society, nor can they mean, obviously, a nationally controlled and self-sustained capitalist expansion, which are the two aspects emphasized as prerequisites of development by the structuralists.

An important methodological point which Cardoso and Faletto raise in dealing with situations of dependency is the relationship between structure and history. For them

> it is necessary to recognize from the beginning that social structures are the product of man's collective behaviour. Therefore, although enduring, social structures can be, and in fact are, continuously transformed by social movements. Consequently our approach is both structural and historical: it emphasizes not just the structural conditioning of social life, but also the historical transformation of structures by conflict, social movements, and class struggles. Thus our methodology is historico-structural.[51]

This is the reason why dependency cannot be conceived as a stable and permanent situation but can change and be challenged. At the same time, structures do have a certain objective conditioning and limiting effect which means that human beings cannot make history as they wish and that not all options are socially viable. A historico-structural explanation, therefore, takes into account both the relative rigidity and enduring quality of structures and the fact that they should also be seen as processes, as the result and crystallization of human practices and class struggles. Hence a historico-structural analysis must explore the historical process of the formation and change of structures. This is best accomplished by means of periodization, that is to say, the determination of certain stages in history where structures change.[52] This is precisely the strategy which Cardoso and Faletto follow in studying the Latin American situations of dependency and which I shall briefly summarize further below.

Prior to that, it is useful to list some of the main theses which we have encountered in other dependency theories and which Cardoso and Faletto specifically reject as errors in order to achieve a more complete, if negative, synthesis of their own methodological position.[53] First, the notion which identifies dependency with stagnation; second, the idea that capitalism is non-viable at the periphery; third, the notion which identifies capitalist development with the resolution of social contradictions and the national control of the economy; fourth, the ethical distinction between growth and development. These four mistakes have been sufficiently analysed above and need no additional comment. Fifth, the thesis that dependent capitalism necessarily entails the superexploitation of labour and that this is a precondition of capitalist accumulation and development in the centres. It should be already clear that this is a mistake (a) because in the most advanced economic sectors of the periphery the dynamic of capital accumulation is based on increasing organic composition and relative surplus-value extraction,[54] which means that in this respect the periphery is no different from the centre, and (b) because the main forces of central capital accumulation are endogenous.

Sixth, the notion that national bourgeoisies in the periphery no longer constitute active social forces, that they are 'lumpen', unable to accumulate and prone to conspicuous consumption. The mistake here is a confusion between bourgeois ideology and the class itself. As Cardoso points out 'what ceased to have any function was the "ideology of national-bourgeois development", not the local bourgeoisies.'[55] The fact that Latin American bourgeoisies lack aspirations for political hegemony, are not anti-imperialist and do not oppose backwardness in the countryside, be it because they lack the strength or be it because they do not see those policies in their own interest, does not mean to deny that

> the form adopted by dependent development benefits the local bourgeoisies and promotes their expansion, *on the condition that they become associated with or 'feudalized' by the multinational oligopolies and the State*. Within these limitations, the national bourgeoisies continue to play an active role in political domination and social control of the subjected classes.[56]

Cardoso lists two other mistaken theses which are mainly propounded by two Latin American authors. The first, found in Marini,[57] states that due to the penetration by multinational firms and the restricted character of the Latin American internal markets some local states like Brazil are driven to pursue the export of manufactures and a politically expansionist policy, typically 'sub-imperialist'. Cardoso rejects this thesis because it is by no means clear that there is a clear-cut relation between all those factors. He shows, for instance, that in Brazil 'it is difficult to uphold the hypothesis that the export of manufactures took place in order to compensate for the restricted size of the internal market. The domestic market is continuing to expand, and the growth of firms and the increase of urban-industrial employment has its own dynamic.'[58] The expansion of exports does not express a tendency to sub-imperialism, but rather results from the need to get international currency to pay for the importation of capital goods. This is no more than what can be expected from a process of dependent development.

The second thesis, found in T. dos Santos, states that as Latin American capitalism is non-viable and in deep crisis, the political alternatives for Latin America are either 'a profound social revolution' leading to socialism or 'the victory of the most barbarous and reactionary forces of our time' leading to fascism.[59] This is complemented by V. Bambirra's thesis that

> The only alternative of wide development that is presented to Chile, Colombia and Uruguay . . . is out of the capitalist system and is the socialist alternative. Socialism then presents itself to them as the only development option, ceasing to be a doctrinaire ideal and becoming a historical necessity.[60]

There are several mistakes in these theses. First, as has already been seen, capitalism is far from being non-viable in Latin America. Second, although there was an expansion of authoritarian regimes in Latin America in the late 1960s and 1970s, they tended not to be fascist in so far as they did not organize state parties or mobilise the masses but destroyed the trade union movement and tried to depoliticize the population. Moreover they are now receding and being replaced by democratic regimes. Third, even at the height of the period of dictatorships, there were many capitalist Latin American countries with more or less formal democratic regimes, such as Venezuela, Colombia, Costa Rica and Ecuador.[61] I would add a fourth error: socialism can never be a historical necessity in the sense of the only option for a country, least of all an option purely determined by the economic necessity of development. Socialism is certainly a possibility, a political goal for certain classes and parties to struggle for and construct in their country, but there is no guarantee that they will succeed or that it will bring about the kind of development which capitalism apparently failed to produce.

It is of the essence of Cardoso and Faletto's approach to distinguish stages and situations of dependency in the context of the Latin American development process. In so far as the main historical stages common to most countries in Latin America are concerned they propose a first period of colonial rule after the beginning of the sixteenth century, which incorporated Latin America into the world market and which was brought to an end by the independence wars (1810–25). A second period of 'outward expansion' is distinguished which spans from the end of colonialism in 1825 to the end of the nineteenth century. Then from 1900 to 1930 there is a period of transition which is characterized by the crisis of the oligarchic system and the political incorporation of the middle classes. A fourth period of expansion and consolidation of the internal market (inward expansion) by means of import-substituting industrialization and politically characterized by nationalism and populism starts in 1930 and goes up to the mid 1950s. From then on a fifth period is distinguished, the so-called 'new nature of dependency', which is characterized by the increased internationalization of the Latin American economies through the direct investment of multinational corporations, which now control the most dynamic parts of the industrialization process.

In the context of these five historical stages Cardoso and Faletto distinguish two situations of dependency which exist prior to the last stage: the situation of 'enclave', that is to say, that which exists in countries where the main exporting activities were foreign-owned; and the situation where the productive system was nationally controlled. During the last stage, the situation of all Latin American countries with a dependent industrialization process, whether former enclaves or countries with nationally controlled economies, becomes more uniform by the foreign control exercised by multinational corporations. This new situation is not, however, similar to that of the old enclaves because that was characterized by the export of raw materials whereas most of the industrial production controlled by international firms during the last stage is sold on the internal market.

The colonial period channeled the economy of the region into production for export and trade with Europe and therefore created a class of producers and merchants oriented to the international market. Yet because the power and economic significance of Spain systematically declined, to the point that by the end of the eighteenth century it played the role of monopolistic intermediary between the colonies and the rest of Europe, colonial relations soon came to be regarded by the local producers and merchants as an obstacle to a more direct, expanding and profitable trade with Great Britain and other European nations. This problem coupled with the political exclusion of the locally born *criollos* from administrative and governmental tasks was at the centre of the independence wars. The achievement of political independence meant a redefinition of the export economy in respect of a new metropolis, Great Britain, and the consolidation of the class of producers (mainly landowners) as the new rural-based political ruling class. They had to create and organize states and juridical orders guaranteeing their political power and the conditions for the continuation of export-oriented production. This task of creating new national states was not easy after a prolonged war and lasted, with many upheavals and disruptions, from 1825 to 1850.

Some mining countries like Mexico, Peru and Bolivia were plunged into years of anarchy and war which led to economic stagnation and almost permanent political instability. Other countries such as Argentina and Chile prospered by exporting agricultural products and, in the case of Chile, also silver and copper. In these latter cases the political stability was achieved earlier by means of alliances between the traditional landowners and the exporting and/or mining interests. At any rate, from the 1850s onwards, practically all Latin American countries expanded and consolidated their exporting economies and their participation in international trade. Most governments followed free trade policies at the behest of the ruling groups exporting primary products. The new international demand for agricultural products led almost everywhere in Latin America to the private appropriation of Indian lands and church properties and to the reimposition of semi-servile extra-economic pressures on the peasants. The scarcity of labour was dealt with by immigration from China, Portugal, Spain and Italy. Cardoso and Faletto describe this stage of outward expansion in the following terms:

> The Latin American countries were linked to the international market through a variety of products: the wheat and copper of Chile; the wool and livestock of the River Plate; the guano of Peru; the coffee of Venezuela, Brazil, Colombia, and Central America; and the sugar of the West Indies, Brazil, Mexico, and Peru. It is interesting to note that these products could still be developed with national capital and that there were sufficient local resources to finance diversified and large-scale undertakings.[62]

Not all Latin American countries, though, were able to keep national control of their main productive sectors and two types of enclave, mining and plantation, were formed. In the case of the first, the national producers are displaced because of their inability 'to compete in the production of commodities requiring technology, marketing systems, and heavy capital investment'.[63] Thus towards the end of the nineteenth century Chile and Peru lost their control over the production of nitrates and guano respectively, which began to be exploited by foreign companies. In the case of the second, national producers for the international market were almost non-existent and the enclave was formed by the direct expansion of the central economies. Thus Central American republics had their economies, and most of their political life too, dominated by plantations controlled by big North American companies. These examples present a different situation of dependency from that of countries like Argentina or Brazil which kept national control over their agricultural production. In the enclaves the main process of capital accumulation was in the hands of a foreign company which controlled labour, technology, investment and the international marketing of the produce. Local ruling groups had to withdraw from the international market and cater for the internal market.

In locally controlled economies, the national producers kept control of investment, labour and technology although the marketing and international prices were beyond their control. Their social and political basis was an alliance between, on the one hand, the exporting, 'modern' groups, plantation and mineowners, merchants and bankers and, on the other, the more traditional, 'oligarchic', landowning groups. This alliance did not exclude contradictions and struggles between them whenever their interests clashed. In the case of the enclaves the social and political basis of the system was more complicated because it entailed not just internal alliances between the oligarchies and the exporting groups but also between them and the external sector. In the case of plantations in Central America the local oligarchies had almost no weight and were dominated by the foreign company. In the mining enclaves of the south, where considerable exporting class were displaced, the internal coalition of those sectors and the landowners were more powerful and able, through the state they controlled, to negotiate and demand better conditions (in terms of taxes and re-investment of profits) from the foreign company.

The expansion and diversification of the export economy led, towards the end of the nineteenth century, to the emergence of a middle class all over Latin America. During the first thirty years of the twentieth century, the period of transition, the political domination of the so-called 'oligarchy' begins to crumble as a consequence of the decline of the export economy which was accelerated by the first world war and the big depression of 1930. Thus the incorporation of the middle classes as a new force into the political system was linked to the necessity of complementing the export economy with the development of the internal market which could be satisfied by local industry. Industrialization began to be seen as the key to providing new sources of employment as the export industries declined. But the transition took various forms. In nationally controlled economies, an important entrepreneurial and bourgeois sector was created. In the case of Argentina there was a clear dominance of the Buenos Aires bourgeoisie which controlled the financial and exporting system. In the case of Brazil, the bourgeoisie was more a federation of various groups, none of which was hegemonic, and this allowed the oligarchic classes to be seen to continue to dominate, although this was more apparent than real.[64]

In the case of Argentina, therefore, the middle classes were directly incorporated into the hegemony of the exporting bourgeoisie. In Brazil, on the contrary, the new emerging middle classes could form alliances with sectors of the bourgeoisie to set up a new kind of political leadership. Still, in a third type of situation, in some countries like Colombia, 'the limited differentiation within social groups, and the monolithic character of the oligarchic-bourgeois classes, blocked access of the middle groups to power and helped maintain the oligarchic pact.'[65] This is why, confronted with the 1930 depression, some countries altered their political and social system whereas others, like Colombia, kept their agro-export oligarchic system   stable until 1945. This is a typical example of how Cardoso and Faletto's approach allows for the same external factors to have different repercussions depending on the internal class structure and balance of power.

In enclaves, the transition was different from that of the nationally controlled economies and was also carried out in a variety of ways which depended on the type of enclave (mining or plantation), the degree of diversification of the national sector of the economy and complex political processes whereby internal alliances between the various groups and relations with the external sector were established. According to Cardoso and Faletto, in enclaves 'the economic weakness of national groups of power obliged these groups to maintain a more exclusive form of domination'[66] and this situation determined that the middle sectors found that their incorporation into the political system was more difficult and they had to resort to alliances with peasants and workers to breach the system. Given the nature of the enclave, peasants and workers were 'concentrated in centers of potential protest' and this represented political risks even for the middle classes.

In some countries like Mexico, Venezuela and Bolivia, with large peasantries, where an oligarchy of traditional hacienda owners clearly dominated, the middle classes were totally excluded and resorted to mobilizing the peasants in order to break the oligarchic system by means of revolutionary movements. Where domination was not purely oligarchic, like Chile and Peru, the middle classes entered into alliances with urban popular sectors and peasants. In Chile they succeeded by taking advantage of the struggles between the ruling groups and pursuing populist policies which attracted urban masses. Thus they won political rights and even the control of the executive branch of government, through which they implemented a policy of industrialization. In Peru, they failed because the populism of the main middle-class party (APRA) was more radical and its violent efforts to break the oligarchic system were repressed by the army. Thus the middle classes lost strength and they were forced into partial alliances with the ruling groups and their popular support was debilitated. A third situation is represented by the plantation enclaves of Central America where middle classes were systematically excluded by the local oligarchies in close alliance with North American companies.

In the 1930s, the transitional stage gave way to a period of consolidation of the internal market. A process of import-substituting industrialization took place that was led by governments in which the middle classes and the industrial and commercial bourgeoisie had a growing participation. In those countries like Argentina where the export economy had remained under national control and where industrialization was already well on its way, the new policies were based on the expansion of private enterprise. However, in Brazil, where the entrepreneurial groups were not hegemonic, the state assumed a more important role in the creation and regulation of industries. In enclave countries like Chile and Mexico, the state was used 'as an instrument in the formation of an industrial class, which eventually would share entrepreneurial functions with the state-owned enterprises.'[67]

Despite these different emphases, in both cases the private sector grew and there was an important participation by the state in the creation of basic industry and infrastructure and in protecting the new industries behind tariff barriers. A new urban proletariat emerged but so did a growing sector of 'marginalized' urban dwellers without employment because the creation of new jobs by the industrialization process always lagged behind the demographic pressures and the internal emigration from the countryside. The developmentalist policies of the state and the growing aspirations of the urban masses were best expressed in nationalist and populist ideologies which represented conflicting interests. The most typical cases were the ideologies fostered by Peron in Argentina and Vargas in Brazil.

The success of this populist stage was necessarily tied up with a growing process of industrialization. The process was dynamic enough during the substitution of non-durable consumer goods, but entered into a difficult phase when trying to go into the production of capital goods.

The crisis of the industrialization process was also the crisis of populism which, in any case, contained contradictory elements which wanted to serve both bourgeois and popular interests. This crisis opens up the last stage of dependency around the mid-1950s, when increasingly a solution was propounded by bourgeois sectors which linked the industrialization process to direct investment by foreign companies. This new strategy of 'associated dependent development' entailed a growing concentration of wealth, the marginalization of vast masses (and also of important sectors of the national bourgeoisie) and the curbing of the trade union movement and of the populist distributivist excesses in order to provide guarantees to the incoming foreign capital. So it is not surprising that it frequently, but with some important exceptions (Mexico, Venezuela, Colombia), led to military take overs like the ones which occurred in Brazil, Argentina, Chile and Uruguay. However, Cardoso and Faletto are careful not to attach 'any inevitability to capitalist development through external control or participation'[68] just as much as they had refused to attach any inevitability to capitalist underdevelopment through external dependence.

I have already said that Cardoso and Faletto's approach seems to me the most balanced and cogent attempt to analyse Latin American dependency. Although it shares some premises with other dependency studies, it differs from them in some substantial respects: it is not an attempt to substitute a tautological and static conceptual frame for the concrete analysis of situations of dependency, nor an approach which substitutes the nation for class analysis. The fact that, because of this, Cardoso and Faletto's position is not subject to the most common pitfalls which usually beset dependency theories, does not mean that it can escape from criticism. On the one hand there is a number of questions and problems about the status and role of the concept of dependency within Marxist studies of development. But this discussion I reserve for the next chapter. On the other hand there are some particular and also more general criticisms which arise on issues ranging from Cardoso's notion of dependency to his conception of the relationship between history and structure.

Certain authors have criticized Cardoso for his ambiguity and vacillation in defining the theoretical and methodological status of his notion of dependency. J. Quartim de Moraes, for instance, would like to know whether it is a theory, a concept or what.[69] Weffort, in his turn, accuses Cardoso of trying to present a 'totalizing concept which would give us the principle of understanding society as a whole', a concept which 'inevitably oscillates, from the theoretical point of view, between a national approach and a class approach.'[70] Cardoso accepts as valid de Moraes's criticism and acknowledges that he has not been clear in defining the theoretical discourse within which he is situated,[71] but he flatly rejects Weffort's criticism, asserting that he never presented a totalizing concept nor did he want to substitute a national approach for a class approach. What he did try to show was that 'in dependent countries, class contradictions are mediated through a national contradiction.'[72] In the context of these two polemics, Cardoso is able to clarify (a) that, strictly speaking, it is not possible to think of a 'theory' of dependence, and (b) that the concept of dependency has a subordinated status in relation to the central categories of the (Marxist) theory of capitalism.

In relation to the first point I think it is very important to accept Cardoso's point that there cannot be a theory of dependency as such and that what he has tried to do is to carry out an analysis of Latin American historical development by basically using Marxist theory. True, dependency is a new category which did not exist in Marx's writings and which in Cardoso's analysis seems to be crucial to the analysis. But so was the concept of imperialism when it was developed not as an alternative theory to Marxism but as the conceptual complement necessary to understand a new historical situation derived from the evolution of capitalism. As for the second point, even if the concept of dependency is given a subordinated status within a wider theory, it is still incumbent on the author who proposes this subsumption to clarify the role of the concept in the new theoretical context. One has to say in this respect that Cardoso has not very rigorously established the theoretical place of the concept of dependency in relation to other categories which pertain to the Marxist analysis of capitalism.

Rodríguez, in his turn, has taken the relationship between history and structure as the focus of his criticism. He maintains that Cardoso 'lacks a coherent methodological position' because he 'varies in the degree of indeterminacy he introduces in historical analysis'.[73] On the one hand, Rodríguez avers, in certain studies Cardoso emphasizes history at the expense of structure to the point that he 'recedes to a form of historicism' and becomes merely descriptive and not explanatory. Bienefeld supports this analysis and points out that because Cardoso and Palma are 'driven back to a study of the uniqueness of each case' they are guilty of a methodological abdication.[74] According to Rodríguez, this historicist bias is responsible for the lack of a general conceptualization of the relationships between internal and external factors and limits Cardoso's analyses to being a 'teleological reconstruction of past events'. The external factors are dissolved into the internal political struggle and have no independent theoretical existence. Thus

> the degree of historical indeterminacy Cardoso introduces makes it impossible to speak of 'laws of movement' within the discourse; if *processes* such as accumulation are but a *fixed* point that influences class struggle, these laws can only be found in the real political action of real social agents and not in the structures and processes that are constituted in a conceptualized manner in the discourse. In conclusion, the methodology of Cardoso's approach . . . means that the issue of the industrialization prospects of peripheral societies. . . cannot be posed. . . we cannot determine whether some degree of industrial development, or indeed a full blown industrialization, is possible, until it becomes an event that can be described *a posteriori*.[75]

On the other hand, Rodríguez goes on, in other writings Cardoso gives greater weight to structural determinations and he is able to conceptualize the link between internal and external factors so that the latter appear as constraints on the process of accumulation. Thus for instance he quotes Cardoso's idea, referred to above, that in terms of the Marxist account of capital accumulation, sector I (production of means of production) is virtually non-existent in dependent economies. However, although this emphasis seems to put right Cardoso's former indeterminacy, Rodríguez is still critical of the fact that the argument 'seems to rest on an international division of labour which is already being undermined', a fact that Cardoso himself acknowledges when he 'offers evidence that the development of a capital good sector is already taking place'.[76]

I have found no trace of the evidence which Cardoso is supposed to have offered in this respect, nor does Rodríguez give any. He only quotes Cardoso as saying that

> it is even possible that in the future the dynamics of the economic system will cease to be based only on the sectors of consumer durables production (controlled by multinationals) and will shift in the direction of a large-scale steel industry and the export of semi-processed and mineral products.[77]

But this is a long way away from offering evidence that the sector which produces capital goods is developing in dependent countries. What Rodríguez does not realize is that the problem is not that the new international division of labour is undermining Cardoso's assertion but rather that there is a confusion in Cardoso about the meaning of sector I (production of means of production). As Castañeda and Hett point out, Cardoso is obviously and mistakenly excluding raw materials from the concept of means of production because otherwise he could not correctly say that their production is virtually non-existent in Latin America. According to Marx, sector I did include raw materials, and Latin American countries are traditionally producers of raw materials.[78] Castañeda and Hett are right in believing that what Cardoso means is not the Marxist concept of 'sector I' but rather the more restricted sector which produces capital goods. In fact, in a different article Cardoso comes close to formulating it thus: 'in the new international division of labour, sector I, or at least those branches which have to do with the creation of new technologies are increasingly concentrated in central economies, especially in the United States.'[79]

This is why the passage cited by Rodríguez does not prove what he thinks. At any rate, the logic of Rodríguez's criticisms is somewhat surprising because by surreptitiously shifting the ground it ends up defeating itself. First he accuses Cardoso of historicism and of not conceptualizing external factors as constraints on capital accumulation. But when Cardoso does conceptualize some structural external constraints, then Rodriguez accuses him of not realizing that they are being undermined. So it appears that after all structures and constraints are not stable and do change as well. This precisely illustrates Cardoso's point that it is not possible to conceive of structures as invariable, and separate from social movements and class struggles. And yet it is not true to say, as Bienefeld does, that Cardoso is driven back to a study of the uniqueness of each case, because he distinguishes periods and situations of dependency which are shared by groups of countries and he does acknowledge the existence of common elements among dependent countries.

After criticizing Cardoso's ambiguity in respect of the concept of 'sector I', Castañeda and Hett go further and argue that even if it is true that Latin America imports almost the totality of its capital goods, it is also true that practically no country in the world produces all its means of production and that all capitalist countries need to import capital goods in order to keep production going. In this sense this would be a problem of capitalist production in general and not exclusively a problem of poor countries.[80] But this is disingenuous. True, all countries import capital goods, but it is not so difficult to see that the way in which say Germany depends on those imports is qualitatively different from the way in which Chile depends on them. The process of capitalist accumulation would survive in Germany without those imports. The disruption to capitalist accumulation which the absence of those imports would produce in Chile would be of a nature such that the system would probably collapse.

6

LATIN AMERICAN DEPENDENCY AND HISTORICAL MATERIALISM: A THEORETICAL CHALLENGE

THE CRITIQUE OF DEPENDENCY THEORY

I have discussed a wide variety of dependency theories, shown their main differences and separately considered their most relevant criticisms. To a certain extent though, it has been inevitable that the mere acceptance or use of the concept of dependency by many authors, however differently the term may be interpreted or defined by them, has led many critics to treat their writings as if they were slightly different versions of a single theory whose fundamental premises were universally shared. Thus quite a few critics, both liberal and Marxist, speak of and criticize 'dependency theory' or a certain 'dependency approach', in general and without making many distinctions, sometimes even conflating the category of dependency with the category of underdevelopment and referring to an abstract entity called 'Underdevelopment and dependency theory' (UDT),[1] or simply 'underdevelopment theory'.[2] Others consider dependency theory as a new scientific paradigm in the Kuhnian sense.[3] More often than not they take A.G. Frank to be its prototypical representative. Because the criticisms made from this perspective are not exactly the same as or have a similar objective to those expressed in the case of individual theories, and, above all, because in spite of their oversimplification of the problematic of dependency they allow a more streamlined confrontation between basic theoretical options, they deserve to be treated separately as a way of introducing ourselves into the major discussion topic of this last chapter.

For convenience I shall distinguish two strands of this general kind of critique. First there is a non-Marxist, general sort of critique which scrutinizes dependence as a testable theory, that is to say, it wants to examine the logic, internal consistency, operationalization of variables, construction of hypotheses and quality of the empirical evidence provided by dependency theory. Here one finds authors like O'Brien and Lall. Second, there is a Marxist critique which in its turn can be divided into two currents. On the one hand, there are the critics of dependency and underdevelopment who emphasize the traditional Marxist position about the inherent developing capabilities of capitalism. Here one finds authors such as Warren, Leys, Bernstein, Taylor, Phillips, Mandle, Kitching and Booth. On the other hand, there is the so-called 'articulation of the modes of production' theory, developed by French anthropologists whose main representative is Rey, which not only criticizes the idea of dependency from a traditional Marxist standpoint but goes on to propose an alternative explanation of underdevelopment which draws on Rosa Luxemburg and which, while safeguarding the belief in the developing qualities of capitalism seeks to explain how capitalism, can be hindered by other modes of production.

DEPENDENCY AS A TESTABLE THEORY

It may seem odd to include O'Brien within this strand because he starts by defending dependency theory against the accusation of triviality and irrelevance (derived from a 'positivist hypothetical-deductive methodology') and characterizes it as an attempt to establish a new general framework or paradigm, whose mission 'is to guide and make more coherent at an abstract level, lower level explanations.'[4] His first criticism is therefore not concerned with the failure of the theory in the face of any particular empirical test, but with its abstract and totalizing characteristics. In the course of his analysis O'Brien drifts towards a different kind of critique which may well derive from a positivist methodology. But before going into that, let us see the first kind of criticism whereby he warns that 'in unsophisticated hands'

> dependency can easily become a pseudo-concept which explains everything in general and hence nothing in particular. In the hands of some Latin American writers, the theory of dependency is used as a *deus ex machina* explanation for everything which seems to be wrong with Latin American society.[5]

Although this criticism is appropriate when addressed to the Wallerstein–Frank–Emmanuel–Amin school and very much evokes the judgment which Cardoso repeatedly passes on their abstract and ahistorical conception of dependency, O'Brien seems to believe that the problem is the misuse of the paradigm 'in unsophisticated hands' rather than the very attempt to construct one. One must conclude that in 'sophisticated hands' there should be no problem with dependency theory. Yet, as Cardoso observed, it was this very totalizing and abstract conception of dependency, the belief in a new universal paradigm, and not its misuse, that necessarily led to the pitfalls recognized by O'Brien.

Be this as it may, it seems somehow paradoxical that once O'Brien has established dependency theory as a paradigm which must be judged in terms of its adequacy as a framework for the articulation of certain relationships, he should criticize it for (a) not enumerating the essential characteristics of dependency and giving instead the following circular argument: 'dependent countries are those which lack the capacity for autonomous growth and they lack this because their structures are dependent ones;'[6] (b) not spelling out in detail the actual mechanisms of dependency; (c) providing 'casual', 'thin' and 'scanty' empirical evidence in support of its hypotheses; and (d) leaving policy conclusions very general and vague.[7] He seems suddenly to revert to the 'positivist hypothetical-deductive methodology' which he had discarded at the beginning, to conceive of 'theory' as a set of formal and testable propositions. Thus he now demands from the theory not just adequacy as a framework for the articulation of certain relationships, but also formal definitions of concepts and enumeration of variables, a set of hypotheses deduced from them, substantial and conclusive empirical evidence to prove the hypotheses and specific policy conclusions derived from it all. Not surprisingly, the 'theory' of dependency, previously defined as a totalizing paradigm, is found to falter on all these aspects.

On the same formal methodological premises, but with more concrete evidence and detailed analysis, Lall presents a devastating critique of the concept of dependency. Two aspects of the analysis found at the beginning of his article provide a clue to his methodological stand. First, his original idea had been 'to produce a working definition of "dependence"'[8] but ended up being a critique. Just like O'Brien, Lall had the impression that dependence was defined in a circular fashion: 'less developed countries . . . are poor because they are dependent, and any characteristics that they display signify dependence.'[9] Consequently, he was looking for a way, through the current literature of his time, to lay down 'certain characteristics of dependent economies which are not found in non-dependent ones'.[10] He found that this could not be done to satisfaction, and concluded that it was impossible to define the concept. Second, he treats dependency as an attempt at a new explanation of underdevelopment and therefore implicitly identifies the concept with the basic premise of Frank's school. According to this logic, dependency 'must be shown to affect adversely the course and pattern of development of dependent countries'.[11] Again, and not surprisingly, Lall concludes that dependence is not causally related to underdevelopment.

In order to draw these two conclusions Lall analyses both static and dynamic characteristics of dependence given by dependency authors. Among the former he mentions cultural and political penetration, inequalities in income distribution, unequal exchange, specialization in primary products, use of capital-intensive technologies and heavy penetration of foreign capital. Among the latter he lists blocking or inhibition of economic growth and various undesirable consequences of dependent growth such as inequality, squandering of resources, lack of technology, etc. After a brief analysis Lall shows how cultural and political penetration occurs in the developed world as well, how all countries, including the developed ones are increasingly dominated by international capital, how some developed countries also depend on foreign technology, how some underdeveloped countries also export industrial goods, grow, and improve the standard of living of their poorest sectors, how there is also marginalization and inequality in non-dependent economies and, in general, how these and other undesirable effects 'are features of *capitalist* growth in general - in certain stages and in certain circumstances - and are not confined to the present condition of the less developed countries'.[12] In this way Lall is able to conclude 'that the concept of dependence as applied to less developed countries is impossible to define and cannot be shown to be causally related to a continuance of underdevelopment.'[13]

There is little doubt that if one examines the theory of dependency from the point of view which O'Brien has called the 'positivist hypothetical-deductive methodology', that is to say as a testable theory with precisely defined variables and concepts whose characteristics are exclusive and apply only to dependent countries and one requiring measurable empirical evidence which substantiates its hypotheses, then the theory of dependency does not seem to pass the test. Even less so when its tenets are so closely associated with and reduced to Frank's position. But one wonders whether this attempt to judge the theory of dependence in accordance with such a formal pattern is really worthwhile. Such an attempt is bound to abstract from and miss what had been the essence of the theory in its origins and in the intention of its best representatives: the historical analysis of Latin American processes 'as the result of struggles between classes and groups that define their interests and values in the process of expansion of a mode of production' and which 'in the struggle for control or for the reformulation of the existing order (through parties, movements, ideologies, the state, etc.) are making a given structure of domination historically viable or are transforming it'.[14]

'Dependency' for such an approach is not a formalized 'theory' separate from the theory of the capitalist development of certain underdeveloped regions, it cannot be defined in terms of a number of static and dynamic characteristics which take into account only external relations between countries and bear no relation to internal contradictions and class struggles. Furthermore, in this perspective dependency is perfectly compatible with growth, with export of some industrial products and with equal exchange, and yet there will be technological subordination and heavy foreign control of capital investment. Lall counterargues that other developed countries, too, suffer technological dependence and foreign investment and that perhaps it is possible to 'quibble' about the 'degree' or scale of dependence but not about the absolute presence or absence of dependence.[15] For a start there seems to be little sense in trying to ascertain 'degrees' of dependency which could be measured by means of quantifiable variables, because, as I have already said, that attempt leaves out the consideration of essential class struggles and opposition of interests through which alone dependency exists.

But even if for the sake of argument one were to accept a limited definition of dependence in terms of measurable foreign capital penetration and technological subordination, and even if one were to recognize that all countries to a certain extent inter-depend on each other for capital and technology, it would still be true that to put Latin American countries on the same level as the European ones and to speak of quibbles about 'degrees' of dependence is disingenuous. Surely Lall must have heard of the possibility of quantitative differences becoming qualitative ones. So one could perfectly well say that the relative scale of technological dependency and foreign penetration of, say, Bolivia, Peru or Chile and that of Germany, Japan or the United States differ so much as to constitute qualitatively separate phenomena. The problem with Lall's conception of dependency is that he assumes that all forms of dependency have common features. He is not aware, for instance, that in Latin America itself, the period of inward-oriented development meant a progressive income distribution and a widening of democratic structures and social participation whereas in the outward-oriented period and in the last period controlled by international firms the opposite features predominated.

On the other hand, part of Lall's problem is that he conceives of dependence in Frankian terms as inevitably leading to underdevelopment. Thus by comparing the technological dependence of Canada, Belgium or Denmark with that of Brazil, India, Taiwan or Colombia, he is not aware that according to the best dependency authors like Cardoso, Faletto and Hinkelammert the former countries may be as dependent as the latter ones, even though they are fully developed as well. So one cannot say, as Lall pretends that dependency theory does, that certain countries like Brazil or Indonesia are more dependent than others like Canada.[16] They may be equally dependent according to formal and quantifiable criteria (if one were to accept them for a moment) and yet these countries have a very different and uneven pattern of development due to their internal class dynamics and other historical peculiarities which redefine their dependence in different directions. The very premise from which Lall starts, namely that dependence is 'a particular explanation of underdevelopment'[17] is erroneous and misleading and can only be predicated of the first group of dependency theories (Frank, Wallerstein, Amin, Emmanuel) which I have identified in chapter 4.

THE ARTICULATION OF THE MODES OF PRODUCTION

Although Clammer has argued that 'there is a complementarity between the work of Andre Gunder Frank and that of recent French economic anthropology'[18] because they both explore the relations of dependence between centre and periphery from different angles, there is little doubt that these approaches are radically different. The school of dependency represented by Frank, Wallerstein, Amin and Emmanuel clearly blamed capitalism, as a world system, for underdevelopment of third world countries and gave pride of place to international market relations through which the exploitation of underdeveloped countries is effected. The French anthropologists (Rey, Dupré, Terray, Meillassoux), on the contrary, assess the potentialities of capitalism in a totally different manner. As Rey makes absolutely clear, capitalism should not be blamed

for underdevelopment, nor should the bourgeoisie be accused of ill will.
There is a

> fundamental law of capitalism, as true today as on the day when Marx
> discovered it: capitalism has as its final goal the destruction of the former
> modes of production and relations of production all over the world in order
> to substitute its own mode of production and production relations for
> them.[19]

> Let us cease to reproach capitalism with the one crime that it has not
> committed, that it could not think of committing, constrained as it is by its
> own laws always to enlarge the scale of production. Let us keep firmly in
> mind that all the bourgeoisies of the world burn with desire to develop the
> 'underdeveloped' countries.[20]

On the other hand, the French anthropologists play down the international
market mechanisms and emphasize the notion of mode of production as
the basis of analysis and explanation of underdevelopment. In this they
are influenced by the work of Althusser and Balibar, particularly their
distinction between mode of production and social formation. The mode
of production is an analytical or abstract concept which has no direct
empirical referent in reality but which indicates a totality comprising a
particular combination of connections between three elements: the
worker, the means of production and the non-worker. The main articulated
connections are the relation of real appropriation which determines the
system of productive forces and the property relation which defines the
relations of production.[21] A social formation, on the contrary, exists in
reality as a concrete and historically determined society, which comprises
a complex articulation of modes of production, one of which is dominant.
As Rey puts it, 'all real social formation is never the place of only one
mode of production, but the articulation of several modes of production.'[22]
I shall concentrate on Rey's account of articulation since it is the most
sophisticated and elaborated of the group.

The combination of the belief in the transforming dynamism of
capitalism everywhere, on the one hand, and the presence of an articulation
of modes of production in concrete societies, especially the
underdeveloped ones, on the other, provides the clue for this approach.
Rosa Luxemburg is credited with being the first to put the accent on the
analysis of the capitalist penetration of new social formations where it
has to destroy old modes of production in order to survive. However, she
did not treat these old modes of production as 'entities susceptible of

resisting for a long time their dismantling by capitalism and of articulating themselves with it'.[23] This idea is expressed in Meillassoux's tenet that pre-capitalist modes of production are 'both undermined and perpetuated at the same time'.[24] Rey puts it thus:

> capitalism can never immediately and totally eliminate the preceding modes of production, nor above all the relations of production which characterize these modes of production. On the contrary, during an entire period it must reinforce these relations of exploitation, since it is only this development which permits its own provisioning with goods coming from these modes of production, or with men driven from these modes of production and therefore compelled to sell their labour power to capitalism in order to survive.[25]

In other words, despite its mission and willingness to substitute itself for the old modes of production, capitalism needs these modes for a long time in order both to get supplies and labour power from them and, as Meillassoux emphasizes, to subsidize and cheapen the reproduction of labour in the capitalist sector. This means that for as long as this occurs capitalism must coexist articulated with these modes of production. The articulation between two modes must be understood not as a static or stable situation, but as a process, that is to say as 'a combat between the two modes of production, with the confrontations and alliances which such a combat entails: confrontations and alliances essentially between the classes which these modes define.'[26] The case of the transition from the feudal to the capitalist mode of production which Rey describes in terms of three stages provides a general model. In the first stage capitalism is still subordinated to feudalism and depends on landed property to get both raw materials and workers. Feudal landlords are instrumental in providing these, both because they expel peasants from their lands and because, needing money, they sell a large proportion of their production on the market.[27] There is then a coincidence of interests and a class alliance between the feudal landlords and the capitalists.

In the second stage capitalism becomes dominant, although it still makes use of feudalism. Capitalism destroys all peasant handicrafts and forms of production and provides the agricultural means of production, but it still depends on the pre-capitalist sector for its provisioning with food and sometimes for obtaining extra labour power.[28] Most 'underdeveloped' countries are in this intermediate stage where capitalist relations of exploitation are combined with pre-capitalist forms of exploitation. This articulation does not necessarily leave the precapitalist modes unchanged but often they are reconstituted into new ones, still non-capitalist, but more amenable to living with capitalism. The class alliance continues and is concretely manifested 'by the sharing of the surplus-value extracted from the dominated class of the dominated mode of production between the bourgeoisie and the non-capitalist ruling class'.[29] This means that in the articulation between traditional modes of production and capitalism the domination of the latter entails a transfer of value from the dominated modes to capitalism. On this point there is a certain formal similarity with Frank's contradiction of expropriation and appropriation of economic surplus. But, of course, this was not conceived as a transfer between modes of production but between regions.

Finally, in the third stage, which has been reached by very few countries, feudalism becomes an obstacle to the development of capitalism and is dismantled. The pre-capitalist mode of production disappears even in the countryside and agriculture becomes mechanized and fully capitalist. The peasantry is finally destroyed and capitalist relations of production are adopted in all economic activities. According to Rey the third stage has not yet been reached anywhere in the third world and it is unlikely that any underdeveloped country will ever reach it because they are likely to experience a socialist revolution before getting to that point. Such a revolution will mobilize the exploited masses against both the bourgeoisie and the ruling classes of the old modes of production, because if capitalism and traditional modes sustain each other it is impossible to struggle for the abolition of pre-capitalist forms of oppression without at the same time seeking to overthrow capitalism.

Although the articulation between the feudal and capitalist modes of production serves as a general model for the articulation of other pre-capitalist modes of production with capitalism, there are important differences in the latter case. The question arises as to why there are countries where the transition seems to progress so slowly or never gets to the third stage. Because Rey started from the premise that capitalism cannot be blamed for lack of dynamism or willingness to accomplish the full transformation of social relations everywhere, the answer must necessarily point to the peculiarities of the old modes of production which it has had to articulate itself with. If capitalism

> has not been able to proceed as rapidly as it believed (and Marx himself expected in 1853) it is not because of lack of will on its part: it is because the former social and economic structures, which it had to substitute itself

for, have proved to be infinitely more resilient than the European pre-capitalist structures . . . Generally speaking, non-western countries, apart from Japan, have shown themselves and still show themselves to be wretched environments for the development of capitalist relations of production. Capitalism only expanded rapidly in those places where it was protected in its youth by feudalism.[30]

This means that in non-Western countries landed property plays a different role which does not facilitate the emergence and consolidation of capitalism, or, what is the same thing, the alliance between the bourgeoisie and the pre-capitalist ruling class cannot be implemented. According to Rey, not to have realized this essential point was an important mistake of Rosa Luxemburg. She continued to attribute a dominant role to landed property in processes of transition to capitalism which did not start within a feudal mode of production.[31] Although Marx failed to realize that ground rent was not an integral part of the capitalist mode of production but a sign of an articulation between the feudal and capitalist mode of production,[32] at least he confined his analysis of the transition only to Western Europe.[33] Rey concludes that in social formations without a preceding feudal mode of production, capitalism cannot take root so naturally as it did in Western Europe. In these cases the stability of the pre-capitalist mode of production must be destroyed by violence. Capitalism can only emerge

thanks to the implanting of transitional modes of production, which will be born in the womb of the colonized social formation and will dissolve themselves when the moment comes to give way to capitalism. Of course, the economic revolution thus provoked is more violent than that produced by the first appearance of capitalism in the world, for the dissolution of the ancient modes of production takes place against the will of their ruling classes . . .[34]

So, during the first stage of the transition, while capitalism is still not dominant, the reproduction of a social formation is dominated by the reproduction of a mode of production which could be feudal, traditional or colonial. The latter is a transitional mode of production whose mission is to break the resistance of the traditional modes of production. After doing that by using force, the colonial mode of production will dissolve itself. During the second stage, which coincides with the end of the colonial mode of production, capitalism becomes dominant. But there are some fundamental differences between the situation of those social formations whose transition started from a predominant feudal mode of production in Marx's time and the present situation of those social formations which Rey calls 'neo-colonial'. In the latter the second stage commences much later and quite often the traditional modes of production are not thoroughly dominated by capitalism. Another crucial difference lies in the fact that the neo-colony is dependent on foreign capital, and, above all, in the fact that 'the essential moment of the process of reproduction of this capital is controlled by metropolitan financial capital, or, increasingly, by international finance capital.'[35] In this way Rey ends up recognizing a situation which is precisely the basis of Cardoso's concept of dependency. But Rey does not elaborate or even mention dependency as a distinct category, he seems to prefer the notion of 'neo-colonialism'.

Rey's theory of articulation of modes of production has been criticized from a variety of points of view. Bradby, for instance, has rejected the idea that violence is a necessary element in the establishment of capitalism and dissolution or reconstitution of pre-capitalist modes. She does not deny that violence has historically existed, but she denies that it has always been necessary. There are cases, she argues, 'where absolutely no extra-economic force has been used to expel the country population, but where capital is embarrassed by an all-too-great potential labour-force.'[36] Foster-Carter follows this point up by asking 'if violence is not essential to the argument, then why is the articulation of capitalism with all other modes of production except feudalism so prolonged and problematic?'[37] My interpretation of this criticism is as follows: if violence by the autochthonous ruling class or the colonial power is not necessary to expel the peasants from their land, then this means that the traditional modes of production, instead of mounting resistance to, seem to facilitate the introduction of capitalism. If this is so, then there is a problem in Rey's argument, for there would be no difference between these modes and feudalism. The whole explanation of underdevelopment would collapse.

Rey's idea that capitalism works always with the same methods and in the same direction, whether it arises endogenously or is externally imposed, is also questioned by Foster-Carter in the context of Rey's own admission that capital in underdeveloped countries was not only introduced from the outside but also has its reproduction controlled by metropolitan or international capital. If this is so, Foster-Carter argues, then there is a level of analysis at which the homology of goals and methods is not true. This difference in the origin and operation of capitalism, Foster-Carter goes on, has been the claim of dependency theory and consists in the fact that

> capitalism comes to the 'Third World' from the outside, as *foreign* capitalism, indeed as *colonial* capitalism; and the *extraversion* thus created *persists*, defining the character of *contemporary* underdevelopment, viz. as an *externally oriented, distorted* and indeed *disarticulated* 'part-economy' subordinated (now, as ever) to *metropolitan* capital.[38]

Although some of Rey's passages seem to move in the direction of accepting a few points emphasized by dependency theory, they are not really well integrated with the rest of the theory and remain isolated remarks. Rey's analysis is really based on the idea that there are no differences in the way in which capitalism works everywhere and that what is different in the case of underdeveloped countries is given by the specificity of their traditional modes of production and by the particularity of their patterns of transition to capitalism. Foster-Carter thinks that Rey is right to emphasize the specificity of traditional modes of production but wrong not to see the dependent nature of capitalism itself. I think it is possible to go further in the critique, if one does not take for granted, as Foster-Carter seems to do, that underdevelopment necessarily entails the existence of traditional modes of production. There are some Latin American countries (Chile, Uruguay, Argentina) where one would be hard put to it to find traditional modes of production of any significance, even in the countryside. And yet those countries remain underdeveloped. It is one thing to criticize Frank for believing that Latin America has been fully capitalist since the sixteenth century, quite another is to believe that the old modes of production still survive everywhere in Latin America at the end of the twentieth century. To blame underdevelopment solely on the resistance of traditional modes of production is to evade the question about the persistence of underdevelopment in fully capitalist countries.

   In this sense it is not really surprising to find that Rey's theory was constructed and is best suited to understand the situation of African countries, in particular the case of Congo-Brazzaville. There Rey finds that a 'lineage' mode of production, reconstituted and reformed by the colonial mode of production, still hinders the process of development even after the end of colonialism.[39] But apart from the fact that at present the survival of traditional modes of production can be found in Africa more easily than in Latin America, there are even greater problems when one considers the Latin American old modes of production in relation to colonial power. The contrast with Congo-Brazzaville, for instance, could not be sharper. Colonial rule in Congo-Brazzaville started with conquest by a capitalist country in 1920 and lasted until 1934. The conquest of Latin America started in the 1500s and colonial rule lasted until 1825. Spain and Portugal in the sixteenth and seventeenth centuries were still feudal countries.[40]

If anything, what the Spaniards brought with them to Latin America were feudal institutions which were articulated with the Indian modes of production. Even if it were right and possible to conceive of a 'colonial mode of production' which was violently imposed in order to break the resistance of the Indian modes of production, this situation cannot be understood as a way of introducing the capitalist mode of production, for it was a way of introducing servile institutions like the *encomienda* and the *latifundia* or *hacienda* system. If there was an articulation it was one between the traditional Indian modes of production and feudalism. When capitalism in Latin America began to expand, much later, and not as a consequence of the facts of conquest and colonization, it had to contend and articulate itself with these semi-feudal institutions. One has to remember that even the Latin American process of independence, far from bringing about the dissolution of the predominantly slave and feudal modes of production, meant their strengthening.[41] This poses serious problems to Rey's theory for as Brewer points out

> If Latin America has been feudal, we must either explain underdevelopment there by some cause other than the pre-existing mode of production, or say that feudalism is not a favourable environment for capitalism, and that the origins of capitalism are to be sought in the *dissolution* of feudalism. Either would undermine Rey's overall account.[42]

Additionally there are many problems in Rey's concepts of 'transitional modes of production' and 'colonial modes of production'. He never clarifies the theoretical status of a transitional mode of production nor does he properly define a colonial mode of production. They remain exceedingly vague and ambiguous categories which are resorted to in order to explain a transitional period where neither capitalism nor other modes seem to be dominant. But this may be more apparent than real, and in any case, although there may be a real problem in the interpretation of the transition, the solution provided by a colonial mode of production is achieved at the cost of neglecting the very definition of mode of

duction which Rey had taken from Althusser and Balibar. I would have thought colonialism is a category which could be best predicated of a social formation and has very little to do with a mode of production. One may ask, what are the specific relations of production which define a colonial mode of production? What system of classes and what kind of domination is determined by those relations of production? These questions have no answers in Rey's writings. But in addition to this I tend to agree with Brewer that it is unnecessary to describe colonialism as a mode of production and that it is possible to solve the problem of the transition in other ways.[43]

MARXISM VERSUS DEPENDENCY THEORY

Perhaps the strongest critique of dependency theory has been advanced by a group of authors influenced by Marxism, in some cases of an Althusserian persuasion. I refer to Warren, Bernstein, Phillips, Taylor, Mandle, Booth, Banaji, Kitching and Leys.[44] Although they differ in many respects, they tend to share Marx's early optimistic belief in the inherently dynamic and developmental capabilities of capitalism and are therefore very suspicious of the concepts of underdevelopment and dependency – which they sometimes put together in the same package labelled 'Underdevelopment and dependency theory' (UDT) – for they cast doubtson the progressiveness of capitalism. Given the number of authors involved and the variety of their opinions, I shall summarize their most representative critique into the following claims:

1   Dependency theory is 'fatally flawed on logical grounds' and vitiated by tautological reasoning.[45] This is exemplified by Frank's proposition that satellites experience more development when their ties to their metropolises are weakest. The crucial flaw is the definition of development as self-sustained industrial growth, so that, by definition, underdevelopment becomes the fate of satellites which lack self-sustained industrial growth. Hence, Frank's assertion is only illustrated but not corroborated by the historical material adduced. The attempted empirical demonstration of the proposition is nothing but an exercise in tautology. The conceptual couple 'development' and 'underdevelopment', where 'development' is a non-problematic model and 'underdevelopment' is conceived as its reverse, necessarily leads to a kind of circular reasoning

which can only produce explanations already contained in the definitions of the terms.[46]

✦ 2   Dependency theory is conceptually loose and theoretically weak. Not only is it not Marxist[47] but also it 'is not rooted in *any* rigorous body of deductive-type theory.'[48] This is shown by its adherence to outdated economic ideas like the consistent deterioration of the terms of trade or the conception of development as self-sustained growth. Another example is the notion of underdevelopment proposed by Baran and Frank which, according to Taylor, is inherently teleological: 'the present is simply "explained" by relating it to a different, "potential" state of utilization of the economic surplus.' Although it is useful to have an indication of the type of economy that could exist without the imperialist drain of surplus, 'teleological axioms provide us with very little basis for *explaining the existence of the present itself.*'[49]

✦ 3   The theory of underdevelopment is contradictory and therefore impossible. On the one hand development is defined as a process of autocentric accumulation which leads to self-sustained growth, but on the other hand this is contradicted by the proposition that the underdevelopment of the periphery is a condition of the development of the centre. As Bernstein puts it,

> Underdevelopment theory cannot have it both ways. If the field of analysis is world economy, if the centre needs the periphery for modes of exploitation that off-set the tendency of the rate of profit to fall, if the circuit of capital in general is realized on the international plane, then there is *no* capitalist formation whose development can be regional autonomous, self-generating or self-perpetuating. Development cannot be conceptualized by its self-centred nature and lack of dependence, nor 'underdevelopment' by its dependence and lack of autonomy.[50]

✦ 4   The theory of underdevelopment provides an ideological and deterministic conception of underdevelopment which replicates the errors of modernization theory. Both theories propose an ideal model of development and assess the situation of the periphery in relation to it. Just as modernization theory assures the development of the periphery by a historical repetition of the process undergone by the 'model' developed countries, underdevelopment theory assures the impossibility of peripheral development within the capitalist world system.[51] As Leys points out, 'it is not really an accident that these simplistic pairings, developed/ underdeveloped, centre/periphery, dominant/dependent resemble those of bourgeois development theory (traditional/modern, rich/poor, advanced/backward, etc.); they are basically polemical *inversion* of them.'[52] Dependency theory may be critical of modernization theory but it has remained within the same 'problematic'.

5   Dependency and underdevelopment theory, especially the kind elaborated by Baran and Amin, has been related to a form of 'third worldist' ideology to the extent that 'it has accepted that the process of accumulation can proceed in the advanced countries in a relatively uninterrupted manner, and that the major locus of contradiction has now shifted to the underdeveloped countries.'[53] Thus these authors have managed out of existence all possibility of crises and class struggles in the centre.

6   Dependency theorists do not properly theorize capitalism: 'the only categories made available for defining capitalism are those of commodity production, market relations and profit, none of which are peculiar to the capitalist mode of production and its *social relations of production.*'[54]

7   Dependency theory is static, economistic and mechanistic. Static in the sense 'that it takes dependency, however defined, as *given*, only its form changing; it conjures away the possibility that dependency may be a declining phenomenon.'[55] Economistic 'in the sense that social classes, the state, politics, ideology figure in it very noticeably as derivatives of economic forces';[56] in fact 'detailed analyses of the nature and focus of existing class struggles are few and far between, while analyses of the relationships between national and international capital are in abundant supply.'[57] Mechanistic 'in the sense that processes tend to be presented as resulting from a "logic" of mechanism, a system of vicious circles reinforcing each other.'[58] Thus underdevelopment appears inevitable.

8   Dependency theory 'incorrectly assumes that imperialism is a monolithic structure. This empirically and historically incorrect contention enables dependency theorists, for example, to minimize the widening range of options open to Latin American societies.'[59] Furthermore, the policies of imperialist countries have generally favoured the economic development of underdeveloped countries and with the rise of indigenous capitalism the ties of dependency 'are being markedly loosened'.[60]

9   Dependency theory is stagnationist and underestimates the prospects of successful capitalist development in the periphery. According

to Warren, empirical evidence shows that 'substantial advances' have already been achieved in industrialization and agrarian transformation in the third world.[61]

10 Dependency theory tries to explain the exploitation and underdevelopment of the third world by a drain of surplus which has two sources: an outflow of capital in terms of repatriation of profits, dividends etc. considerably greater than the inflow of foreign capital (Frank, Wallerstein), and unequal exchange (Emmanuel, Amin). But in order for such a drain to produce underdevelopment, Warren argues, 'it must be an *absolute drain*, not simply an unequal "transaction" that nevertheless leaves both sides better off than before.'[62] As foreign investment usually creates new values, salaries and state revenues which would not have existed otherwise and as trade is not a zero–sum game in which one side's gain must be the other's loss, 'it is thus highly unlikely at first glance that either foreign investment or unequal exchange (supposing it to exist) causes any absolute drain of surplus compared to the situation that would pertain in the absence of the investment or trade.'[63] A related but different criticism by Jenkins maintains that 'critical accounts of the "drain of surplus" are unsatisfactory in that they remain at the level of appearances, being content to show the existence of a net outflow of capital without providing an adequate theoretical explanation.'[64] Bettelheim, Castañeda and Hett also make the point that to speak of the 'exploitation' of poor countries by rich countries is to conceal the true exploitation of workers or to relegate it to a position of secondary importance.[65]

11 Dependency theorists seem to believe that socialism is desirable because capitalism can no longer produce development. The problem with this premise is that if it were to be shown that capitalism could produce development, then the case for socialism would collapse. As Phillips puts it, 'if the necessity of socialism lies in the impossibility of a capitalist solution to the problems of national development, any suggestion that there may be a capitalist solution seems to be establishing a "case for capitalism".'[66] Socialism is treated as a national necessity because it promises to produce the goods that capitalism fails to deliver, but dependency theory does not discuss whether socialism is possible nor does it 'disclose the potential class forces on which a revolutionary struggle can be based'.[67] Thus socialism ceases to be a movement for the liberation of the working class and becomes a movement for the modernization of underdeveloped societies.[68]

12   Dependency theory is 'inherently incapable of breaking loose from the platform of national capitalism'.[69] The idea of a national development which dependency theory uncritically accepts is advanced by bourgeois theory 'as an apolitical concept which transcend class interests'[70] and has subordinated the working-class movements in the periphery to nationalist and populist ideologies which substitute the struggle against alleged external enemies for internal class struggle.[71] Kitching, as we saw in chapter 4, has compared underdevelopment and dependency theory with the position held by the Russian populists such as Vorontsov, Danielson and Flerovsky in the nineteenth century and concluded that they shared a pervasive nationalism coupled with pessimism about the possibilities of indigenous capitalist development.[72] Mandle goes further and argues that 'In the world capitalist economy, for development to occur, a nation must be prepared to forego a considerable amount of its sovereignty, especially as that sovereignty relates to economic decision-making. Similarly it must be prepared to accept relatively high levels of income inequality and unemployment.'[73] While acknowledging the negative effects of dependent development, Mandle assimilates them to other contradictions typical of capitalism. Loss of sovereignty, just as much as inequality, are today part of the necessary and heavy cost of economic development.

13   Dependency theory is vitiated either by lack of empirical evidence or by empirical fallacy. Mandle makes the point that the expansion or lack of expansion of productive forces, which was for Marx the central issue of development, is empirically testable. Because dependency theories lack conceptual precision about this central issue, they advance 'their pessimistic hypothesis without subjecting it to an empirical test. They construct their argument assuming that development is not occurring. But the assumption of stagnation may be false.'[74] Empirical fallacy occurs because dependency theory fails to substantiate its hypotheses that increased marginalization, authoritarian politics, cultural alienation, inappropriate technology and regressive income distribution are caused by dependency: 'no systematic effort was made to distinguish the effects of transnationalization *per se* from those of the local social and political context, the prevailing economic policy regime and so on.'[75]

14   Dependency theory performs a negative ideological role in respect of Marxism:

On one side there is historical materialism, on the other there is the variety of theoretical and ideological currents in bourgeois philosophy and social sciences. The blurring of the incompatibility and antagonism between the two through the medium of a radical sociology of underdevelopment, or any other radicalization of social science, can only result in the subversion of Marxism to the benefit of the bourgeois order.[76]

For Booth, on the contrary, one cannot simply oppose Marxism to dependency theory because even within Marx's writings themselves dependency views can be found (for instance in his letters on Ireland). Why then, Booth asks, have dependency perspectives, despite being logically, empirically and theoretically wrong, had such an enduring presence within Marxism? Because, he says, there is a basic problem in Marxist theory which consists in 'its metatheoretical commitment to demonstrating that what happens in societies in the era of capitalism is not only explicable but also in some stronger sense *necessary*.'[77] By following Hindess and Hirst, Booth argues that 'Marxist theory systematically neglects certain kinds of issues because of a belief derived from the methodology of Marx's *Capital* that the significant characteristics of national economies and social formations may be "read off" from the characteristics, especially the "laws of motion", of the capitalist mode of production.'[78]

15   Those dependency views which do not fall into this pitfall are, nevertheless, caught in a different trap, and that is the functionalist and teleological type of explanation. Marxism, according to Booth, is based on functional explanations and therefore, together with structural functionalism, 'reify social institutions of a given type, placing them by metatheoretical fiat further beyond human control than they can be empirically shown to be.'[79] This is why certain dependency approaches are so keen to see the role of less developed countries and their institutions in terms of their contribution to a wider system.

UNDERDEVELOPMENT AND DEPENDENCY: A CHALLENGE TO HISTORICAL MATERIALISM

Many of the criticisms just outlined are quite compelling and adequately fit the first group of dependency theories represented by Frank, Wallerstein, Emmanuel and Amin. However, given the complexity and variety of the so-called theories of dependency, such a critique becomes grossly unfair when applied generally, without any distinctions. This is the main problem of this kind of Marxist critique. With the exception of Warren, the other critics tend to reduce the various strands of dependency analysis to the Frankian 'capitalist world system' paradigm. When one introduces the necessary distinctions then these criticisms can be seen in a different light. Tautology and circular reasoning does occur in the analyses of Frank, Wallerstein and Amin. One can accept that conceptual looseness and ambiguity in the definition of concepts is even more widespread. It is also possible that more empirical evidence and of a better kind would be required.

But to say that dependency analysis in general is not Marxist and, worse still, not rooted in any rigorous body of deductive theory is a wild exaggeration. There is no point in denying the Marxist origins of most dependency approaches. Even Booth, who maintains that the dependency approach 'is obviously at variance with the theoretical *core* of classical Marxism', acknowledges that 'it has clearly had a certain place in Marxist thought not just since Lenin but since Marx himself.'[80] True, Marxist theory is not always rigorously applied and sometimes – particularly in the case of the world system strand – is even misinterpreted. But other authors like Cardoso are far more rigorous in their Marxism and equally critical of catastrophistic and outdated economic ideas such as the permanent and systematic deterioration of the terms of trade or the definition of development as self-sustained growth. Even Warren recognizes 'that Cardoso stands somewhat apart from other theorists'.[81]

The contradictory affirmation of an autocentric accumulation which necessitates third world surpluses; the replication of the errors of modernization theories; the conception of a non-contradictory capitalism in the centre; the lack of a proper theorization of capitalism; static, economistic and mechanistic theorization; a monolithic conception of imperialism and stagnationism are all certainly accurate criticisms of Frank and company. Three qualifications are necessary though. First, to be fair to Baran, he does not simply transfer the locus of contradictions to underdeveloped countries. Both Mandle and Phillips in their criticisms of Baran's theory fail to mention that for him it is not just capitalism in the poor countries that is no longer dynamic but also central capitalism. In this Baran agrees with Lenin's view of a decadent and stagnant capitalism. But, of course, this in itself is also flawed, as Warren has argued.

Second, Warren explicitly includes Cardoso in the criticism that dependency theory is static, not in the sense that it precludes all possibilities of development, but in the sense that dependency appears as given, 'only its form changing', not considering the possibility that it may decline. This is basically true, but if dependency changes its form and is compatible with certain forms of development then the label static is a misnomer. At any rate, going to the nub of the criticism, one has to consider the possibility that if Cardoso does not envisage the decline of dependency it is because, contrary to Warren's opinion, dependency in reality has not declined, at least so far. The point is whether Cardoso's approach can, in principle, accommodate challenges to imperialism and dependency. It seems to me that his approach, based on class analysis, certainly does allow for this possibility. In this sense his analysis does not assume that imperialism is a monolithic structure, but conceives of a wide range of options open to Latin American countries. Warren's perspective, on the contrary, is far more static and deterministic because his approach is not based on class analysis and therefore it cannot allow the possibility of an accentuation of dependency.

Third, stagnationism and underestimation of the prospect of successful capitalist development in the periphery are not only a feature of the Frankian paradigm but characterize several other theories, especially Hinkelammert's and some structuralist approaches (Sunkel, Furtado). Again, Cardoso and Faletto must be excluded from this criticism. However, one cannot fail to notice that Warren's determinism commits the opposite error of systematically overestimating the prospect of capitalism development everywhere in the periphery. To maintain that imperialism is everywhere supposed to favour the industrialization and economic development of the third world is as crass a mistake as to maintain that imperialism necessarily leads to the general stagnation of the underdeveloped world. Statistics show that the new 'export-led' industrialization processes are heavily concentrated in a few less developed countries. Besides, one should keep a sense of proportion. The general enthusiasm about the NICs should not make us forget that although there have been substantial advances in the 'export-led' industrialization of some less developed countries, none of them 'loom as large in the world system as even the smaller more developed countries. The largest exporter of manufactured goods, Taiwan, exports under half what Belgium does. The heart of the global manufacturing system remains overwhelmingly concentrated in the more developed countries.'[82]

As for the drain of surplus, one has to say, in the first place, that it exists, both in terms of unequal exchange and as a net outflow of capital. As unequal exchange the drain of surplus was already recognized by

Marx on several occasions where he even spoke of the exploitation of poor nations:

> nations may continually exchange with one another, may even continually repeat the exchange on an ever expanding scale, without for that reason necessarily gaining in equal degrees. One of the nations may continually appropriate for itself a part of the surplus labour of the other, giving back nothing for it in the exchange.[83]

> Most agricultural peoples are forced, to sell their product below its value whereas in countries with advanced capitalist production the agricultural product rises to its value.[84]

> The relationship between labour days of different countries may be similar to that existing between skilled, complex labour and unskilled, simple labour within a country. In this case the richer country exploits the poorer one, even where the latter gains by the exchange.[85]

Differences in the organic composition of capital, in the degree of development of productive forces, and in the skills of the labour force are bound to determine transfers of surplus from the poor nations to the rich nations when they trade. Even the critics of Emmanuel's version of unequal exchange, like Bettelheim, acknowledge that. Equally, there is recent and substantial empirical evidence which shows that the outflow of capital from developing countries greatly exceeds the inflow of foreign investment. Jenkins, for instance, establishes that 'between 1960 and 1972 repatriated dividend income by US subsidiaries in Latin America exceeded net inflows by over $9000 million, while in Western Europe the inflows of US capital exceeded repatriated dividend income by over $5000 million.'[86]

If one takes developing countries as a whole and foreign investment from all developed countries, there has been a net outflow of capital from the third world every year from 1970 to 1980 apart from 1975. In 1970 the outflow was $3,859 million, in 1976 was $5,869.6 million, and in 1980 was $8,178.8 million.[87] However, Warren's criticism has to do with the significance rather than with the mere existence of the drain of surplus. And here he has a point because it cannot be argued that the surplus drain explains underdevelopment, nor that it is indispensable for the development of central countries. On the one hand, as Warren argues (and Marx's passage from the *Grundrisse* explicitly suggests) the drain does not mean that underdeveloped countries do not benefit from trade or foreign investment, it only means that they gain less than the central economies.

On the other hand, as Hinkelammert argues, the drain of surplus does not exclusively define the situation of exploitation because even if there was no transfer of surplus, the underdeveloped world would still be dependent given its situation of unbalanced periphery.[88] Nevertheless, the fact that the drain of surplus does not explain underdevelopment does not mean that in itself is desirable or has no effects on the rates of growth. Warren's point is entirely based on the idea that without international trade and foreign investment the third world would be worse off. This may be the case, but it should not make us forget that with equal exchange and with more foreign reinvestment of profits the third world would be better off. In other words, the subordinated position of the third world in terms of trade and investment, makes things more difficult and this is still a valid dependency point.

Jenkins makes the related point that the 'drain of surplus' accounts are unsatisfactory because they remain at the level of appearances, and critically questions whether such a drain is the cause of underdevelopment or a consequence. I agree with his implicit suggestion that it is a consequence and not a cause. But in trying to account theoretically for the low level of reinvestment in Latin America, Jenkins proposes an 'internationalization of capital' approach which goes beyond a merely market oriented explanation and according to which the problem resides in the coexistence of pre-capitalist and capitalist modes of production, and more specifically in the supposed fact that in Latin America wage goods are produced under pre-capitalist production relations.[89] Rather surprisingly he is forced to recognize that the argument does not hold in a number of Latin American countries where capitalism has penetrated agriculture rather rapidly. Again, I agree. But then I fail to see the contribution of the 'internationalization of capital' approach which Jenkins proposes, and I am bound to conclude that it is not an adequate explanation either.

The criticisms concerned with the conception of socialism and the dangers of nationalism are also adequate when levelled against the 'world system' paradigm. Cardoso, once more, is to be exempted from this indictment. However, the supposed 'ideological' role of the 'radical sociology of development' proposed by Bernstein deserves a comment. First, the idea that on one side there is historical materialism and on the other there is a variety of ideological bourgeois theories, with the connotation that the former is true and the latter are false, strikes me as

Manichaean and unhelpful, typical of the Althusserian positivist and arrogant conceptions about science and its self-evident truths.[90] Second, the best dependency analyses are clearly an application of historical materialism to the reality of some underdeveloped countries. So they cannot possibly perform the role of 'blurring' the incompatibility between Marxism and bourgeois theories. Third, Bernstein's Althusserian conception of ideology is clearly idealist. For him the problem seems to be that some mistaken ideas subvert Marxism. He resembles the left Hegelians who thought that the real problem was the existence of mistaken religious and philosophical ideas which could be dealt with at the level of criticism. For Marx, on the contrary, the problem is not the existence of mistaken ideas but the real contradictions which originate ideology and which should be dealt with in practice, not by mere criticism.

Booth's final and more profound criticism must also be dealt with. Although I agree with him that one cannot so easily dissociate Marxism from dependency views, his belief (entirely based on Mori's discussion of Marx's writings on India, Poland and Ireland[91]) that Marx 'adopted an almost diametrically opposed position' to his original enthusiastic assessment of the British mission in Asia, and that the new position amounts to a dependency view, must be questioned. It is true that, as we saw in chapter 2, Marx's letters on Ireland take the opposite view to 'The British rule in India', and there is also a change of mind in respect of Poland and other national problems. But Marx's reasons do not amount to a general, systematic and fully worked out intellectual shift. While he criticized the British rule in Ireland, he had no qualms about the North American conquests, interventions and subversions in Latin America. What was crucial for Marx was the advance of socialism; neither moral considerations about the right of all peoples to self-determination nor dependency analyses about the need for new nations to secure more economic autonomy played any role in his thought. In Marx's assessment, socialism in Europe required the liberation of Ireland as a precondition for the liberation of the British working class, just as much as in America the submission of Mexico was required in order to enhance the development of the North American proletariat.

Even if we accept that there is a residual dependentist perspective to be found in Marx on Ireland, this is not the crude and flawed approach Booth is interested in unmasking. There is simply no basis for putting Marx's analyses on the same level as Frank's. But Booth thinks otherwise. For him the root of the problem, which is shared by Marxist critics of dependency such as Warren and Rey, is this supposed metatheoretical and deterministic premise of all Marxisms (also shared by structural functionalism as it turns out) which consists in trying to show that processes within capitalist societies are not only intelligible but also necessary, thus reifying them and placing them beyond human control. This assessment Booth takes rather uncritically from Hindess and Hirst. He seems to be unaware of the existence of any Marxism other than the orthodoxy defended in different but convergent ways by Warren, Althusser and Cohen. He first reduces Marxism to a deterministic economism and then, having constructed the straw man, he proceeds to destroy it. But in doing so Booth ultimately fails to do justice to, and worse still, does not even consider the possibility of Marxism as a theory of practice.

This is no accident but strictly obeys the curious logic of Hindess and Hirst procedures: first, in the name of Althusser, they dismiss all forms of the humanist, ideological and pre-scientific Marxism which emphasizes the determining role of class struggles in history. Then, when Althusserianism has been erected as *the* scientific and rigorous interpretation of Marxism which emphasizes the determining role of structures in a subjectless history, it is in its turn easily destroyed as a contradictory and crass determinism. But then there is no attempt to return to Marx's original theses, there is no withdrawal of the original Althusserian critique of humanism. Marxism can only be a form of structuralism but as such is now pronounced intrinsically flawed. It is ironic, to say the least, that Booth should say that Marxism places social institutions further beyond human control than they are empirically shown to be, by basing himself on Hindess and Hirst's Althusserian interpretation of Marxism which precisely and explicitly started by putting social institutions beyond human control.[92] This was not and has never been a feature of Marxism conceived as a theory of practice.[93]

Yet if one puts aside Booth's reduction of Marxism one can accept that his critique appropriately fits both the Frankian paradigm and its Warrenite opposition. What is common to Amin, Emmanuel, Frank, Wallerstein and other *dependentistas* (excluding Cardoso and Faletto) is the attempt to provide a general abstract mechanism that explains underdevelopment everywhere as a result of similar exploitative market relations controlled by the developed world, thus giving no important theoretical place to the internal processes of class struggle. Warren only changes the content of an equally deterministic structural relationship: imperialism favours industrialization and economic development everywhere. In either case there is no room for the variability and uncertainty which is typical of the outcome of class struggles. In so far as they draw from Marxism, their conception is most compatible with the economistic and deterministic orthodox version of historical materialism which I described in chapter 1. But if the dependency perspective has anything valuable to say to the Marxist analysis of less developed nations, it has to be in connection with, or rather from within, an alternative version of historical materialism: a conception which underlines the increasing scope of human practice and rejects the idea of an immanent drive which leads history towards an inevitable end.

Mavros has made the interesting point that the attempt by the above-mentioned Marxist authors to criticize dependency as a non-Marxist alternative theory to Marxism is entirely misplaced because the two are not comparable. While Marxism is a theory, that is to say, a system of interrelated abstract concepts which supplies the conceptual tools to analyse society, underdevelopment and dependency 'theory' (UD'T') is not a theory but a generalization or model stemming from the concrete analysis of cases. These are two complementary forms of discourse which need one another:

> Marxism as an abstract theoretical system is of limited use without concrete investigations; UD'T' on the other hand, cannot proceed without concepts. It is therefore futile to try to impose a barrier between the two: it will not work. The accumulated wisdom of UD'T' cannot be so easily dismissed, despite its evident and serious shortcomings. Similarly it would be impossible to grasp the specificity of the Third World without the help of the conceptual armoury of Marxism.[94]

However, Mavros deals with UDT in general and therefore does not take into account two things. First, it is not just the Marxist critics, but also some dependency theorists, particularly those from the 'capitalist world system' paradigm, that conceive of dependency as an explanatory theory of underdevelopment which is separate from Marxism. This is especially true of Frank, who explicitly states that he has never claimed to be a Marxist. Second, although I accept that there is a sort of 'accumulated wisdom' of dependency perspectives, this is quite uneven, and the Marxist critics can argue that even if one considers dependency as a generalization or model, the concrete analyses of cases tends to be superficial and weak. In other words, dependency can still be found to be deficient as analysis on its own level. In fact many of the criticisms I have listed point in this direction. Yet, as I have repeatedly argued, one cannot generalize and damn all dependency analyses as inadequate. By doing this, the Marxist critics systematically blind themselves to, and refuse even to consider, the specificity of capitalist development in the periphery. This is why I think Mavros's distinction between the discursive level of Marxism and that of dependency is still valuable and coincides with some of Cardoso's intuitions, especially when he argues that

> rigorously it is not possible to think of a 'theory of dependency'. There may be a theory of capitalism and classes, but dependency, as we characterize it, is no more than the political expression, in the periphery, of the capitalist mode of production when it is driven to international expansion.[95]

and that 'analyses of situations of dependency imply theories and require the use of methodologies.'[96]

I think that to a great extent this clarifies what the status of dependency analyses should be in relation to Marxism. The issue of dependency arises in the study of the development of capitalism in the periphery. It does not replace a Marxist analysis of classes, relations of production and productive forces, it only contextualizes it. This contextualization is necessary from the moment one accepts the reality of the centre–periphery distinction. This distinction is hinted at by Marx in all but name when he argues that 'a new and international division of labour, a division suited to the requirements of the chief centres of modern industry springs up, and converts one part of the globe into a chiefly agricultural field of production, for supplying the other part which remains a chiefly industrial field.'[97] Dependency analysis is constructed on the centre–periphery paradigm, that is to say, on the assumption that peripheral capitalist economies are not only not identical to central capitalist economies, but are in a position of subordination.

The question arises as to what the origin is of this situation of subordination. Foster-Carter has argued that it comes from the colonial imposition of capitalism from outside and the persistence of the extraversion thus created.[98] Marx's passage about the international division of labour comes in a context that seems to support this perspective: 'East India was *compelled* to produce cotton, wool, hemp, jute, and indigo for Great Britain,' and foreign lands are said to be '*converted* into settlements for growing the raw material of the mother country; just as Australia, for example was *converted* into a colony for growing wool.'[99] However, I want to argue that it is simply wrong to generalize the claim that capitalism is imposed from the outside, as colonial capitalism, on the whole of the third world. The colonization of Latin America did not mean the introduction of the capitalist mode of production but created semi-feudal and slave institutions everywhere. True, these Latin American predominantly pre-capitalist modes of production were externally oriented and extraverted by the colonial power, but this integration into the international market did not make them capitalist.

Capitalism began to develop in Latin America much later in the nineteenth century, even after the process of independence. It was also extraverted when it began to expand, not because of any colonial imposition, but because of the legacy of the colonial exporting economy which was well articulated with the renewed exporting interests of the ruling classes. It was in the interest of the ruling classes which controlled the exporting economy to open their frontiers to allow the penetration of British and European goods whose competition destroyed handicraft industries and hindered the emergence of an autochthonous modern industry. So, although it is still true that 'by ruining handicraft production in other countries, machinery forcibly converts them into fields for the supply of its raw material,'[100] this was done not against the will of the already independent Latin American ruling classes but with their accord, because the consolidation of the international division of labour referred to by Marx worked in their own interest as exporters of raw materials.

Thus the dependent nature of Latin American capitalism cannot be explained by its original imposition from without but must be explained by the particular development of its structures of class domination, which in the nineteenth century were articulated with the interests of the European industrial bourgeoisie. The situation of Africa, India and the Caribbean is very different because there capitalism was directly imposed by British colonial rule. In a more general way then one can say that the capitalist periphery was originally formed as a result of the expansion of European capitalism which, either through colonization processes or through trade and international class alliances, reorganized the economic structures of the colonized or already independent third world countries and integrated or reintegrated them into the world market in a subordinated position.

Warren does not deny that there are differences between centre and periphery, but he criticizes the fact that this assumption remains unexamined in the light of empirical evidence.[101] What he wants to show is that economic power is being effectively redistributed in favour of peripheral economies. I believe, on the contrary, that empirical evidence shows that economic power has largely remained under the control of central economies. This can be clearly seen in the centre's undisputed primacy and leadership in the production of capital goods and in the technological and financial sectors which are crucial for capital accumulation. I think very few people would deny this. However, I fully agree with Cardoso that the acceptance of a centre–periphery paradigm should not lead to a 'theory of dependent capitalism', like the one proposed by Amin, not only because 'it seems senseless to search for "laws of movement" specific to situations that *are dependent*,'[102] but more specifically because it leads to a basically flawed distinction between a non-contradictory and developing capitalism in the centre and a contradictory and stagnant capitalism in the periphery.

I start from the premise that capitalism is inherently contradictory and that as such it produces development both in the centre and the periphery. Dependency does not alter this premise. What dependency analysis does is to account for the specific kind of development and the particular character, strength and variety of the contradictions which are found in the periphery. But here a warning must immediately be issued: the fact of dependency in itself does not determine a general and universal type of development and contradictions. In this sense Hinkelammert's distinction between balanced and unbalanced peripheries, so long as it does not denote a fixed pattern of stagnation for the latter, is a useful classification.[103] The character and specificity of the process of development and its contradictions in the periphery is determined by the historically specific processes of internal class struggles and by other peculiar historical and geographical circumstances.

The subordinated position may be common to all dependent countries but whether it is accepted or actively fought against, negotiated, redefined or passively opposed, whether it allows full employment and accelerated development or not, varies in accordance with the internal political processes and other historical peculiarities. In order to evaluate the contribution of dependency analyses one has to explore whether these analyses do convincingly show, in a variety of ways which correspond to a variety of situations of dependency, the specific character and peculiar contradictions of the process of capitalist development in the periphery. For instance, a differentiated analysis of various situations of dependency in Latin America by Cardoso and Faletto has already been presented in chapter 5. In principle a similar analysis might be done for African and Asian countries or even for dependent developed countries. But my concern in this book has been the Latin American case. However, despite the variety of dependency situations in Latin America, I think it is legitimate to ask whether dependency analyses of Latin America detect in a more global manner some common and recurrent features of its capitalist development which may allow an interesting contrast with the development of capitalism in central economies.

In trying to answer this question I must emphasize two aspects. First, there are some common features of Latin American countries which, using Evers's words, 'can be analysed at an "intermediate level" of the *specific*, between the *general* of the abstract laws of capital and the *particular* of its concrete functioning in each country.'[104] Second, I reaffirm the idea, against Amin, that there cannot exist two qualitatively different models of capitalism which work in essentially different ways, according to different laws, in the centre and in the periphery. But I contend that one can find different emphases which specify the Latin American situation and which must be theoretically accounted for by historical materialism. The laws of capitalism may be the same, but the historical conditions in which they operate are different. Marxism is right to reject all dependency-oriented attempts to understand capitalism as a world system which inherently excludes some areas from development or splits the operation of capitalism into two different models, but it is also, in its turn, rightly challenged by dependency analyses to account for the specificity of the Latin American capitalist development. Strictly speaking, the expressions 'peripheral capitalism' or 'dependent capitalism' are not entirely felicitous because they may induce the idea that it is not just the historical conditions of application, but also the very laws of movement that change. Wherever I use them I only mean capitalism in the specific historical conditions of the periphery.[105]

The first point some dependency analyses rightly make is to remind us of the fact that capitalism emerged as the dominant mode of production in Latin America rather late, in the last 30 or 40 years of the nineteenth century, precisely when it was entering in its monopoly and imperialist phase in the industrial centres. Three aspects of this process are relevant. First, the emergence of capitalism in Latin America is not unconnected with the enormous expansion of the demand for raw materials, the export of capital and the revolution in the means of transportation which central monopolistic capitalism brings about. Capitalism in Latin America is extraverted, that is to say, it is born not so much seeking the development of the internal market, as seeking to export. Second, although capitalism subordinates the old modes of production, these are not immediately and totally destroyed and carry on in a subordinated form well into the twentieth century. Third, the exploitation and looting of foreign lands and the enslavement of their indigenous populations, described by Marx as the 'idyllic proceedings' which constituted the 'chief momenta' of the European primitive accumulation,[106] were not of course available to Latin American capitalism. Primitive accumulation had to be carried out on a purely internal basis, by the massive expropriation of church and Indian lands, and, in certain countries like Brazil, by the freeing of the slaves.[107]

The slow but consistent penetration of capitalism in the countryside seems to have followed the 'Junker' pattern described by Lenin:

> the old landlord economy, bound as it is by thousands of threads to serfdom, is retained and turns slowly into purely capitalist, 'Junker' economy. The basis of the final transition from labour-service to capitalism is the internal metamorphosis of feudalist landlord economy. The entire agrarian system of the State becomes capitalist and for a long time retains feudalist features.[108]

In this way the Latin American *hacienda* survived for a long time on the basis of the extraction of absolute surplus-value. Hence the development of productive forces tended to be necessarily slow and, as Cueva points out, the bourgeoisie was born closely bound up with the landowning aristocracy.[109] So by the 1930s, Latin American capitalism was characterized by its extraversion and relatively low degree of development of economic activities catering for the internal market and also by its very slow penetration of the countryside, where it survived articulated with semi-servile institutions. The so-called 'oligarchic' state, characterized by authoritarian features and a restricted franchise, was the political linchpin of capitalism's incipient expansion. Of this situation it can be perfectly said, using Marx's words, that

> the bourgeoisie, at its rise, wants and uses the power of the state to "regulate" wages, *i.e.*, to force them within the limits suitable for surplus-value making, to lengthen the working-day and to keep the labourer himself in the normal degree of dependence.[110]

The emergence of an industrial bourgeoisie proper after the 1930s did not mean any significant rupture of the export-led model of accumulation. On the contrary, the process of industrialization remained dependent on the export of primary products and the import of machinery. One of the most important characteristics of the Latin American capitalist development is the non-existence or relative insufficiency of the sector which produces capital goods. This means that the process of accumulation in Latin America depends on the ability to expand primary exports and is organically linked to the production of capital goods in the industrial centres.

It also means that both the industrial bourgeoisie and the urban proletariat remained numerically small and both politically and organizationally weak. True, they participated in the struggles against the oligarchic state, but neither of them was in a commanding position. On the contrary, in the case of the industrial proletariat an incongruency and tension arose between their economic struggles against the bourgeoisie and their political struggles against the oligarchic system. Both the bourgeoisie and the proletariat were at times uneasy partners in wider populist coalitions and neither could impose its interests on the rest of society. These populist governments dismantled the most undemocratic features of the oligarchic political order and changed the course of economic and social policies. They granted some organizational rights and defensive legislation to the working class while using the state to promote industrialization policies which favoured the industrial bourgeoisie.

Two consequences ensue from this. First, the role of the state became much more important for the formation and development of the essential classes of the capitalist mode of production than it had ever been in central countries. This particularly affected the development of the working class. As Mouzelis puts it,

> the state's well entrenched incorporative tendencies and its leading role in the industrialization process meant that it could easily undermine the autonomy of working-class organizations and bring the growing number of industrial workers into the post-oligarchical political arena in a vertical, dependent manner.[111]

But this was not yet a state fully representative of bourgeois interests as the more backward landowing interest managed to keep important positions within it, especially by controlling parliaments and vetoing all legislation which sought to modernize the countryside. Second, as Mouzelis has argued, in contrast to the European pattern, Latin America experienced popular mobilization and achieved widespread political participation before the development of industrial capitalism: 'the demise of oligarchic politics and the transition from political "clubs" to parties occurred before these countries experienced large-scale indus-trialization.'[112]

Still, in the stage following the crisis of the oligarchic state, a process of industrialization promoted and defended by the state began to take place. However, in most Latin American countries this process acquired some importance and became dynamic only after the second world war, when it was helped by an improvement in the terms of trade of primary products. Cueva quotes statistics that show that between 1945 and 1955 industrial production grew approximately 50 per cent in Argentina, 120 per cent in Uruguay, 30 per cent in Chile, 100 per cent in Mexico and 123 per cent in Brazil.[113] It is in this post-war period up to 1955 that industrialization was able to provide new sources of employment and increases in real wages. From then onwards the process lost its dynamism until the late 1960s and early 1970s when, under military regimes and in alliance with transnational corporations and foreign capital, industrialization restarts its process of expansion at least in some countries. But this time it does not entail increases in salaries and a significant expansion of employment. The new industries are capital-intensive and the military regimes everywhere secure the dismantling of working-class organizations and a drastic fall in the value of real wages in order to attract foreign capital. Accumulation of capital goes on but now in a highly exclusive manner and on the basis of reversing many of the political and economic rights achieved by labourers since the 1930s.

What is peculiar to the Latin American process of capitalist development is not the existence of cleavages, cycles and contradictions in itself. By definition all processes of capitalist development, in the industrial centres as much as in the periphery, are cyclical and contradictory. What is peculiar is the specific character and the degree of accentuation and accumulation of the contradictions typical of capitalism. These specific features are determined by the following factors which in one way or another have been studied by dependency analyses:

1   The absence or insignificance of the crucially important industrial sector which produces capital goods and machinery. Although there has been some small relocation of capital good industries in Latin America, particularly in so far as transport equipment is concerned, in general the process is very limited. Industrial centres control more than 60 per cent of world production and more than 90 per cent of world exports.[114] In any case the capital goods industry that has been emerging is heavily dependent technologically from the industrial centres.

2   The original extraversion of Latin American capitalism which up until today has made the process of industrialization dependent on the export of primary products and/or heavy indebtness.

3   Not even at the peak of industrial expansion and when wages and employment were expanding did the process of industrialization in Latin America affect, let alone reconstruct, the whole of society. The paramount importance of the service sectors and the relatively small or declining size of the industrial working class have been permanent features of Latin American capitalism, whereas they constituted new features in central economies where manufacturing industry had already been the most important economic activity and the main employer and where the working class had been the strongest class numerically. Neo-liberal policies can dramatically accentuate this problem. A typical example is Chile. According to Tironi the numerical weight of the Chilean workers is only a third of what it was at the beginning of the 1970s and between 1971 and 1984 industrial workers have been reduced by 60 per cent. This decline in numbers is coupled with a dramatic weakening of the trade union movement: whereas in 1973 the unemployed were a tenth of the unionized workers,[115] in 1983 there were three times as many unemployed as workers in trade unions.

4   The relative smallness and the political and organizational weaknesses of both industrial bourgeoisie and industrial proletariat are correlated with the over-development of the state, the lack of a fully developed and autonomous civil society and the crucial role of the military institutions.

5   The fact that in Latin America popular mobilization and the erosion of the oligarchic state occurs before large-scale industrialization reverses the situation of Western Europe, where 'capitalist industrialization was one of the main processes leading to the transition from a restrictive/ oligarchic system of government based on clubs of notables to one based on broadly organized political parties.'[116] The Latin American early mobilization against the oligarchy without strong bourgeoisies and working classes and without a firm economic basis was a contributory factor in the formation of populist political movements, and the eventual accentuation of economic contradictions.

6   Structural unemployment which goes beyond the cyclical fluctuations of the labour reserve army and which permanently affects and marginalizes a very high proportion of the active population. Twenty

per cent is a conservative estimate for Latin America as a whole.[117] This problem is compounded in certain countries by the existence of ethnic groups and Indian communities which are marginalized as a whole.

7 Massive foreign control of the most modern and technologically sophisticated industry. The share of manufacturing industry controlled by foreign firms was 44 per cent in Brazil (1977); 66 per cent in Ecuador (1971–3); 31 per cent in Argentina (1972); 35 per cent in Mexico (1970); 36 per cent in Venezuela (1975); 43 per cent in Colombia (1974) and 40 per cent in Trinidad and Tobago (1968).[118] This creates what has been called 'structural heterogeneity', that is, the concentration of technology, finance and high salaries in the transnational capitalist sector, and the subsistence of secondary national capitalist sectors with low technology, little finance and very low salaries. This segments not just the bourgeoisie but also the working class to an extent unknown in central economies.

8 Enormous inequalities in income distribution, not just in relative terms which are also typical of central countries, but in the absolute sense of wide sectors having no income at all. This not only produces a widespread problem of destitution, poverty and starvation but in its turn negatively affects the development of an internal market. In a report to Latin American governments Prebisch estimated that in Latin America

around half of the present population has an exiguous average personal income of 120 dollars per year. And this vast social number represents approximately only one fifth of the Latin American total personal consumption, with the highest coefficients of undernourishment, ill clothing and even worse housing, as much as of disease and illiteracy; and also with the highest rates of reproduction.[119]

9 Absence, recent dismantling or lack of sufficient development of the welfare state benefits which could help alleviate the problems created by marginality and widespread poverty.

Some of these factors not only explain the specific character and strength of contradictions but also pose problems for the traditional Marxist approach to the study of capitalist societies. One of them is, for instance, the problem of class analysis in societies where there is a permanent and significant number of people without employment. Marxism usually limits its analysis to the traditional classes and the social movements and political parties which represent them. Questions arise about the political, social and economic impact of marginal sectors and about the theoretical categories and relations which account for it. It no longer seems adequate to deal with this problem in terms of concepts such as 'lumpen proletariat', 'relative surplus population' or 'industrial reserve army'. There have been a few attempts to work out a theoretical place for the concept of marginality within Marxism.[120] The results have not always been very successful.[121] On the other hand, Johnson's optimistic analysis of the revolutionary potential of 'marginal underclasses' and 'internal colonies'[122] may have grossly overestimated the political role of these groups. Still, all these attempts certainly draw our attention to a real and recurrent problem of dependent capitalist development which traditional Marxist analysis does not seem to have the theoretical instruments to deal with.

In conclusion, the dependency approach, in so far as it constitutes the application of historical materialism to the analysis of peripheral capitalist countries, is not dead. It has certainly been gravely ill, especially by virtue of the efforts of some of its practitioners to convert it into a fully fledged and autonomous theory which (a) conceives of underdevelopment as a form of permanent stagnation, and (b) explains such stagnation as a necessary result of the world capitalist system. The reaction against such a conception was swift and devastating. However, the critique of dependency went too far and threatened to throw away the baby with the bathwater. In trying to emphasize the developing capabilities of capitalism everywhere it tended to neglect the specificities and peculiarities of capitalist development in the periphery. In reaffirming the contradictory nature of capitalism in the industrial countries, it tended to overlook the particular character, force and accumulation of contradictions in the third world. In describing new dynamic processes of industrialization in certain less developed countries it hastily jumped to the conclusion that the third world was disappearing.[123] In denying that capitalism can have a qualitatively different mode of operation in the centre and in the periphery, it abandoned the very idea of centre and periphery.

All this is very reassuring for the conscience of developed countries and constitutes very good news for the supporters of capitalism. But if one were to accept the total homogeneity of the historical conditions of capitalist development and if one were to scrap distinctions such as centre and periphery, one would be depriving oneself of the sole basis on which the dramatic differences in the present world system can begin to be understood. When Leys criticizes the 'simplistic pairings' developed/ underdeveloped, dominant/dependent, centre/periphery and concludes 'that "underdevelopment" and "dependency" theory is no longer serviceable and must now be transcended',[124] one wonders what is to take their place. The critics hardly ever propose an alternative and hence one is left with the impression that either they find nothing specific in the situation of the third world which is worth analysing or, if they find it, they refuse to understand it for lack of an adequate conceptual apparatus. In either case one is left with a vacuum which neo-liberal theories are only too happy to fill.

In effect, while Marxists like Leys, Bernstein, Warren and others are busy dismantling 'underdevelopment and dependency theory', neo-liberals take advantage of their aid and sing the praises of capitalism, the free market forces and the brilliant industrial prospects of the whole of the third world. Just as the 'world system' theorists made the mistake of confusing the critique of capitalism with its non-viability in the periphery, many of their Marxist critics make the mistake of confusing the viability of capitalism in the periphery with its historical necessity and the universal homogeneity of its conditions of application. If the former neglected all contradictions in central economies, the latter play down the particular character and virulence of the contradictions in the periphery. This is why the idea of dependent capitalist development and its specificity must be maintained in any analysis of the third world.

NOTES

INTRODUCTION

1   See M. Dobb, *Economic Growth and Underdeveloped Countries* (London: Lawrence & Wishart, 1963), p. 8; and R. Brenner, 'The agrarian roots of European capitalism', in T.H. Aston and C.H.E. Philpin, eds, *The Brenner Debate* (Cambridge : Cambridge University Press, 1985), p. 214.

2   K. Marx and F. Engels, *Manifesto of the Communist Party*, in *Selected Works in One Volume* (London: Lawrence & Wishart, 1970), p. 38.

3   R. Brenner, 'Agrarian class structure and economic development in pre-industrial Europe', in Aston and Philpin, eds, *The Brenner Debate*, p. 38.

4   K. Marx, *Theories of Surplus-Value* (London: Lawrence & Wishart, 1969), vol. III, p. 501.

5   See 'Afterword to the second German edition' of *Capital* (London: Lawrence & Wishart, 1974), vol. I, pp. 24–6, and p. 85, note 1.

6   Marx, *Theories of Surplus-Value*, vol. I, p. 285. A good explanation of this principle and its methodological importance can be found in K. Marx, 1857 'Introduction' to *The Grundrisse* (Harmondsworth: Penguin, 1973), pp. 85–8.

7   I loosely follow the terminology proposed by E. Mandel, *Late Capitalism* (London: New Left Books, 1975), chapter 2.

8   F. S. Weaver, *Class, State, and Industrial Structure* (Westport: Greenwood Press, 1980), p. 16.

9   Marx, *Theories of Surplus-Value*, vol. III, p. 470.

10 See on this, C. Palloix, *L'Économie Mondiale Capitaliste et les Firmes Multinationales* (Paris: Maspero, 1975), vol. I, chapter 4.

11 Marx, *Theories of Surplus Value*, vol. III, p. 55.

12 Ibid., p. 501.

13 See Weaver, *Class, State, and Industrial Structure*, p. 17.

14 See on this, C. Napoleoni, *Economic Thought of the Twentieth Century* (London: Martin Robertson, 1972), chapter 1, and O. Sunkel and P. Paz, *El subdesarrollo latinoamericano y la teoría del desarrollo* (Mexico: Siglo Veintiuno, 1970), chapter IV.

15 See on this, I. Bradley and M. Howard, *Classical and Marxian Political*

Economy (London: Macmillan, 1982), p. 8.

16 G.M. Meier and G.M. Baldwin, *Economic Development* (New York: John Wiley & Sons, 1957), pp. 10 and 66. See also J.A. Schumpeter, *History of Economic Analysis* (New York: Oxford University Press, 1954), p. 892.

17 Palloix, *L'Économie Mondiale Capitaliste*, p. 98.

18 Weaver, *Class, State, and Industrial Structure* , p. 4.

19 See on this, S. Schram and H. Carrère D'Encausse, *El Marxismo y Asia, 1853-1964* (Buenos Aires: Siglo Veintiuno Editores, 1974), pp. 257–9.

20 Mandel, *Late Capitalism*, p. 63.

21 W.W. Rostow, *The Stages of Economic Growth, A Non-Communist Manifesto* (Cambridge: Cambridge University Pres, 1985).

22 D. McClelland, *The Achieving Society* (New York: Van Nostrand, 1961).

23 B. F. Hoselitz, *Sociological Aspects of Economic Growth* (Glencoe, Ill: The Free Press, 1960).

24 G. Germani, *Política y Sociedad en una Época de Transición* (Buenos Aires: Editorial Paidos, 1965).

25 See P. A. Baran, 'On the political economy of backwardness', in A.N. Agarwala and S.P. Singh, eds, *The Economics of Underdevelopment* (New Delhi: Oxford University Press, 1975) and *The Political Economy of Growth* (Harmondsworth: Penguin, 1973).

26 See United Nations, Economic Commission for Latin America, *Development Problems in Latin America* (Austin: University of Texas Press, 1969) and *The Economic Development of Latin America and its Principal Problems* (New York: United Nations, 1950). See also R. Prebisch, *Economic Development of Latin America and some of its Principal Problems* (New York: United Nations, 1950).

27 See A.G. Frank, *Capitalism and Underdevelopment in Latin America* (New York: Monthly Review Press, 1969).

28 See F.H. Cardoso and E. Faletto, *Dependency and Development in Latin America* (Berkeley: University of California Press, 1979).

29 See I. Wallerstein, *The Modern World-System* (New York: Academic Press, 1974).

30 See A. Emmanuel, *Unequal Exchange* (London: New Left Books, 1972).

31 See S. Amin, *Le Développement Inégal* (Paris: Les Éditions de Minuit, 1973).

32 See P.P. Rey, *Les alliances de classes* (Paris: Maspero, 1978).

CHAPTER 1   EARLY CAPITALISM

1 K. Marx, *Capital* (London: Lawrence & Wishart, 1974), vol. I, p. 85, note 1.

2 See M. Dobb, *Theories of Value and Distribution since Adam Smith*

(London: Cambridge University Press, 1973) p. 22.

3 See C. Napoleoni, *Smith , Ricardo , Marx* (Oxford: Blackwell, 1975), p. 46.

4 Adam Smith, *The Wealth of Nations* (Harmondsworth: Penguin, 1976), pp. 356.

5 Ibid., pp. 356–8.

6 M. Dobb, *Theories of Value and Distribution*, pp. 55–6.

7 On Adam Smith's concept of development see I. Bradley and M. Howard, *Classical and Marxian Political Economy* (London: Macmillan, 1982); S. Clarke, *Marx, Marginalism and Modern Sociology, from Adam Smith to Max Weber* (London: Macmillan, 1982); G.M. Meier and R.E. Baldwin, *Economic Development* (New York: John Wiley & Sons, 1957); C. Napoleoni, *Smith, Ricardo, Marx* (Oxford: Blackwell, 1975) and *Economic Thought of the Twentieth Century* (London: Martin Robertson, 1972); J.P. Platteau, *Les Économistes Classiques et le Sous-Développement* (Namur: Presses Universitaires de Namur, 1978), vol. I, and J.A. Schumpeter, *History of Economic Analysis* (New York: Oxford University Press, 1954).

8 Smith, *The Wealth of Nations,* p. 472.

9 Ibid., pp. 429–30.

10 Ibid., p. 121: 'As it is the power of exchanging that gives occasion to the division of labour, so the extent of this division must always be limited by the extent of that power, or, in other words, by the extent of the market.'

11 Clarke, *Marx, Marginalism and Modern Sociology*, p. 30.

12 D. Ricardo, *The Principles of Political Economy and Taxation* (London: J.M. Dent, 1955), p. 1.

13 Smith, *The Wealth of Nations*, pp. 483 and 462–3. As M. Dobb has pointed out, this conception reflects the early time at which Smith was writing, some 40 years before Ricardo, when capitalism had not yet entered the stage of 'machinofacture' and when the most notable progress in capitalist investment was effectively made in agriculture. See Dobb, *Theories of Value and Distribution*, p. 55.

14 Schumpeter, *History of Economic Analysis*, p. 571.

15 D. Ricardo, 'Funding System', in *The Works and Correspondence of David Ricardo* , ed. P. Sraffa, (London: Cambridge University Press, 1951), vol. IV, p. 179.

16 Ricardo, letter to Trower, 21 July 1820, in *The Works and Correspondence of David Ricardo*, vol. VIII, p. 208.

17 K. Marx, *The Poverty of Philosophy* (Moscow: Progress, 1976), p. 115.

18 For this section I have greatly benefited from the reading of the definitive work on the classics and underdevelopment by J. P. Platteau, *Les Économistes Classiques et le Sous-Développement* (two volumes). Although I disagree with his general conclusion that there is a theory of underdevelopment in classical political economy, his detailed analysis of classical economists and compilation of their references to backward societies is immensely

useful.

19 A. Smith, *An Inquiry into the Nature and Causes of the Wealth of Nations*, ed. J.R. M'Culloch (Edinburgh: Adam and Charles Black, 1863), book IV, chapter 1, p. 196.

20 Ibid., book IV, chapter VII, part III, p. 275.

21 Ibid., p. 273.

22 Ibid., book IV, chapter IX, p. 307.

23 Ibid., p. 303.

24 See Platteau, *Les Économistes Classiques et le Sous-Développement*, vol. I, p. 103.

25 Ibid., p. 192. Quoted from J.B. Say, *Cours Complet d'Économie Politique Pratique* (Rome: Edizioni Bizzarri, 1968), part 4, chapter XXVI, p. 311.

26 James Mill, *The History of British India* (London: Baldwin, Cradock, and Joy, 1820), vol. II, book II, chapter IX, p. 88.

27 Ibid., vol. II, book II, chapter X, p. 195.

28 D. Ricardo, letter to J. Mill, 6 January 1818, in *The Works and Correspondence of David Ricardo*, vol. VII, p. 243.

29 T. R. Malthus, *An Essay on Population* (London: J.M. Dent, 1952), vol. 2, book III, chapter IV, p. 30.

30 Ibid., vol. 1, book II, chapter XIII, p. 305.

31 T. R. Malthus, *Principles of Political Economy* (London: International Economic Circle, Tokyo and the London School of Economics and Political Science, 1936), book II, section IV, pp. 337–41.

32 Ibid., book II, section IX, p. 403.

33 J. S. Mill, 'A Few Words on Non-intervention' in *Dissertations and Discussions* (London: Longmans, Green, Reader, and Dyer, 1875), vol. III, pp. 167-8.

34 K. Marx, Afterword to the second German edition of *Capital*, vol. I, p. 25.

35 K. Marx, *Theories of Surplus Value* (London: Lawrence & Wishart, 1969), vol. II, p. 500.

36 Marx, *The Poverty of Philosophy*, pp. 47–8.

37 Marx, *Theories of Surplus Value*, vol. II, p. 166.

38 K. Marx, *Grundrisse* (Harmondsworth: Penguin, 1973), p. 105.

39 See Marx, *The Poverty of Philosophy*, p. 112: 'Economists have a singular method of procedure. There are only two kinds of institutions for them, artificial and natural. The institutions of feudalism are artificial institutions, those of the bourgeoisie are natural institutions. In this they resemble the theologians, who likewise establish two kinds of religion. Every religion which is not theirs is an invention of men, while their own is an emanation from God.'

40 K. Marx, letter to P.V. Annenkov, 28 December 1846, in K. Marx and F. Engels, *Selected Correspondence* (Moscow: Progress Publishers, 1975), p. 34.

41   See Marx, *Theories of Surplus Value*, vol. II, pp. 527–9 and *The Poverty of Philosophy*, p. 115.

42   Marx, *Theories of Surplus Value*, vol. II, p. 165.

43   Ibid., pp. 397–8.

44   Marx, *Capital*, vol. III, p. 259.

45   See next chapter.

46   For such a discussion see J. Larrain, *A Reconstruction of Historical Materialism* (London: Allen & Unwin, 1986); G.A. Cohen, *Karl Marx's Theory of History, a Defence* (Oxford: Clarendon Press, 1978); H. Fleischer, *Marxism and History* (London: Allen Lane, 1973); W.H. Shaw, *Marx's Theory of History* (London: Hutchinson, 1978) and J. McMurtry, *The Structure of Marx's World-View* (Princeton NJ: Princeton University Press, 1978).

47   See J. Stalin, *Dialectical and Historical Materialism*, in *Problems of Leninism* (Peking: Foreign Languages Press, 1976).

48   Larrain, *A Reconstruction of Historical Materialism*, p. 32.

49   K. Marx, Preface to *A Contribution to the Critique of Political Economy*, in K. Marx and F. Engels, *Selected Works in One Volume* (London: Lawrence & Wishart, 1970), p. 181–2.

50   Marx, *The Poverty of Philosophy*, p. 102.

51   Marx, *Capital*, vol. I, p. 320.

52   K. Marx and F. Engels, *The German Ideology, in Collected Works* , vol. 5 (London: Lawrence & Wishart, 1976), p. 54.

53   Marx, *Grundrisse*, p. 706.

54   Marx, letter to P.V. Annenkov, 28 December 1846, in *Selected Correspondence*, p. 30. (All emphases in quotes are those of the original unless otherwise stated.)

55   Marx and Engels, *The German Ideology*, p. 54.

56   See R. Brenner, 'The social basis of economic development', in John Roemer, ed., *Analytical Marxism* (Cambridge: Cambridge University Press, 1986), pp. 40–5.

57   Ibid., p. 36.

58   R. Brenner, 'Agrarian class structure and economic development in pre-industrial Europe', in T.H. Aston and C.H.E. Philpin *The Brenner Debate* (Cambridge: Cambridge University Press, 1985), p. 30.

59   Larrain, *A Reconstruction of Historical Materialism*.

60   Marx, Preface to the first German edition of *Capital*, vol. I, p. 21.

61   Marx, Afterword to the second German edition of *Capital*, vol. I, p. 27.

62   Marx, Preface to *A Contribution to the Critique of Political Economy*, p. 182.

63   Marx, Preface to the first German edition of *Capital*, p. 19.

64   K. Marx, Letter to Vera Zasulich, 8 March 1881, in *Selected Correspondence*, p. 319.

65   Marx, Letter to the Editorial Board of the *Otechestvenniye Zapiski*, November

1877, in *Selected Correspondence*, p. 293.

66 Marx, *Grundrisse*, p. 107.

67 See F. Engels, *The Peasant War in Germany* (London: Lawrence & Wishart, 1969), pp. 42–8.

68 A. Schmidt, *The Concept of Nature in Marx* (London: New Left Books, 1971), p. 121.

69 K. Marx, Preface to *A Contribution to the Critique of Political Economy*, p. 182.

70 K. Marx, letter to S. Meyer and A. Vogt, 9 April 1870, in *Selected Correspondence*, p. 223.

71 K. Marx, letter to F. A. Sorge, 27 September 1877, in *Selected Correspondence*, p. 289.

72 For a detailed analysis of these texts see Haruki Wada, 'Karl Marx and revolutionary Russia', *Annals of the Institute of Social Science* (University of Tokyo), no. 18 (1977), pp. 106–20.

73 Ibid.

74 From N.G. Chernyshevsky, *Essays on Communal Ownership of Land* (Geneva, 1872), quoted by Wada, 'Karl Marx and Revolutionary Russia', p. 100.

75 M. Löwy, *The Politics of Combined and Uneven Development* (London: Verso, 1981), chapter 1.

76 Ibid., p. 27

77 Ibid.

78 Ibid., p. 105

79 Ibid., p. 1.

80 Ibid., p. 104.

81 Ibid., p. 88.

82 K. Marx and F. Engels, *The Holy Family* (Moscow: Progress Publishers, 1975), p. 94.

83 The most obvious difference between them, apart from their historical separation, is that whereas a 'traditional society' is pre-capitalist and not usually aware of being 'traditional' (before knowing of advanced industrialization a society can hardly conceive of itself as 'traditional'), an 'underdeveloped society' is capitalist and fully conscious of its backwardness as it comes into being when industrially developed societies are already in existence. See on this, F. Hinkelammert, *Dialéctica del Desarrollo Desigual* (Valparaiso: Ediciones Universitarias de Valparaiso, 1972), pp. 9–11.

84 See Larrain, *A Reconstruction of Historical Materialism*, p. 98.

85 Marx and Engels, *The German Ideology*, p. 31.

86 Marx, *Capital*, vol. I, p. 188.

87 Ibid., p. 303.

88 Ibid., vol. III, pp. 212–31 and 249–59.

89 Ibid., p. 249.

90 Ibid., p. 237.
91 Marx, *Theories of Surplus-Value* , vol. II, p. 437.
92 Marx, *Capital*, vol. III, p. 106.
93 Ibid., p. 237.
94 Marx, *Grundrisse*, pp. 407-8.
95 Marx, *Theories of Surplus-Value*, vol. III, p. 470.
96 Marx, *Capital*, vol. I, p. 705.

CHAPTER 2   THE EXPANSION OF CAPITALISM

1   K. Marx, *The Poverty of Philosophy* (Moscow: Progress Publishers, 1976), p. 126.
2   K. Marx, *Capital* (London: Lawrence & Wishart, 1974), vol. I, p. 703.
3   K. Marx, letter to F. Engels, 8 October 1858, in K. Marx and F. Engels, *Selected Correspondence* (Moscow: Progress Publishers, 1975), pp. 103–4.
4   K. Marx, 'The British rule in India' (1853), in K. Marx, *Surveys from Exile*, ed. D. Fernbach (Harmondsworth: Penguin, 1973) pp. 306–7.
5   K. Marx, 'The future results of the British rule in India' (1853), in *Surveys from Exile*, p. 320.
6   Ibid., p. 322.
7   Ibid., p. 323.
8   K. Marx, letter to F. Engels, 14 June 1853, in *Selected Correspondence*, pp. 78–9.
9   B. Sutcliffe, 'Imperialism and industrialization in the Third World', in R. Owen and B. Sutcliffe, eds, *Studies in the Theory of Imperialism* (London: Longman, 1972), p. 181.
10 M. Barrat Brown, 'A critique of Marxist theories of imperialism', in Owen Sutcliffe, eds, *Studies in the Theory of Imperialism*, p. 47.
11 S. Amin, *Accumulation on a World Scale* (New York: Monthly Review Press, 1974), p. 148.
12 F. Hinkelammert, *Dialéctica del Desarrollo Desigual* (Valparaiso: Ediciones Universitarias de Valparaiso, 1972), pp. 11 and 76–7.
13 See B. Warren, *Imperialism, Pioneer of Capitalism* (London: Verso, 1980). Warren seems to enjoy scandalizing and shocking fellow Marxists with passages like this: 'Imperialism was the means through which the techniques, culture, and institutions that had evolved in Western Europe over several centuries – the culture of the Renaissance, the Reformation, the Enlightenment, and the Industrial Revolution – sowed their revolutionary seeds in the rest of the world . . . we must accept the view that the epochal imperialist sweep was indeed a titanic step towards human unity . . . But the imperialist achievement seems greeted only by a shower of abuse from these beneficiaries' (pp. 136–7).

14 See P. Scaron, 'A modo de Introducción', in Marx and Engels, *Materiales para la Historia de América Latina* (Mexico: Cuadernos de Pasado y Presente, 1980), pp. 5–19.

15 See K. Mori, 'Marx and "underdevelopment": his thesis on the "Historical roles of British free trade" revisited', *Annals of the Institute of Social Science* (University of Tokyo), no 19 (1978), and H.B. Davis, *Nationalism and Socialism* (New York: Monthly Review Press, 1967), chapter 3.

16 K. Marx, letter to N.F. Danielson, 10 April 1879, in *Selected Correspondence*, pp. 298–9.

17 Marx, 'The future results of the British rule in India', *Surveys from Exile*, p. 320.

18 K. Marx, Brief an V.I. Sassulischt, Dritter Entwurf, 1881, *Werke*, 19, Bd., S. 402, quoted by Mori, 'Marx and "Underdevelopment"', p. 50.

19 K. Marx, letter to F. Engels, 30 November 1867, in *Selected Correspondence*, pp. 184–5.

20 Marx, 'The future results of the British rule in India', pp. 324–5.

21 F. Engels, letter to K. Marx, 23 May 1856, in *Selected Correspondence*, p. 87.

22 K. Marx, 'Outline of a report on the Irish question to the Communist Educational Association of German Workers in London', 16 December 1867, in K. Marx and F. Engels, *Ireland and the Irish Question* (Moscow: Progress Publishers, 1978), p. 142.

23 Marx, *Capital*, vol. I, p. 708.

24 Ibid., pp. 424–5.

25 K. Marx, *Grundrisse* (Harmondsworth: Penguin, 1973), p. 872.

26 K. Marx, *Theories of Surplus-Value* (London : Lawrence & Wishart, 1969), vol. III, pp. 105–6.

27 Ibid., vol. II, p. 474–5.

28 K. Marx, 'Speech on Poland', 9 December 1847, in K. Marx, *The Revolutions of 1848*, ed. D. Fernbach (Harmondsworth: Penguin, 1973), p. 100.

29 K. Marx, letter to F. Engels, 10 December 1869, in *Selected Correspondence*, p. 218.

30 K. Marx, letter to F. Engels, 2 November 1867, in *Selected Correspondence*, p. 182.

31 K. Marx, letter to F. Engels, 10 December 1869, in *Selected Correspondence*, p. 218.

32 K. Marx, 'For Poland', speech, 24 March 1875, in K. Marx, *The First International and After*, ed. D. Fernbach (Harmondsworth: Penguin, 1974), p. 391.

33 See K. Mori, 'Marx and "Underdevelopment"', p. 46, and P. Scaron, 'A modo de Introducción', p. 8.

34 Marx, *Capital* , vol. I, p. 421.

35 Ibid., p. 406.

36 Ibid., p. 424.
37 Ibid., p. 428.
38 Ibid., p. 708.
39 Ibid., p. 361.
40 Ibid.
41 Ibid., pp. 361–3
42 F. Hinkelammert, *Dialéctica del Desarrollo Desigual*, p. 84–5. Here and elsewhere where no English language source is given, the translation is mine – Jorge Larrain.
43 For a good and balanced account of this kind of abuse see H. B. Davis, *Nationalism and Socialism*, especially chapter III.
44 F. Engels, 'Die Bewegungen von 1847', *Deutsche Brüsseler Zeitung*, 23 January 1848, in *Materiales para la Historia de América Latina*, p. 183.
45 F. Engels, 'Democratic pan-Slavism', *Neue Rheinische Zeitung*, 15 February 1849, in *The Revolutions of 1848*, p. 230.
46 K. Marx, 'Intervention in Mexico', *New York Daily Tribune*, 23 November 1861, in *Materiales para la Historia de América Latina*, p. 256.
47 K. Marx, letter to F. Engels, 20 November 1862, in *Materiales para la Historia de América Latina*, p. 286.
48 K. Marx, 'Bolívar y Ponte', *The New American Cyclopaedia*, vol. III, 1858, in *Materiales para la Historia de América Latina*, p. 76–93.
49 G.W.F. Hegel, *The Philosophy of History* (New York: Dover Publications, 1956), pp. 79–87. The penultimate sentence omitted by the English translation has been taken from the Spanish version, *Lecciones sobre la filosofía de la historia universal* (Madrid: Alianza Editorial, 1982), p. 172. Hegel's description of the indolence of American Indians goes so far as to record that in the Jesuit mission in Paraguay 'at midnight a bell had to remind them [the indians] even of their matrimonial duties' (p. 82, English version).
50 F. Engels, 'Democratic pan-Slavism', p. 231.
51 K. Marx and F. Engels, 14th article of the series entitled 'Germany, revolution and counter-revolution', *New York Daily Tribune*, 24 April 1852, in *Materiales para la Historia de América Latina*, p. 199.
52 J. Aricó, *Marx y América Latina* (Lima: CEDEP, 1980), p. 105.
53 G. Haupt and C. Weill, 'Marx y Engels frente al problema de las naciones', in G Haupt, M. Löwy and C. Weill, eds., *Los Marxistas y la cuestión Nacional* (Barcelona : Fontamara, 1982), p. 152.
54 R. Rosdolsky, *El problema de los Pueblos sin Historia* (Barcelona: Fontamara, 1981), p. 160.
55 K. Marx, letter to S. Meyer and A. Vogt, 9 April 1870, in *Selected Correspondence*, p. 223.
56 J.A. Hobson, *Imperialism* (Ann Arbor: The University of Michigan Press, 1972); R. Hilferding, *Finance Capital* (London: Routledge & Kegan Paul, 1981); R. Luxemburg, *The Accumulation of Capital* (London: Routledge &

Kegan Paul, 1963) and *The Accumulation of Capital – An Anti-Critique* , in K.J. Tarbuck, ed., *Imperialism and the Accumulation of Capital* (London: Allen Lane, 1972); N. Bukharin, *Imperialism and World Economy* (London: Merlin Press, 1976) and *Imperialism and the Accumulation of Capital* in Tarbuck, ed., *Imperialism and the Accumulation of Capital;* V.I. Lenin, *Imperialism, the Highest Stage of Capitalism* (Peking: Foreign Languages Press, 1975).

57 See for instance T. Kemp, *Theories of Imperialism* (London: Dobson, 1967); A. Brewer, *Marxist Theories of Imperialism*, (London: Routledge & Kegan Paul, 1980); C.A. Barone, *Marxist Thought on Imperialism* (London: Macmillan, 1985); M. Barrat Brown, *Essays on Imperialism* (London: The Spokesman, 1972); Owen and Sutcliffe, eds., *Studies in the Theory of Imperialism.*

58 Lenin, *Imperialism, the Highest Stage of Capitalism*, p. 20 and 105.

59 Ibid., p. 131. See also pp. 129–30.

60 Ibid., p. 125.

61 Ibid., p. 106.

62 R. Hilferding, *Finance Capital*, pp. 301–7.

63 Ibid., p. 335.

64 N. Bukharin, *Imperialism and World Economy*, p. 110n.

65 Luxemburg, *The Accumulation of Capital*, p. 446.

66 Ibid. (my emphasis).

67 Ibid., pp. 295–6.

68 According to Luxemburg this was due to the fact that Marx believed that the capitalists themselves realized the increasing surplus-value in order to expand production. She rejects this possibility because its result 'is not accumulation of capital but an increasing production of producer goods to no purpose whatsoever'. Ibid., p. 335.

69 Ibid., pp. 351–2.

70 Ibid., p. 416.

71 Luxemburg, *The Accumulation of Capital – An Anti-Critique*, pp. 61.

72 Hobson, *Imperialism*, p. 27 and 38.

73 Ibid., p. 35 and 85. Brewer has argued that Hobson's theory is underconsumptionist in so far as the reason for the imperialist expansion is the fact that capitalists cannot sell their commodities at home because the low level of wages and over-saving of profits negatively affect demand (*Marxist Theories of Imperialism,* p. 112). Hobson does indeed make these points. However, he cannot be put in the same category as Luxemburg because for him this is not a necessary process and, on the contrary, with the right economic policy 'there will be no need to fight for foreign markets or foreign areas of investment.' *Imperialism*, p. 86.

74 Bukharin, *Imperialism and the Accumulation of Capital*, pp. 243 and 246.

75 Marx, *Capital*, vol. III, p. 256

76 Bukharin, *Imperialism and the Accumulation of Capital*, p. 254.
77 Hilferding, *Finance Capital*, pp. 314 and 365.
78 Ibid., p. 322.
79 Ibid., p. 331.
80 Hobson, *Imperialism*, p. 94.
81 Hilferding, *Finance Capital*, p. 334.
82 Lenin, *Imperialism, the Highest Stage of Capitalism*, pp. 73–4.
83 Brewer, *Marxist Theories of Imperialism*, p. 112.
84 Lenin, *Imperialism, the Highest Stage of Capitalism*, p. 73.
85 Hobson, *Imperialism*, p. 367. See also pp. 53 and 107.
86 Lenin, *Imperialism, the Highest Stage of Capitalism*, chapter VIII.
87 Hilferding, *Finance Capital*, p. 318.
88 Ibid., p. 370.
89 Luxemburg, *The Accumulation of Capital*, p. 417.
90 Luxemburg, *The Accumulation of Capital – An Anti-Critique*, p. 76.
91 Bukharin, *Imperialism and the Accumulation of Capital*, p. 260.
92 Ibid., p. 261.
93 Ibid., p. 266.
94 Hobson, *Imperialism*, p. 69.
95 Ibid., p. 227.
96 Ibid., p. 234. See also pp. 228–33.
97 Hilferding, *Finance Capital*, pp. 318 and 322.
98 Luxemburg, *The Accumulation of Capital*, pp. 370–1 and 395.
99 Ibid., p. 419.
100 Lenin, *Imperialism, the Highest Stage of Capitalism*, p. 76.
101 Barrat Brown, *Essays on Imperialism*, p. 38. However, Barrat Brown makes
    it clear in a another essay further on that the adverse effects of imperialism
    for underdeveloped countries are not so much the result of an actual flow of
    resources out of them as the consequence of the distortions of their
    dependent economies by the artificial division of labour imposed on them,
    according to which central economies concentrate on manufacturing and
    peripheral economies concentrate on primary production. See p. 84.
102 F.H. Cardoso, 'Dependency and development in Latin America', *New Left
    Review*, no. 74 (July–August 1972), p. 87.
103 Warren, *Imperialism, Pioneer of Capitalism*, pp. 57–67.
104 Hinkelammert, *Dialéctica del Desarrollo Desigual*, p. 78
105 Ibid., pp. 76–8.
106 Warren, *Imperialism, Pioneer of Capitalism*, pp. 67–8.
107 See J. Larrain, *A Reconstruction of Historical Materialism* (London: Allen
    & Unwin, 1986).
108 Warren, *Imperialism, Pioneer of Capitalism*, pp. 82–3.
109 Brewer, *Marxist Theories of Imperialism*, p. 131.
110 'Theses on the revolutionary movement in colonial and semi-colonial

countries', in J. Degras, ed., *The Communist International, 1919–1943: Documents* (London: Oxford University Press, 1960), vol. 2, 1923-28, p. 533.

111 Warren, *Imperialism, Pioneer of Capitalism*, pp. 82–3.

112 F.H. Cardoso, 'The originality of the copy : CEPAL and the idea of development', *CEPAL Review*, no. 2 (second half 1977), p. 11. CEPAL is the Spanish acronym for ECLA.

113 'Theses on the revolutionary movement in colonial and semi-colonial countries', p. 532 (my emphasis).

114 Warren, *Imperialism, Pioneer of Capitalism*, p. 83.

115 It was not the first time this possibility was considered within Marxism. Marx himself toyed with the idea in his answer to Vera Zasulich about the prospect of Russian socialism. See letter, 8 March 1881, in *Selected Correspondence*, p. 319.

116 Marx, 'Future results of the British rule in India', in *Surveys from Exile*, p. 323 (my emphasis).

117 G. Palma, 'Dependency and development : a critical overview', in D. Seers, ed., *Dependency Theory, A Critical Reassessment* (London: Francis Pinter, 1981), p. 40. The same idea could be found in Warren, *Imperialism, Pioneer of Capitalism*, pp. 82–3; F.H. Cardoso, 'The originality of the copy: CEPAL and the idea of development', p. 11, and Sutcliffe, 'Imperialism and industrialization in the Third World', in Owen and Sutcliffe, eds., *Studies in the Theory of Imperialism*, pp. 183–4.

118 'Theses on the revolutionary movement in colonial and semi-colonial Countries', p. 533.

119 Ibid., p. 535.

120 P. Baran, *The Political Economy of Growth* (Harmondsworth: Penguin, 1973), pp. 267–8.

121 In order to carry out his analysis Baran introduces the concept of economic surplus. There are three variants: (1) Actual economic surplus: the difference between society's actual current output and its actual current consumption; (2) Potential economic surplus: the difference between the output that could be produced in a given natural and technological environment with the help of employable productive resources, and what might be regarded as essential consumption. It appears under 4 headings: (a) society's excess consumption; (b) output lost through the existence of unproductive workers; (c) output lost through the irrational and wasteful organization of the productive apparatus; (d) output lost through unemployment (ibid., pp. 132–4). (3) Planned economic surplus: the difference between society's optimum output attainable in a historically given natural and technological environment under conditions of planned optimum utilization of all available productive resources, and some chosen optimum volume of consumption (ibid., p. 155).

122 This view was first clearly expressed in 1966 by P.A. Baran and P.M. Sweezy in *Monopoly Capital* (New York: Monthly Review Press, 1968), p. 178, before A. G. Frank made it popular.

123 Baran, *The Political Economy of Growth*, p. 118.

124 Ibid. p. 120: 'what is decisive is that economic development in underdeveloped countries is profoundly inimical to the dominant interests in the advanced capitalist countries.'

125 Marx, Preface to the first German edition of *Capital*, p. 19.

126 Baran and Sweezy, *Monopoly Capital* , p. 12.

127 Baran, *The Political Economy of Growth*, p. 276.

128 And yet Baran is also aware that 'socialism in backward and underdeveloped countries has a powerful tendency to become a backward and underdeveloped socialism.' *The Political Economy of Growth*, p. 14.

129 Ibid., p. 284.

130 Ibid., p. 294.

131 Ibid., p. 276.

132 Ibid., pp. 316–17.

133 Brewer, *Marxist Theories of Imperialism*, p. 138.

134 Baran, *The Political Economy of Growth*, p. 14. For an argument that it is impossible to construct socialism in materially poor and deprived societies see G. Kitching, *Rethinking Socialism* (London: Methuen, 1983).

CHAPTER 3   MODERNIZATION AND THE ECONOMIC COMMISSION FOR LATIN AMERICA

1   S. N. Eisenstadt, 'Social change, differentiation and evolution', *American Sociological Review*, vol. 29, no. 3 (June 1964), p. 376.

2   M. Weber, 'The social psychology of the world religions', in *From Max Weber: Essays in Sociology*, ed. H.H. Gerth and C.W. Mills (London: Routledge & Kegan Paul, 1970), p. 296.

3   T. Parsons, *The Social System* (Glencoe, Illinois: The Free Press, 1951), pp. 58–67.

4   Ibid., pp. 176–7.

5   B. F. Hoselitz, *Sociological Aspects of Economic Growth* (New York: The Free Press, 1965), p. 40.

6   Ibid., p.36.

7   Ibid., pp. 66 and 61–2.

8   G. Germani, *Politica y Sociedad en una Epoca de Transición* (Buenos Aires: Editorial Paidos, 1965).

9   Ibid., p. 72.

10   Ibid. p. 56. Germani's distinction is more general than Weber's because both elective and prescriptive actions can be either habitual or rational.

11   However, Germani is quite aware of research that shows that the nuclear

family existed in Europe before the transition. So he suggests that the nuclear family might have been one of the pre-conditions which facilitated the emergence of the industrial society. Ibid., p. 89.

12 Ibid., p. 104.

13 Ibid., p. 108.

14 Ibid., p. 147.

15 G. Germani, *Sociología de la Modernización* (Buenos Aires: Paidós, 1969), pp. 51–8.

16 D. McClelland, 'The achievement motive in economic growth', in B.F. Hoselitz and W.E. Moore, eds., *Industrialization and Society* (UNESCO – Mouton, 1966), p. 74.

17 Ibid., p. 76.

18 Ibid., p. 78.

19 Ibid., p. 79.

20 Ibid., see table on p. 82.

21 W.W. Rostow, *The Stages of Economic Growth, A Non-Communist Manifesto* (Cambridge: Cambridge University Press, 1985).

22 Ibid., p. 2. See also *The Process of Economic Growth* (Oxford: Oxford University Press, 1960), p. 12.

23 W.W. Rostow, *The Stages of Economic Growth, A Non-Communist Manifesto*, p. 21.

24 Ibid., p. 139.

25 W.W. Rostow, *Estrategia para un mundo libre* (Buenos Aires: Ed. Troquel, 1966), p. 133.

26 A.G. Frank, 'Sociology of development and underdevelopment of sociology', in J.D. Cockcroft, A.G. Frank and D.L. Johnson, eds., *Dependence and Underdevelopment* (New York: Anchor Books, 1972).

27 See for instance F.H. Cardoso, *Cuestiones de Sociología del Desarrollo de América Latina* (Santiago: Editorial Universitaria, 1969); A. Solari, R. Franco and J. Jutkowitz, *Teoría, Acción Social y Desarrollo en América Latina* (Mexico: Siglo Veintiuno, 1976); I. Roxborough, *Theories of Underdevelopment* (London: Macmillan, 1979) and J. G Taylor, *From Modernization to Modes of Production* (London: Macmillan, 1979).

28 A. Leon and R. Recacoechea, 'Un alcance crítico a la necesidad de logro y su relación con el crecimiento económico', *Boletin ELAS*, Año 2, no. 4 (December 1969), pp. 7–18.

29 A.M.M. Hoogvelt, *The Third World in Global Development* (London: Macmillan, 1982), p. 116.

30 Solari, Franco and Jutkowitz, *Teoría, Acción Social y Desarrollo en América Latina*, p. 187.

31 Germani, *Sociología de la Modernización*, p. 37.

32 Ibid., p. 36–7.

33 R. Prebisch, *The Economic Development of Latin America and its Principal*

Problems (New York: United Nations, 1950).

34 R. Prebisch, 'El desarrollo económico de la América Latina y algunos de sus principales problemas', in ECLA *El pensamiento de la CEPAL* (Santiago: Editorial Universitaria, 1969), p. 49.

35 Ibid.

36 ECLA, *El pensamiento de la CEPAL* , p. 18.

37 ECLA, 'Estudio Económico de América Latina, 1949', in *El pensamiento de la CEPAL*, p. 52.

38 ECLA, *La cooperación internacional en la política de desarrollo latinoamericana* (September 1954), in *El pensamiento de la CEPAL* , p. 91.

39 ECLA, *Introducción a la técnica de programación* (Julio 1955), in *El pensamiento de la CEPAL* , p. 98.

40 *El pensamiento de la CEPAL* , p. 33.

41 ECLA, *La cooperación internacional en la política de desarrollo latinoamericana*, in *El pensamiento de la CEPAL*, pp. 137–61.

42 ECLA, *Contribución a la política de integración económica de America Latina* (Junio 1965), in *El pensamiento de la CEPAL*, pp. 163–70.

43 Ibid., pp. 181–6.

44 ECLA, 'Tres aspectos sociológicos del desarrollo económico', *Revista de la Comisión Económica para América Latina*, número especial (Agosto 1955), in *El pensamiento de la CEPAL* , p. 245.

45 Ibid., pp. 260–1.

46 ECLA, *El desarrollo Social de América Latina en la Postguerra* (Buenos Aires: Solar/Hachette, 1966).

47 Ibid., p. 93.

48 A.O. Hirschman, *A Bias for Hope* (Boulder: Westview Press, 1985), p. 289.

49 F.H. Cardoso, 'The originality of the copy: CEPAL and the idea of development', *CEPAL Review* , no. 2 (second half 1977), p. 14. CEPAL is the Spanish acronym for ECLA.

50 G. Harberler, 'Terms of trade and economic development', in H.S. Ellis, ed., *Economic Development for Latin America* (London: Macmillan, 1963), pp. 275–97.

51 Ibid., p. 287.

52 Cardoso, 'The originality of the copy: CEPAL and the idea of development', p. 17.

53 Ibid., p. 38.

54 See for instance F.H. Cardoso, 'Dependency and development in Latin America', *New Left Review*, no. 74 (July–August 1972).

55 See for instance T. dos Santos, 'The crisis of development theory and the problem of dependence in Latin America', in H. Berstein, ed., *Underdevelopment and Development* (Harmondsworth: Penguin, 1973).

56 R. Prebisch, *Towards a Dynamic Development Policy for Latin America* (New York: United Nations, 1963), p. 71.

CHAPTER 4   DEPENDENCY, UNEQUAL EXCHANGE AND UNDERDEVELOPMENT

1   See F.H. Cardoso, 'The consumption of dependency theory in the United States', in *Latin American Research Review*, XII (3) (1977), p. 8.
2   The most popular definition of dependence has been provided by T. dos Santos: 'dependence is a *conditioning situation* in which the economies of one group of countries are conditioned by the development and expansion of others. A relationship of interdependence between two or more economies or between such economies and the world trading system becomes a dependent relationship when some countries can expand through self-impulsion while others, being in a dependent position, can only expand as a reflection of the expansion of the dominant countries, which may have positive or negative effects on their immediate development.' T. dos Santos, 'The crisis of development theory and the problem of dependence in Latin America', in H. Bernstein, ed., *Underdevelopment and Development* (Harmondsworth: Penguin, 1973), p. 76.
3   G. Palma, 'Dependency and development: a critical overview', in D. Seers, ed., *Dependency Theory, A Critical Reassessment* (London: Francis Pinter, 1981) p. 42–3.
4   J. Larrain, *A Reconstruction of Historical Materialism* (London: Allen & Unwin, 1986), p. 100.
5   A.G. Frank, *Capitalism and Underdevelopment in Latin America* (New York: Monthly Review Press, 1969), pp. 146–7.
6   Ibid., p. 147.
7   A.G. Frank, *Latin America: Underdevelopment or Revolution* (New York: Monthly Review Press, 1970), p. 150.
8   Ibid., p. 163.
9   Frank, *Capitalism and Underdevelopment in Latin America*, p. 240.
10   Ibid., p. 242.
11   Ibid., p. 239.
12   Ibid., pp. 126–7.
13   The *encomienda* was a servile system whereby a group of Indians was allocated to a Spanish *conquistador* who had the right to exact tribute from them, in goods, money or personal services in his lands or mines during part of the year.
14   A.G. Frank, *Dependent Accumulation and Underdevelopment* (London: Macmillan, 1978), pp. 43 and 43–69.
15   A.G. Frank, *World Accumulation, 1492-1789* (London: Macmillan, 1978), p. 254.
16   Ibid., p. 240.
17   R.M. Marini, 'Dialéctica de la dependencia: la economía exportadora", *Sociedad y Desarrollo*, no. 1 (January–March 1972).
18   Frank, *Capitalism and Underdevelopment in Latin America*, p. 270.

19 Ibid., p. xv.
20 Frank, *Latin America: Underdevelopment or Revolution*, p. 127.
21 Ibid., p. 371.
22 A.G. Frank, *Critique and Anti-Critique* (London: Macmillan, 1984), p. 92.
23 A.G. Frank, 'Crisis and transformation of dependency in the world system', in R.H. Chilcote and D.L. Johnson, eds., *Theories of Development* (Beverly Hills: Sage, 1983), p. 194–5.
24 Ibid., p. 195.
25 Frank, *Critique and Anti-Critique*, pp. 212 and 213.
26 Ibid., p. 215.
27 Ibid., p. 216.
28 Ibid., p. 217.
29 Ibid.
30 Ibid., p. 219. Frank's general negative assessment of export-led industrialization does not significantly differ from the conclusions reached by 'the new international division of labour' theory of Fröbel et al. According to them 'this process of industrialization ... actually intensifies the tendency towards uneven and dependent development in the underdeveloped countries ... The more this process of industrialization oriented to the world market expands and deepens ... the more the development of the underdeveloped countries will manifest itself as continued underdevelopment.' See F. Fröbel, J. Heinrichs and O. Kreye, *The New International Division of Labour* (Cambridge: Cambridge University Press, 1980), p. 403.
31 I. Wallerstein, *The Modern World System* (New York: Academic Press, 1974), p. 86.
32 Ibid., p. 87.
33 Ibid., p. 92.
34 I. Wallerstein, 'The rise and future demise of the world capitalist system: concepts for comparative analysis', *Comparative Studies in Society and History*, 16 (4) (January 1974), p. 394.
35 Wallerstein, *The Modern World System*, p. 126.
36 Wallerstein is rather vague in the definition of these terms. Still, in *The Modern World System*, p. 102, he states that 'the semi-periphery represents a midway point on a continuum running from the core to the periphery.'
37 I. Wallerstein, 'The present state of the debate on world inequality', in I. Wallerstein, ed., *World Inequality* (Montreal: Black Rose Books, 1975), p. 23.
38 Wallerstein, *The Modern World System*, pp. 15–16.
39 Ibid., p. 350.
40 Ibid., p. 349. In a more recent book Wallerstein explains this process of transfer more simply in terms of 'unequal exchange' 'made possible by the existence of an interstate system containing a hierarchy of states.' See *Historical Capitalism* (London: Verso, 1983), p. 61.

41 Wallerstein, *Historical Capitalism*, p. 60.

42 Ibid., pp. 60–1.

43 Palma, 'Dependency and development: a critical overview', p. 45. Palma repeats almost word for word the observation of R. Brenner, 'The origins of capitalist development: a critique of neo-Smithian Marxism', *New Left Review*, no. 104 (July–August 1977), p. 27. Similar criticisms can be found in T. dos Santos, 'The crisis of development theory and the problem of dependence in Latin america', and B. Cabral et al., 'Importancia y evaluación del trabajo de A.G. Frank sobre el subdesarrollo Latinoamericano', mimeo, Escuela Nacional de Economía, UNAM (Mexico 1969).

44 Frank, *Capitalism and Underdevelopment in Latin America*, p. xv.

45 A.G. Frank, *Lumpenbourgeoisie: Lumpendevelopment* (New York: Monthly Review Press, 1972).

46 Frank, *Capitalism and Underdevelopment in Latin America*, p. 94.

47 Frank, *Lumpenbourgeoisie: Lumpendevelopment*, p. 13.

48 Ibid., pp. 1–12.

49 Frank, *Critique and Anti-Critique*, p. 262.

50 A rigorous and cogent presentation of such arguments can be found in G.A. Cohen, *Karl Marx's Theory of History: a Defence* (Oxford: Clarendon Press, 1978).

51 See P. Gonzalez Casanova, *Sociología de la Explotación* (Mexico: Siglo XXI, 1969). Gonzalez Casanova distinguishes between 'class exploitation' which he defines more or less in Marxist terms and 'regional exploitation' which was neglected by Marxism and consists in the appropriation of part of the surplus generated in one region by the population of another region. Within each region it is necessary to distinguish the classes which benefit from or suffer the regional exploitation (p. 126). From this Gonzalez Casanova derives the existence of two models of capitalism. The classical model where class exploitation is more important than regional exploitation and the neo-capitalist model where class inequalities are smaller than regional inequalities.

52 Brenner, 'The origins of capitalist development: a critique of neo-Smithian Marxism', p. 39.

53 Frank, *Capitalism and Underdevelopment in Latin America*, p. 264.

54 E. Laclau, *Politics and Ideology in Marxist Theory* (London: New Left Books, 1977), pp. 22–3. There is also a postscript dealing with Wallerstein, pp. 42–50.

55 Brenner, 'The origins of capitalist development: a critique of neo-Smithian Marxism', pp. 70–3.

56 Peasants occupying land in the *haciendas* who were personally obliged to pay rent to, or work the land of, the landowner.

57 Laclau, *Politics and Ideology in Marxist Theory*, p. 31.

58 This he tries to do in *Dependent Accumulation and Underdevelopment*,

pp. 43–69.

59 J. Banaji, 'Gunder Frank in retreat?', in P. Limqueco and B. McFarlane, eds., *Neo-Marxist Theories of Development* (London: Croom Helm and St Martin's Press, 1983), p. 104.

60 Wallerstein, *The Modern World System*, p. 126.

61 Ibid., p. 127.

62 Brenner, 'The origins of capitalist development: a critique of neo-Smithian Marxism', p. 72.

63 See on this J. Castañeda and E. Hett, *El Economismo Dependentista* (Mexico: Siglo XXI, 1985), pp. 50–8.

64 Ibid., pp. 59–60.

65 Palma, 'Dependency and development: a critical overview', p. 44.

66 F.H. Cardoso, 'The originality of a copy: CEPAL and the idea of development', *CEPAL Review*, no. 2 (second half 1977), p. 32.

67 Brenner, 'The origins of capitalist development: a critique of neo-Smithian Marxism', p. 91.

68 Frank, 'Crisis and transformation of dependency in the world system', p. 197.

69 B. Warren, *Imperialism, Pioneer of Capitalism* (London: Verso, 1980), p. 171.

70 Banaji, 'Gunder Frank in retreat?', p. 109.

71 Warren, *Imperialism, Pioneer of Capitalism*, pp. 163–4.

72 F.H. Cardoso, 'Dependency and development in Latin America', *New Left Review*, no. 74 (July–August 1972), p. 94.

73 C. Hamilton, 'Capitalist industrialization in the four little tigers of East Asia', in Limqueco and McFarlane, eds., *Neo-Marxist Theories of Development*, p. 161.

74 S. Corbridge, *Capitalist World Development* (London: Macmillan, 1986), p. 181.

75 Ibid., p. 187.

76 See on this D. Booth, 'Andre Gunder Frank, an introduction and appreciation' in I. Oxaal et al., eds., *Beyond the Sociology of Development* (London: Routledge & Kegan Paul, 1975), p. 51.

77 A. Emmanuel, *Unequal Exchange* (London: New Left Books, 1972), p. xxx.

78 Ibid., p. xxxi.

79 Organic composition is a concept within Marxist economic theory which refers to the proportion of the total investment capital which is laid out for means of production (machinery, capital goods, raw materials) as against the capital laid out for paying labour. In other words, it is the proportion of constant capital relative to variable capital (wages). The greater the proportion of constant capital, the higher the organic composition of capital.

80 Emmanuel, *Unequal Exchange*, pp. 60 and 160–3. In spite of denying that this form of non-equivalence is unequal Emmanuel calls it unequal exchange

in the 'broad sense'.

81 Ibid., p. 61. It is worthwhile having a look at the mathematical examples provided by Emmanuel in chapter 2 which quantify the amount of value transferred in each case and clarify the premises and the process of unequal exchange.

82 Ibid., p. 64.

83 Ibid., p. 265.

84 Ibid., p. 148.

85 Ibid., p. 267.

86 Ibid., pp. 150 and 267. Emmanuel even mentions, as a possibility of reducing the transfer of value abroad, a tax on exports which will transfer the excess surplus value to the state. But he also abandons it as impractical.

87 Ibid., p. 148.

88 Ibid., p. 179.

89 Ibid., p. 180.

90 Ibid.

91 C. Bettelheim, 'Theoretical comments', in Emmanuel, *Unequal Exchange*, p. 288.

92 Ibid., pp. 288–9.

93 Ibid., p. 292.

94 A. Brewer, *Marxist Theories of Imperialism* (London: Routledge & Kegan Paul, 1980), p. 227. For a similar argument see G. Kitching, *Development and Underdevelopment in Historical Perspective* (London: Methuen, 1982), p. 171.

95 Bettelheim, 'Theoretical comments', p. 310.

96 S. Amin, 'The end of a debate', in *Imperialism and Unequal Development* (Brighton: Harvester Press, 1977), p. 181.

97 Ibid., p. 206. See also pp. 191–4 and 205.

98 Ibid., p. 211.

99 Ibid., p. 215.

100 S. Amin, *Accumulation on a World Scale* (New York: Monthly Review Press, 1974), pp. 22–3.

101 Amin, 'The end of a debate', p. 222.

102 Amin, *Accumulation on a World Scale*, pp. 24–5.

103 Amin, 'The end of a debate', p. 185.

104 S. Amin, 'Accumulation and development: a theoretical model', *Review of African Political Economy*, no. 1 (August–November 1974), p. 10.

105 S. Amin, *Le Développement Inegal* (Paris: Les Editions de Minuit, 1973), pp. 60–5. See also a summary in 'Accumulation and development: a theoretical model', pp. 10–12.

106 Amin, *Le Développement Inegal*, p. 64.

107 Ibid., pp. 164–9. See also a summary in 'Accumulation and development: a theoretical model', pp. 12–16.

108 Amin, *Accumulation on a World Scale*, p. 598.

109 Amin, *Le Développement Inegal*, p. 64.

110 Amin, *Accumulation on a World Scale*, p. 599.

111 Amin, *Le Développement Inegal*, p. 168.

112 Ibid., p. 169. See also *Accumulation on a World Scale*, p. 600.

113 This theory will be analysed in chapter 6. Its main representative, P.P. Rey, author of *Les Alliances de Classes* (Paris: Maspero, 1978) is quoted by Amin.

114 Amin, 'The end of a debate', p. 190.

115 Kitching, *Development and Underdevelopment in Historical Perspective*, p. 152.

116 Amin, 'The end of a debate', p. 190.

117 Ibid., p. 191.

118 S. Smith, 'Class analysis versus world system: critique of Samir Amin's typology of underdevelopment', in Limqueco and McFarlane, eds., *Neo-Marxist Theories of Development* , p. 73

119 Amin, *Accumulation on a World Scale*, p. 393.

CHAPTER 5   DEPENDENCY, INDUSTRIALIZATION AND DEVELOPMENT

1   A. Pinto, *Chile, un caso de desarrollo frustrado* (Santiago: Editorial Universitaria, 1962).

2   C. Furtado, *Subdesarrollo y estancamiento en America Latina* (Buenos Aires: EUDEBA, 1966).

3   O. Sunkel, 'Cambio social y frustración en Chile', in H. Godoy, ed., *Structura Social de Chile* (Santiago: Editorial Universitaria, 1971). The article was originally published in *Economía*, Año 23 (3° y 4° trimestre, 1965).

4   Pinto, *Chile, un caso de desarrollo frustrado*, pp. 129–30. See also pp. 11 and 82 for other formulations of the same idea. This thesis is also developed in 'Desarrollo económico y relaciones sociales' in A. Pinto et al., eds., *Chile Hoy* (Santiago: Siglo XXI, 1970), p. 5. N. Mouzelis has elaborated a similar thesis for the wider context of the semi-periphery, including Latin America, Greece and the Balkans. For him the semi-periphery has had an early political and social development which has come before economic development. The adoption of liberal ideas and parliamentary institutions contributed to the early mobilization of non-oligarchic political groups and the broadening of political participation before the advent of industrialization. This mobilization without strong bourgeoisies and working classes and without a firm economic basis led to the formation of populist political movements, the accentuation of economic contradictions and eventually to authoritarian forms of government. See N.P. Mouzelis, *Politics in the Semi-*

Periphery (London: Macmillan, 1986), pp. 6–7, 13, 15, 72, 98 and 122.

5 Pinto, *Chile, un caso de desarrollo frustrado*, p. 81.
6 Ibid. p. 88.
7 Ibid., p. 128.
8 Sunkel, 'Cambio social y frustración en Chile', p. 523.
9 Ibid., p. 533.
10 Furtado, *Subdesarrollo y estancamiento en America Latina*, p. 106.
11 Ibid., p. 97.
12 A. Pinto, 'Naturaleza e implicaciones de la 'heterogeneidad estructural' de la América Latina', *El Trimestre Económico*, XXXVII (1), no. 145 (Enero-Marzo 1970), p. 85. See also 'Concentración del progreso técnico y de sus frutos en el desarrollo Latinoamericano', *El Trimestre Económico*, XXXII (1), no. 125 (Enero-Marzo 1965), pp. 7–8.
13 Pinto, 'Naturaleza e implicaciones de la 'heterogeneidad estructural' de la América Latina', p. 93.
14 Ibid., p. 88.
15 Ibid., p. 90.
16 C. Furtado, *Desarrollo y Subdesarrollo* (Buenos Aires: EUDEBA, 1965), p. 177.
17 O. Sunkel and P. Paz, *El Subdesarrollo Latinoamericano y la Teoría del Desarrollo* (Mexico: Siglo XXI, 1970), p. 39.
18 D. Seers, 'What are we trying to measure?', in 'Communications', *IDS Reprints*, no. 106, Brighton, Institute of Development Studies (1972), p. 3.
19 See O. Sunkel, 'Political nacional de desarrollo y dependencia externa', *Revista de Estudios Internacionales* , 1 (1) (Abril 1967).
20 Seers, 'What are we trying to measure?', p. 3. However Seers does not want to put these requirements on the same level as the first three in order to keep his analysis at the level of the basic economic needs of the poorest countries.
21 Furtado, *Subdesarrollo y estancamiento en America Latina*, p. 27.
22 A. Pinto, 'Notas alrededor del sistema centro-periferia', ECLA/IDE/DRAFT/ 5 (Nov. 1970), p. 19.
23 This new character or modality of dependency is also detected by authors of other tendencies like dos Santos and Cardoso.
24 C. Furtado, *Economic Development of Latin America* (London: Cambridge University Press, 1970), p. 173 and more generally pp. 166–78.
25 Pinto, 'Notas alrededor del sistema centro-periferia', pp. 2–10. See also A. Pinto and J. Knakal, 'The centre–periphery system twenty years later', *Social and Economic Studies*, 22 (1) (March 1973), pp. 44–8.
26 Furtado, *Subdesarrollo y estancamiento en America Latina*, chapter 2.
27 O. Sunkel, *Capitalismo Transnacional y Desintegración Nacional en América Latina* (Buenos Aires: Ediciones Nueva Visión, 1972), p. 81.
28 F.H. Cardoso, 'The originality of a copy: CEPAL and the idea of Development', *CEPAL Review* , no. 2 (second half 1977), p. 32.

29 F. Hinkelammert, *Dialéctica del Desarrollo Desigual* (Valparais: Ediciones Universitarias de Valparaiso, 1972), p. 15.

30 See G. Palma, 'Dependency and development: a critical overview", in D. Seers, ed., *Dependency Theory, A Critical Reassessment* (London: Francis Pinter, 1981) p. 47.

31 Hinkelammert, *Dialéctica del Desarrollo Desigual*, pp. 28–57.

32 Ibid., pp. 41-2.

33 Ibid., pp. 58-9.

34 Ibid., p. 82.

35 See K. Marx, *Capital* (London: Lawrence & Wishart, 1974), vol. I, pp. 361–3. See my analysis in chapter 2.

36 Hinkelammert, *Dialéctica del Desarrollo Desigual*, p. 84.

37 Ibid., pp. 88–9.

38 This point is not beyond contestation though. For an argument that industrialization is indispensable for all forms of development see G. Kitching, *Development and Underdevelopment in Historical Perspective* (London: Methuen, 1982), p. 179: 'industrialization cannot be avoided or run away from. Those who try to do so, in the name of loyalty to the peasantry and the poor (an effective rural development requires as a prerequisite a dynamic and growing industrial sector of certain sort) are likely to end up offering no effective help to the people, and seeing the process of industrialization occur in any case, under the anarchic sway of international capital.'

39 Hinkelammert, *Dialéctica del Desarrollo Desigual*, pp. 113–14.

40 On this point see chapter 6.

41 F.H. Cardoso and E. Faletto, *Dependency and Development in Latin America* (Berkeley: University of California Press, 1979), p. x.

42 F.H. Cardoso, '"Teoría de la dependencia" o análisis concretos de situaciones de dependencia?', in *Estado y Sociedad en América Latina* (Buenos Aires: Ediciones Nueva Visión, 1972), p. 138.

43 Cardoso and Faletto, *Dependency and Development in Latin America*, p. xvii.

44 Cardoso, ''Teoría de la dependencia" o análisis concretos de situaciones de dependencia?', p. 139.

45 F.H. Cardoso, 'Notas sobre el estado actual de los estudios sobre dependencia', in J. Serra, ed., *Desarrollo Latinoamericano, Ensayos Críticos* (Mexico: Fondo de Cultura Económica, 1974), p. 340.

46 Cardoso and Faletto, *Dependency and Development in Latin America*, p. xxi.

47 F.H. Cardoso, 'Dependency and Development in Latin America', *New Left Review*, no. 74 (July–August 1972), p. 90.

48 Cardoso and Faletto, *Dependency and Development in Latin America*, p. xxi.

49 Cardoso, 'Dependency and development in Latin America', p. 94.
50 F.H. Cardoso, 'Associated-dependent developmen: theoretical and practical implications', in A. Stepan, ed., *Authoritarian Brazil* (New Haven: Yale University Press, 1973), p. 149.
51 Cardoso and Faletto, *Dependency and Development in Latin America*, p. x.
52 Cardoso, 'Notas sobre el estado actual de los estudios sobre dependencia', p. 336–9.
53 See on this F.H. Cardoso, 'Some new mistaken theses on Latin American development and dependency' (MS1973). Also reprinted as 'Current theses on Latin American development and dependency: a critique', *Occasional Paper* no. 20, Ibero–American Language and Area Centre, New York University (1976). I shall quote from the manuscript.
54 Ibid., p. 9. See also F.H. Cardoso, 'The consumption of dependency theory in the United States', in *Latin American Research Review*, XII (3) (1977), p. 19; and Cardoso, 'Notas sobre el estado actual de los estudios sobre dependencia', pp. 346–50.
55 Cardoso, 'Some new mistaken theses on Latin American development and dependency', p. 12.
56 Ibid.
57 See R.M. Marini, 'Dialéctica de la dependencia: la economía exportadora', *Sociedad y Desarrollo*, no. 1 (January–March 1972); and 'Brazilian subimperialism', *Monthly Review*, IX (23) (Feb. 1972).
58 Cardoso, 'Some new mistaken theses on Latin American development and dependency', p. 38.
59 See T. dos Santos, *Socialismo o Fascismo: Dilema Latinoamericano* (Santiago: Ediciones Prensa Latinoamericana, 1969), p. 35.
60 V. Bambirra, *El Capitalismo Dependiente Latinoamericano* (Mexico: Siglo XXI, 1975), pp. 178–9.
61 See on this Cardoso, 'Some new mistaken theses on Latin American development and dependency', p. 18, and 'On the characterization of authoritarian regimes in Latin America', in D. Collier, ed., *The New Authoritarianism in Latin America* (Princeton: Princeton University Press, 1979).
62 Cardoso and Faletto, *Dependency and Development in Latin America*, p. 59.
63 Ibid., p. 70.
64 Ibid., p. 78.
65 Ibid., pp. 98–9.
66 Ibid., p. 102.
67 Ibid., p. 128.
68 Ibid., p. 153.
69 J. Quartim de Moraes, 'Le statut théorique de la rélation de dépendence', IV Seminaire Latino Americaine, CETIM, Genève (April 1972).

70 F.C. Weffort, 'Notas sobre la teoría de la dependencia: ¿teoría de clase o ideología nacional?', FLACSO, 2° Seminario para el Desarrollo, Santiago (Noviembre 1970), pp. 10 and 7.

71 Cardoso, 'Notas sobre el estado actual de los estudios sobre dependencia', p. 339.

72 Cardoso, 'Teoría de la dependencia' o análisis concretos de situaciones de dependencia?', p. 141.

73 E. Rodríguez, 'The articulation of external and internal variables and the industrial prospects of peripheral societies', in 'Is dependency dead?', *IDS Bulletin*, 12 (1) (December 1980), p. 11.

74 M. Bienefeld, 'Dependency in the eighties', in 'Is dependency dead?', *IDS Bulletin*, 12 (1) (December 1980), p. 7.

75 Rodríguez, 'The articulation of external and internal variables and the industrial prospects of peripheral societies', p. 12.

76 Ibid., p. 13.

77 Cardoso, 'Some new mistaken theses on Latin American development and dependency', p. 42.

78 J.G. Castañeda and E. Hett, *El Economismo Dependentista* (Mexico: Siglo XXI, 1985), pp. 29–34.

79 Cardoso, 'Notas sobre el estado actual de los estudios sobre dependencia', p. 349.

80 Castañeda and Hett, *El Economismo Dependentista*, p. 31.

CHAPTER 6   LATIN AMERICAN DEPENDENCY AND HISTORICAL MATERIALISM

1 Terminology introduced by C. Leys, 'Underdevelopment and dependency: critical notes', *Journal of Contemporary Asia*, 7 (1) (1977), p. 92.

2 H. Bernstein, 'Sociology of underdevelopment vs. sociology of development?', in D. Lehmann, ed., *Development Theory, Four Critical Studies* (London: Frank Cass, 1979), p. 85, and A. Phillips, 'The concept of "development"', *Review of African Political Economy*, no. 8 (Jan–April 1977), p. 9.

3 For instance P.J. O'Brien, 'A critique of Latin American theories of dependency', in I. Oxaal et al., eds., *Beyond the Sociology of Development* (London: Routledge & Kegan Paul, 1975), p. 12.

4 Ibid., pp. 11–12.

5 Ibid. p. 12.

6 Ibid., p. 24.

7 Ibid., pp. 19-24.

8 S. Lall, 'Is "dependence" a useful concept in analysing underdevelopment?', *World Development*, 3 (11–12) (1975), p. 799.

9 Ibid., p. 800.

10 Ibid.
11 Ibid.
12 Ibid., p. 808.
13 Ibid.
14 F.H. Cardoso, 'The Consumption of dependency theory in the United States', *Latin America Research Review*, XII (3) (1977), pp. 15–16.
15 Lall, 'Is "dependence" a useful concept in analysing underdevelopment?', p. 804.
16 Ibid., p. 802.
17 Ibid., p. 799.
18 J. Clammer, 'Economic anthropology and the sociology of development: "liberal" anthropology and its French critics', in I. Oxaal et al., eds., *Beyond the Sociology of Development*, p. 208.
19 P.P. Rey, *Les Alliances de Classes* (Paris: Maspero, 1978), pp. 10–11.
20 Ibid., p. 16.
21 L. Althusser and E. Balibar, *Reading Capital* (London: New Left Books, 1975), pp. 209–16. See also Rey, *Les Alliances de Classes*, pp. 93–102, and E. Terray, *Marxism and 'Primitive' Societies* (New York: Monthly Review Press, 1972), pp. 97 105.
22 Rey, *Les Alliances de Classes*, p. 179. See also C. Meillassoux, 'From reproduction to production', *Economy and Society*, 1 (1) (February 1972), p. 98.
23 Rey, *Les Alliances de Classes*, p. 28.
24 Meillassoux, 'From reproduction to production', p. 103.
25 Rey, *Les Alliances de Classes*, pp. 15–16.
26 Ibid., p. 15.
27 Ibid., pp. 74–5.
28 Ibid., pp. 85 and 81.
29 P.P. Rey, *Capitalisme Négrier* (Paris: Maspero, 1976), p. 63.
30 Rey, *Les Alliances de Classes*, p. 11.
31 Ibid., p. 89.
32 Ibid., p. 15.
33 K. Marx, letter to Vera Zasulich, 8 March 1881, in K. Marx and F. Engels, *Selected Correspondence* (Moscow: Progress, 1975), p. 319: 'the "historical inevitability" of this process is *expressly* limited to the *countries of Western Europe* .'
34 Rey, *Les Alliances de Classes*, p. 159. The expulsion of the peasants from their land by the feudal lords was also violent. But to dissolve a mode of production against the will of its ruling class requires even more violence.
35 Ibid., p. 164.
36 B. Bradby, 'The destruction of natural economy', *Economy and Society*, IV (2) (May 1975), p. 151.
37 A. Foster-Carter, 'The modes of production controversy', *New Left Review*,

no. 107 (January–February 1978), p. 62.

38 Ibid., p. 66.

39 See P.P. Rey, *Colonialisme, néo-colonialisme et transition au capitalisme* (Paris: Maspero, 1971). For a good summary see A. Brewer, *Marxist Theories of Imperialism* (London: Routledge & Kegan Paul, 1980), pp. 191–8.

40 See on this K. Glauser, 'Orígenes del régimen de producción vigente en Chile', *Cuadernos de la Realidad Nacional*, no. 8 (June 1971), p. 92. It is an oddity of this otherwise most interesting analysis that it seeks to subsume the original pre-capitalist modes of production in Chile as anomalies within a Frankian model of the Chilean insertion into the capitalist world system.

41 See on this A. Cueva, *El Desarrollo del Capitalismo en América Latina* (Mexico: Siglo XXI, 1978), p. 16.

42 Brewer, *Marxist Theories of Imperialism*, p. 200. This argument is valid only if there was feudalism in Latin America. Glauser's article 'Orígenes del régimen de producción vigente en Chile', tries to show that although the Spaniards had the intention to transfer feudal institutions the resulting articulation with the Indian modes of production and the Spanish crown's interest in avoiding a class of feudal lords – the crown granted most *conquistadores* concessions which included 300 Indians for work but which did not include land – resulted in a different kind of mode of production which he labels the *encomienda* mode of production, and which has only some feudal features. However it is arguable that the feudal features were accentuated as the Spaniards appropriated the land (through land concessions) and big *haciendas* or *latifundia* were formed. In fact servile relations of production within the *hacienda* soon affected poor Spanish peasants, too, who had started as free tenants.

43 Brewer, *Marxist Theories of Imperialism*, p. 201.

44 See B. Warren, *Imperialism, Pioneer of Capitalism* (London: Verso, 1980); Bernstein, 'Sociology of underdevelopment vs. sociology of development?'; Phillips, 'The concept of "development'; J. Taylor, 'Neo-Marxism and underdevelopment – a sociological phantasy', *Journal of Contemporary Asia*, 4 (1) (1974), and *From Modernization to Modes of Production: A Critique of the Sociologies of Development and Underdevelopment* (London: Macmillan, 1979); J.R. Mandle, 'Marxist analyses of capitalist development in the Third World', *Theory and Society*, 9 (6) (1980); D. Booth, 'Marxism and development sociology: interpreting the impasse' in M. Shaw, ed., *Marxist Sociology Revisited* (London: Macmillan, 1985); J. Banaji, 'Gunder Frank in retreat?', in P. Limqueco and B. McFarlane, eds., *Neo-Marxist Theories of Development* (London: Croom & Helm and St Martin's Press, 1983); G. Kitching, *Development and Underdevelopment in Historical Perspective* (London: Methuen, 1982), and Leys, 'Underdevelopment and dependency: critical notes', *Journal of Contemporary Asia*, also published in Limqueco and McFarlane, eds., ibid.

45 Booth, 'Marxism and development sociology: interpreting the impasse', pp. 52–3.
46 Bernstein, 'Sociology of underdevelopment vs. sociology of development?', p. 93.
47 Ibid., p. 94.
48 Booth, 'Marxism and development sociology: interpreting the impasse', p. 55.
49 Taylor, 'Neo-Marxism and underdevelopment – a sociological phantasy', p. 8.
50 Bernstein, 'Sociology of underdevelopment vs. sociology of development?', p. 92.
51 Ibid., p. 93.
52 Leys, 'Underdevelopment and dependency: critical notes', p. 95.
53 Phillips, 'The concept of "development"', p. 9.
54 Bernstein, 'Sociology of underdevelopment vs. sociology of development?', p. 85.
55 Warren, *Imperialism, Pioneer of Capitalism*, p. 163.
56 Leys, 'Underdevelopment and dependency: critical notes', p. 95.
57 Phillips, 'The concept of "development"', p. 20.
58 Leys, 'Underdevelopment and dependency: critical notes', p. 95.
59 Warren, *Imperialism, Pioneer of Capitalism*, p. 164.
60 Ibid., p. 10.
61 Ibid., p. 9.
62 Ibid., p. 141.
63 Ibid., p. 142. Similar arguments can be found in Kitching, *Development and Underdevelopment in Historical Perspective*. For him the simple comparison of money capital inflows with money capital outflows is an inadequate basis on which to assess the benefits of foreign investment. Such a procedure fails to take into account the internal benefits which flow from the initial investment: wages, external economies, etc. Kitching also adds an argument of counter-factuality: had there not been foreign investment, there is no way of deciding whether backward countries would have developed their resources.
64 R. Jenkins, *Transnational Corporations and Uneven Development* (London: Methuen, 1987), p. 98.
65 See C. Bettelheim, 'Theoretical comments', in A. Emmanuel, *Unequal Exchange* (London: New Left Books, 1972), appendix I, p. 301, and J.G. Castañeda and E. Hett, *El Economismo Dependentista* (Mexico: Siglo XXI, 1985), p. 44.
66 Phillips, 'The concept of "development"', p. 20.
67 Leys, 'Underdevelopment and dependency: critical notes', p. 98.
68 Warren, *Imperialism, Pioneer of Capitalism* , pp. 105–9.
69 J. Banaji, 'Gunder Frank in retreat?', p. 109.

70 Phillips, 'The concept of "development"', p. 19.
71 Warren, *Imperialism, Pioneer of Capitalism*, p. 171.
72 Kitching, *Development and Underdevelopment in Historical Perspective*, p. 152.
73 Mandle, 'Marxist analyses of capitalist development in the Third World', p. 874.
74 Ibid., p. 869.
75 Booth, 'Marxism and development sociology: interpreting the impasse', p. 54.
76 Bernstein, 'Sociology of underdevelopment vs. sociology of development?', p. 97.
77 Booth, 'Marxism and development sociology: interpreting the impasse', p. 74.
78 Ibid., p. 75.
79 Ibid., p. 78.
80 Ibid., p. 57.
81 Warren, *Imperialism, Pioneer of Capitalism*, p. 161.
82 N. Harris, *The End of the Third World* (Harmondsworth: Penguin, 1986), p. 99.
83 K. Marx, *Grundrisse* (Harmondsworth: Penguin, 1973), p. 872.
84 K. Marx, *Theories of Surplus-Value* (London: Lawrence & Wishart, 1969), vol. II, p. 475.
85 Ibid., vol. III, pp. 105–6.
86 Jenkins, *Transnational Corporations and Uneven Development*, p. 98.
87 Ibid., p. 97. Data taken from UNCTC, *Transnational Corporations in World Development Third Survey*, New York, UN, ST/CTC/46 (1983), tables II.2 and II.4.
88 F. Hinkelammert, *Dialéctica del Desarrollo Desigual* (Valparaiso: Ediciones Universitarias de Valparaiso, 1972), p. 50.
89 Jenkins, *Transnational Corporations and Uneven Development*, pp. 99–100.
90 This point has been emphasized from various angles by A. Foster-Carter, 'Marxism versus dependency theory?: a polemic', *The University of Leeds Occasional Papers in Sociology*, no. 8 (February 1979).
91 K. Mori, 'Marx and "underdevelopment": his thesis on the "historical roles of British free trade" Revisited', *Annals of the Institute of Social Science* (University of Tokyo), no. 19 (1978).
92 This is why I am astonish to read in an otherwise sensible book by S. Corbridge that Cardoso and Faletto's theory of dependency finds support in the writings of Hindess and Hirst. The mind boggles. See S. Corbridge, *Capitalist World Development* (London: Macmillan, 1986), p. 66.
93 For those interested in a discussion of Marxism as a theory of practice see J. Larrain, *A Reconstruction of Historical Materialism* (London: Allen & Unwin, 1986). See also H. Fleischer, *Marxism and History* (London: Allen

Lane, 1973), and A. Schmidt, *The Concept of Nature in Marx* (London: New Left Books, 1971).

94 E. Mavros,'"Marxism" versus dependency "theory": on the futility of a debate', *The University of Leeds Occasional Papers in Sociology*, no. 17 (January 1984), p. 38.

95 F.H. Cardoso, 'Teoría de la dependencia' o análisis concretos de situaciones de dependencia?', in *Estado y Sociedad en América Latina* (Buenos Aires: Ediciones Nueva Visión, 1972), p. 139.

96 F.H. Cardoso and E. Faletto, *Dependency and Development in Latin America* (Berkeley: University of California Press, 1979), p. xxiii.

97 K. Marx, *Capital* (London: Lawrence & Wishart, 1974), vol. I, pp. 424–5.

98 Foster-Carter, 'The modes of production controversy', p. 66.

99 Marx, *Capital* , vol. I, pp. 424–5 (my emphases).

100 Ibid.

101 Warren, *Imperialism, Pioneer of Capitalism*, p. 163.

102 Cardoso and Faletto, *Dependency and Development in Latin America*, p. xxiii.

103 Underdeveloped not in the sense of stagnant, but in the descriptive sense of a country with little diversification of its productive system.

104 T. Evers, *El Estado en la Periferia Capitalista* (Mexico: Siglo XXI, 1985), p. 38.

105 Ibid., p. 14.

106 Marx, *Capital*, vol. I, p. 703.

107 See on this Cueva, *El Desarrollo del Capitalismo en América Latina*, chapter 4.

108 V.I. Lenin, preface to the second edition of *The Development of Capitalism in Russia* (Moscow: Progress, 1974), p. 32.

109 Cueva, *El Desarrollo del Capitalismo en América Latina*, p. 85.

110 Marx, *Capital*,vol. I, p. 689.

111 N.P. Mouzelis, *Politics in the Semi-Periphery* (London: Macmillan, 1986), p. 51.

112 Ibid., pp. 4–5.

113 Cueva, *El Desarrollo del Capitalismo en América Latina*, p. 187.

114 Harris, *The End of the Third World*, p. 112.

115 E. Tironi, *Los silencios de la revolución* (Santiago: Editorial Puerta Abierta, 1988), p. 67.

116 Mouzelis, *Politics in the Semi-Periphery* , p. 4.

117 D.L. Johnson calculates that 'in Latin America about 25 per cent of the population of major cities earn no regular income and are crowded into the most squalid of slums' and that the situation of peasants in rural areas is no better. See 'On oppressed classes', in J.D. Cockcroft et al., eds., *Dependence and Underdevelopment* (New York: Anchor Books, 1972), p. 269.

118 Data taken from Jenkins, *Transnational Corporations and Uneven*

Development, p. 10.

119 R. Prebisch, 'Estructura socioeconómica y crisis del sistema', *Revista de la CEPAL* (Segundo Semestre de 1978), p. 177. Although the quoted report is from 1963, in 1978 Prebisch regarded it as still valid.

120 See for instance J. Nun, 'Superpoblación relativa, ejército industrial de reserva y masa marginal', *Revista Latinoamericana de Sociología*, 5 (2) (Julio 1969); A. Quijano, 'The marginal pole of the economy and the marginalized labour force', *Economy and Society*, 3 (4) (November 1974), *Notas sobre el concepto the marginalidad social* (Santiago: CEPAL, 1966) and 'Redefinición de la dependencia y proceso de marginalización en América Latina' in A. Quijano and F. Weffort, eds., *Populismo, Marginalización y Dependencia* (San José, Costa Rica: EDUCA, 1973), part 2.

121 See for instance F.H. Cardoso's critique of Nun and Quijano: 'Comentario sobre los conceptos de superpoblación relativa y marginalidad' and 'Participación y marginalidad: Notas para una discusión teórica', in *Estado y Sociedad en América Latina,* chapters 7 and 8.

122 See Johnson, 'On oppressed classes'.

123 Harris, *The End of the Third World*, p. 200.

124 Leys, 'Underdevelopment and dependency: critical notes', pp. 95 and 92.

INDEX